THE COMPLETE BOOK OF
ROSES

THE COMPLETE BOOK OF
ROSES

JOHN MATTOCK, V. M. H.
SEAN McCANN
FRED WITCHELL
and
PETER WOOD

Edited by John Mattock

WARD LOCK

PUBLISHER'S NOTE

Readers are requested to note that in order to make the text intelligible in both hemispheres, plant flowering times, etc. are described in terms of seasons, not months.

The following table provides an approximate 'translation' of seasons into months for the two hemispheres.

Northern Hemisphere				Southern Hemisphere
Mid-winter	=	January	=	Mid-summer
Late winter	=	February	=	Late summer
Early spring	=	March	=	Early autumn
Mid-spring	=	April	=	Mid-autumn
Late spring	=	May	=	Late autumn
Early summer	=	June	=	Early winter
Mid-summer	=	July	=	Mid-winter
Late summer	=	August	=	Late winter
Early autumn	=	September	=	Early spring
Mid-autumn	=	October	=	Mid-spring
Late autumn	=	November	=	Late spring
Early winter	=	December	=	Early summer

First published in Great Britain in 1994
by Ward Lock Limited, Villiers House, 41/47 Strand,
London WC2N 5JE, England
A Cassell Imprint

Text filmset by Method Limited, Epping, Essex

Printed and bound in Spain
by Graficas Reunidas, S.A. Madrid

CIP data for this book is available upon application
from The British Library

ISBN 0 7063 7136 1

CONTENTS

Preface

The rose has been an essential element in the proper appreciation and development of civilization in the past three milleniums. Early Greeks and Romans, together with the Persians, recognized the subtle scents and colours of what today is the most popular garden plant in the world.

Nevertheless the sophisticated, classically formed blooms are a product of intense selection and plant breeding, spanning a short period of two hundred years.

Our forefathers were accustomed and indeed expected a rose to flower for a relatively brief period. The old music hall song 'The Last Rose of Summer' epitomizes the correlation of the rose to the blazing summers with, alas, the last blooms disappearing all too soon.

All this changed when a small insignificant rose plant was discovered in China at the end of the eighteenth century with an ability to flower in a remarkably repetitive fashion throughout the summer and autumn. Brought back to Europe and bred with the gems of the Old World, it immediately passed on to its offspring a similar ability to flower in a recurrent fashion.

Natural selection and the application of modern techniques in plant breeding and genetics have produced in a short space of time the classic bloom we are so familiar with today. In parallel with the evolution of such a beautiful asset to the garden, techniques have also improved in both production and culture.

The modern rose is a sophisticated product of the twentieth century, demanding neither too much cossetting nor cultural knowledge from the grower. It will provide an abundance of colour and bloom inconceivable one hundred years ago, combined with a tolerance of the most blatant abuses to plant life, to give pleasure to garden lovers in a wide range of climatic conditions.

Plant breeders have produced a plant that will clothe the most exotic and extensive arbors, or fit neatly into window boxes which serve as gardens in many of today's smaller houses and flats. No other genus has been so popular and so widely grown.

Many fables and myths have developed in the course of its history and cultivation. The rose world is constantly changing with new techniques in cultivation, new varieties being bred and our knowledge of how to grow them expanding every day.

This book will give the interested gardener the benefit of four experts' vast experience but, just as importantly, it will also share with the reader an enthusiasm for the world's favourite flower.

J.M.

Acknowledgements

The publishers are grateful to the following for granting permission to reproduce the following photographs: Photos Horticultural (pp. i, ii(top), iv, viii, ix, xi, xii, xv, xvii, xix, xx, xxi, xxii, xxiii, xxiv, xxvi, xxvii, xxix(top), and xxx)); John Mattock (pp. ii(lower), v(both), vii(lower), xiii(both), xiv, xvi, xviii(both), xxix(lower) and xxxi(lower)); Harry Smith (pp. iii, xxv, xxviii and xxxi(top); and Pat Brindley (pp. vii(top) and xxxii)).
The line illustrations are by Michael Shoebridge.
The quotations on pp. 9 and 10 are reproduced by permission of the Royal Horticultural Society from the *RHS Dictionary of Gardening* (ed. Fred J. Chittenden); Vol. IV (PT–ZY); pub. 1951.

CHAPTER 1

The World of Roses

The history of the world and the progress of civilization is very conveniently divided into eras, usually for the convenience of historians, but fortunately on occasions for the benefit of botanical commentators. The rose appeared on this earth, according to the paleontologists, well before man, and was distributed throughout the temperate regions of the northern hemisphere.

The Greeks and Egyptians

At the time of the Greeks and Egyptians, the rose had been developed as a plant whose medicinal properties were legion, although modern research has not firmly authenticated this. We are aware that the ripe rose hip is a valuable source of Vitamin C. Early European mythology is both romantic and diverse. Probably the legend of 'sub rosa' is the most familiar. After the Greeks were defeated by Xerxes on land, they retreated to a rose bower to discuss a possible retaliation by sea. The venue for the talks 'under the rose' subsequently connected the idea of confidentiality to the rose. Many meeting places and council chambers have by convention roses embossed or carved on their ceilings. The Egyptians grew large numbers of roses in the Nile delta which were used in religious ceremonies (Fig. 1.1).

The Romans

The development and expansion of the Roman Empire was a tremendous boost to the cultivation of the rose. A banquet (or a debauchery) was not complete without decorations of rose blooms and petals. There is evidence to suggest that the Egyptians created a very lucrative market of exporting rose blooms to Rome.

Confusion has been caused by Victorian painters depicting these feasts with an enthusiasm that stretches botanical credence. Nevertheless there is ample evidence to suggest that the rose was a very significant element in Roman civilization (Fig. 1.2).

The Persians

The advance of Islam into Western Europe played a great part in the spread of the cult of the rose along the caravan routes. There is no doubt that the distribution of the Damask and Gallica roses benefited greatly from this colonial expansion from the East.

Medieval development

The decline and fall of the Roman Empire has been associated with the rose losing its popularity, but it also left a legacy of the

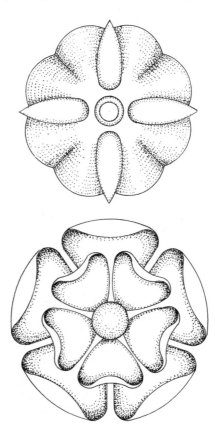

Fig. 1.1 Persian – rosette from a golden bowl of the period of the Persian King, Khusrau II (590-628 A.D.); the decoration consists of three rings with 18 rosettes.

Fig. 1.2 Roman – a form of double rose from the sarcophagus of Celsus Polemaenus; in the Celsus library; *ca.* 135 A.D., founded by Celsus' son in memory of his father who lived to see its completion; also in Ephesus.

genus *Rosa* being accepted as an indigenous plant in many parts of northern Europe. Once the association of the rose with debauchery had been dispelled, the expanding Christian church adopted the rose in many forms as a symbol in architecture, heraldry and nationalism. Rose windows in ecclesiastical buildings were but one part of an expanding art form and the establishment of rosarian collections became fashionable (Fig. 1.3). The Tudor rose of England was an amalgamation of the Gallica and the Alba (Fig.1.4).

The Renaissance

Such was the expansion of culture and the association with the rose that it is difficult to find spheres of influence where it did not appear.

Roses in art

By the sixteenth century the Dutch flower painters had discovered the rose and it was depicted in many forms by a series of artists. Although there is a temptation to identify many of the cultivars painted at that time, there is reason to believe that a

Fig. 1.3 Medieval – (*a*) Notre Dame, Paris, South Transept Rose Window (13th century). (*b*) Detail of the carved roses in the Rose Window, Notre Dame.

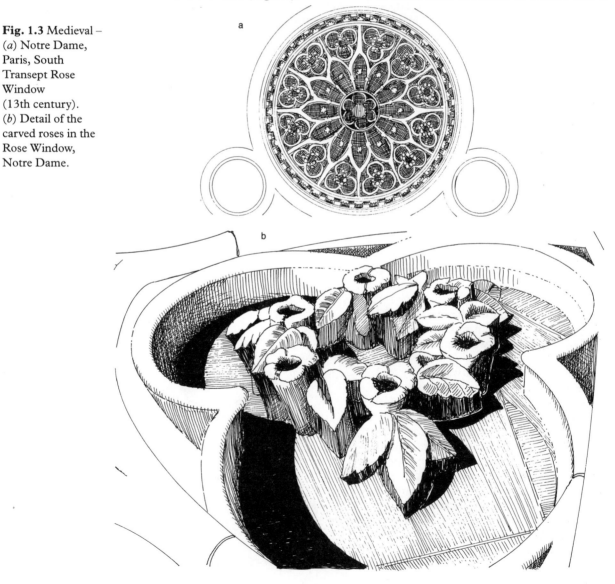

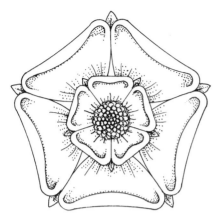

certain amount of artistic licence was used, and apart from recognizing the major group, which were the Centifolias, no degree of accuracy can be guaranteed.

The French influence

The rose as a symbol and as an art form received very high recognition in the glittering courts of Versailles. Madame de Pompadour and her successor Madame du Barry were so enamoured of the rose that it became a fetish. However it was the wife of Napoleon, Empress Josephine, who some one hundred years later assembled an extraordinary collection of extant rose varieties at the palace of Malmaison. The stories of the means whereby she accumulated this collection are legendary.

Redouté

Pierre-Joseph Redouté was a painter of roses which were popular at the end of the eighteenth century and beginning of the nineteenth century. His illustrations are a combination of the cultivars of Europe together with the newest discoveries from the Far East. The technique of watercolour on vellum produced remarkable paintings which are every bit as popular today as they were at the time they were commissioned. Nevertheless it is unfortunate that the botanical accuracy of his illustrations is not matched by the quality of the nomenclature. More recently, the exquisite and very accurate illustrations of Alfred Parsons in Mrs Ellen Wilmott's *Genus Rosa* (1914) are the only paintings of true merit that can be compared to the French artist.

The Chinese influence

Although historians are meticulous in charting the development of the rose in Europe and the Near East it must not be forgotten that the rose was cultivated in China some 2,000 years before the Christian era. It did not, however, enjoy the popularity of the peony or the chrysanthemum and consequently there is a dearth of information from that country of its development. The genus nevertheless was highly prized during the Ming Dynasty.

There is a general presumption that the first recurrent flowering roses were sent back from China to Europe as live plants in about 1760. Although the significance of this was realized, it was not used to good effect until the end of that century. In spite of the fact that the Royal Horticultural Society regularly sponsored plant expeditions to China, many species that we are familiar with in the garden today were not collected until the turn of this century. There is ample evidence to suggest that there are still many botanical treasures to discover.

Rosaceae

The rose family or tribe is a vast collection of plants, many of which are common in the garden today. They include such diverse members as blackberries, medlars, quinces, pears, plums and herbaceous plants including spiraea, potentilla and strawberry. Botanically they are described as Dicotyledons:

A family of 90 genera including about 2000 species of herbs, shrubs and trees found in all parts of the world. Leaves alternate, usually stipulate, the stipules often adnate to the petiole. Flowers usually regular, usually perfect, terminal, in racemes or cymes. Calyx of 5 sepals, often with an epicalyx of small leaves, petals 5, like the sepals usually overlapping in the bud, stamens 2, 3 or 4 times as many as the petals or indefinite, bent inwards in the bud; carpels 2 or 3 times as many as petals or indefinite, rarely 1 or 4, free as a rule, and usually superior but sometimes completely united to the receptacle but inferior.

Fig. 1.4 Tudor – Heraldic Tudor rose.

The genus *Rosa*

Botanically described as a genus of about 125 species but could be as many as 150, of which 95 are Asiatic, 18 American and the remainder European and N.W. African (Fig. 1.5).

Shrubs, generally with prickly stems ranging from a few centimetres (inches) to many metres (feet) in height, in many instances climbers. Leaves alternate, generally deciduous, odd-pinnate and stipulate (except R. persica). Flowers solitary or up to 100 or more in corymbs at ends of short growths of the current year; sepals and petals 5 (except 4 in R. sericea and R. omeinesis); sepals usually persistent on fruit, often pinnate; stamens and styles numerous, later surrounded by receptacle which becomes fleshy at maturity to form the hip, enclosing few to many boney achenes (seeds).

Systematic botanists are currently enjoying a vogue in the horticultural world and re-classifying plants appears to be a never-ending exercise. The genus *Rosa* is no stranger to this phenomenon, but mercifully there appears to be general agreement that some form of stability has been achieved for the moment. The groups described here enjoy common recognition, but it must be understood that future research may revise some of the nomenclature. They are grouped in this chapter in botanical order and are not relevant to garden uses.

Hulthemia. This group of Middle Eastern origin has recently been ostracized and botanically it is no longer in the genus *Rosa*. Some hybridists, particularly Harkness, have been very successful breeding from this family and lines are now being pursued with some remarkable results in Europe.

R. pimpinellifoliae. Natives of Europe and the Far East, this section includes well known species which are familiar in gardens today, including *R. hugonis* and *R. xanthina spontanea* 'Canary Bird' from the Orient, and the Scotch roses of European descent. An interesting member is *R. foetida*, which is largely responsible for the yellow in modern roses (Fig. 1.6).

Fig. 1.5
The world – map showing distribution of the genus *Rosa* exclusively in the northern hemisphere.

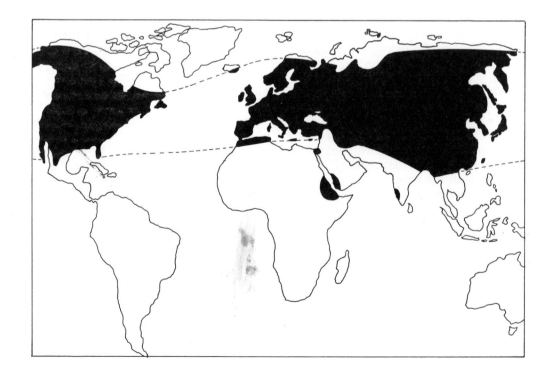

Fig. 1.6 (*Left*) *Rosa pimpinelli-foliae.*

Fig. 1.7 (*Right*) *Rosa carolinae* (*R. virginiana*).

Gallicanae. From Europe and the Near East in origin, the Damasks, Gallicas and Moss roses are the dominant plants.

Caninae. The dog roses, Albas and sweet briars make up the majority of this section.

Carolinae. Found exclusively in North America, *R. virginiana* is probably the most garden worthy, with its unique feature of beautiful autumnal foliage (Fig. 1.7).

Cassiorhodon (Cinnamomeae). A large group whose origins are to be found stretching virtually round the northern hemisphere. The *rugosas* from Japan are their most distinguished members, together with the garden forms of the *R. moyesii* family (Fig. 1.8).

Synstylae. Modern Floribundas can claim to have originated from the genes of *R. wichuriana* and *R. multiflora*, the two most important members of this group collected in Asia. Found also on the eastern seaboard of America and Europe.

Fig. 1.8 *Rosa cassiorhodon.*

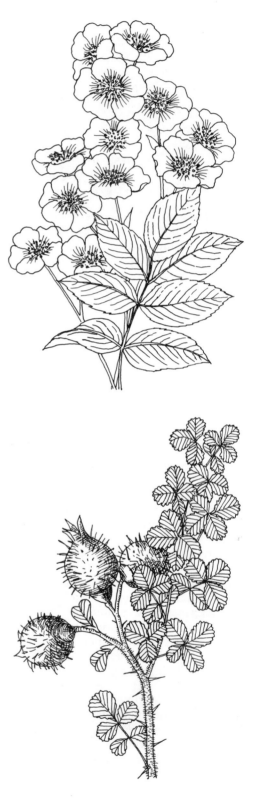

Fig. 1.9 *Rosa bracteata.*

Chinensis. Found exclusively in China, Kashmir and Nepal, the Chinas can claim to be the origin of remontancy (recurrent flower) in the modern rose, together with the classical shape of the Hybrid Tea, which is derived from the Tea roses.

Banksianae. To date there are no records of this group contributing to the modern rose. Originating in China, the Banksians are nevertheless a valuable asset to the warmer gardens with clouds of very early white or yellow small blooms on very vigorous climbing plants.

Laevigatae. A very small group of roses discovered in East China. The semi-hardy plants, producing single flowers, have become naturalized in the Southern States of America, where they are known as the Cherokee Roses.

Bracteata. Of Chinese origin, but grown widely in all rose lovers' gardens in the form of 'Mermaid'. To many connoisseurs, considered the most beautiful rose grown in the garden today (Fig. 1.9).

Platyrhodon. *R. roxburghii*, the sole member of this group, collected in China, this has the distinction of being the only rose specie whose peeling bark in the winter is a distinguishing and beautiful feature in many gardens.

Hesperhodos. *R. stellata* is a native of South-west America and Mexico and its chief claim to fame is the distinct gooseberry-like foliage (Fig. 1.10).

The Rose in the economy

In common with many other plants, the rose was first adopted for its medicinal properties. We are told that Pliny, the famous medical writer of the Roman period, listed some 30 medicines made from roses, most of which he gained from Greek sources. Among many suggestions and prescriptions are cures for ailments of the intestines, the stomach, and bad breath. There is even a suggestion that rose petals

Fig. 1.10 *Rosa stellata mirifica.*

steeped in wine delayed the more soporific effects of alcohol. There is no doubt that scented rose petals were used as an air freshener. Red rose petals by the gallon were recommended as an astringent in the bath, although no mention is made of how to dispose of the inevitable soggy mass before bathing! In this century, rose-hip syrup was produced as an extremely valuable source of Vitamin C during the Second World War, and is now widely given to babies for this purpose.

Rose as a perfume

The production of Attar of Roses contributes to a considerable proportion of the Gross National Product of Bulgaria, and is based in the town of Kazanlik. There are also areas of significant acreage in the Crimea and Krasnodar in Russia and Morocco. *Rosa damascena* 'Trigintipetala' and *Rosa alba* are the two main sources. The statistics of production are quite astonishing. Approximately 1kg (2.2 lb) of Attar can be distilled from 3,000 kg (6,600 lb) of petals. This amount can be collected from about 1 hectare (2.5 acres) in a good season. The petals are picked from half-opened blooms between sunrise and 9am, the time when they are considered to contain their highest concentration of essential oils.

This industry is not highly mechanized, and is of relatively recent origin dating from about 1750. Virtually all the product from Bulgaria is exported to Grasse, the centre of the perfume industry in France.

Pot-pourri

A most pleasant air-freshener (the modern word for *pot-pourri*) may be made using the dried rose petals of the Centifolias and Gallicas. Blended with lavender and other scented garden flowers, the mixture is packed into ornamental bags and jars to make attractive and useful presents.

Rose petal wine

Rose petal wine is a favourite in old country recipe books and will make a dry or sweet wine according to taste. It makes good sorbets, and excellent spritzers.

Ingredients
2½ l (2 quarts) rose petals
3 l (3 quarts) boiling water
50 g (½ oz) citric acid
1 tsp tannin
284 ml (½ pt) grape juice
1 kilo (2½ lb) granulated sugar
Wine yeast
Campden tablet

Method
Using petals from unsprayed plants, select variety according to scent and petal colour. White, yellow and pink roses give a pale straw/peach-coloured wine. Mid-red roses a pink wine, and dark red a darker pink.

Collect rose petals when scent is high; sort petals in a light place to allow pollen beetles or other insects to escape towards the light. To avoid bitterness, carefully remove the petals from the white base. Put petals into a large sterilized container (not aluminium) which can be sealed. Pour on boiling water and crush petals using a wooden spoon or pestle, to extract colour and perfume. Cover and allow to cool at room temperature. Add one campden tablet, plus citric acid dissolved in warm water. At this stage, for better bite and a more professional wine, add tannin. For more body, and the *really* professional wine, add grape juice concentrate, using the correct type according to colour of liquor developed from your petals. Cover and store in a cool place for 7 days. Stir daily with a wooden spoon.

Drain off liquor, add granulated sugar dissolved in minimum amount of water (don't boil). Make up wine yeast according to instructions. Add to liquor and place in a sterilized fermentation bottle, seal, fit an airlock and ferment at room temperature (provided this is not below 16–18°C or 62–65°F). To protect colour, keep out of sunlight. Ferment to finish.

Wine made from flower petals is always better finished slightly sweet to bring out the aroma. If too dry add a small amount of sugar or 'syrup' in the minimum amount of wine. Filter. Stand for 3 weeks to allow pollen to fall. Filter, bottle and serve well chilled.

Rose hip wine

The wine produced from rose hips, it is claimed, has many therapeutic qualities with a combination of the alcoholic contents and the ever present Vitamin C. This recipe has a remarkable affinity in taste to sherry and may be fortified on completion of fermentation with the addition of brandy.

Ingredients

    1 kg (2.2 lb) rose hips
    1 lemon
    1½ kg (3 lb) sugar
    4½ l (1 gal) boiling water
    Sherry yeast and pectic enzyme
    Campden tablet

Method

Collect wild rose hips in the late autumn when fully coloured and after a good frost. After washing, crush and place in a crock or bucket (non-metallic) together with the sugar, and pour boiling water over them, stirring vigorously. When cool, add the prepared yeast, juice of the lemon and the pectic enzyme. Cover and place in a warm room. Two weeks later strain into a demijohn, fit with an air-lock and ferment to finish. Sterilize with a campden tablet, rack and bottle.

This will make a very drinkable wine if kept for about 12 months.

Roses as cut flowers

Although this book is primarily concerned with the cultivation of the garden rose, it is well to consider the contribution that the rose has made to the world of floristry. The majority of roses used in the flower trade are grown in very precisely controlled conditions under glass. The varieties that are used have been bred to criteria that would be impossible in the garden. Length of stem, longevity and production rates, together with form and colour, are of the greatest importance. Many growers would add ability to withstand the rigours of packing and air travel. A top variety propagated on a *R. inermis* stock, planted at a density of about six plants per sq m (sq yd), is expected to have a minimum production rate of about 40 stems per plant per annum. A well-maintained crop should come into flower approximately five times in a season. The cut flower is graded according to the length of stem and quality of bloom.

The breeding lines of these varieties have very little in common with garden roses. Occasionally one or two of the latter are tested and can prove successful, although this is very rare.

Commercial production of garden roses – a few facts

The majority of garden roses are produced in nurseries where they are propagated by budding (see Chapter 6). The average production rate is approximately 52,000 plants per hectare (22,000 per acre). The planting, cultivation and harvesting is a very highly mechanized operation. The principal rose-producing countries of the world are France, Germany, the United Kingdom and the United States. Italy, Hungary, Denmark and Poland also grow considerable quantities. The most recent production figures for the UK are about 20–25 million per annum; for the USA 40 million and for Germany 35 million.

CHAPTER 2

Growing Roses

The range of varieties is so great these days that it is possible to suggest a rose for virtually any position in the garden. Towards the latter half of this book a considerable number of types and varieties are discussed, but here we must pause for a moment and briefly examine the many different classes into which the genus *Rosa* is divided. The World Federation of Rose Societies in their wisdom have attempted to categorize the innumerable divisions and although they may confuse you if you are a novice, take comfort in the fact that they have little relevance to modern commercial practice, and the majority of nurseries tend to categorize their stock in compact, tidy groups more relevant to their function in the garden and selling potential.

The New Classification
Basically the WFRS (World Federation of Rose Societies) has attempted to divide the rose into three major divisions:

> Modern roses
> Old Garden roses
> Wild roses

They have then progressed into dividing each of these groups into their habit of growth and the frequency with which they flower. Thus, among the Modern roses, ground cover roses are divided into recurrent and non-recurrent, the modern shrub by a similar method; but the bush roses, which are all assumed to be recurrent, are divided into large flowered Hybrid Teas and cluster flowered (Floribundas). The modern climbers are divided into recurrent and non-recurrent, with the bonus of differentiating between climbers and ramblers and so on and so on.

The Old Garden roses are divided into shrubs and climbers. For good measure, recently two cultural associations have been formed to promote these types of roses.

One calls itself 'The Historic Roses Group' and is based in the UK and the other is called 'Heritage Roses', based in the USA.

The Wild roses are thankfully only divided into climbing and non-climbing, and their true description, Species Roses, appears to have been ignored.

To summarize, without being specific in descriptions, the WFRS has produced a grand total of some 37 divisions or subdivisions.

Groups discussed in this book
For the purposes of clarity, roses in this book have been divided into a more modest number of categories which may or may not be broken down into smaller sections, but only to give accurate guidance to the reader:

Species, Old Garden Roses, and Modern Shrubs (Chapter 9)
Bush Roses, Hybrid Teas, and Floribundas (Chapter 10)
Climbing Roses and Rambling Roses (Chapter 11)
Miniatures, Patio and Ground Cover Roses (Chapter 12)

Mention has been made of the descriptive phrases 'large flowered' and 'cluster flowered' when referring to Hybrid Teas and Floribundas. Whereas these may well be more accurate descriptions, they do lose a lot in transcription and the reader will have to bear with the old nomenclature. The bulk of rose enthusiasts are born romantics and will appreciate that Hybrid Tea is a far better description than 'recurrent flowering bush roses of the large-flowered type'!

Where will roses grow?
The rose is botanically a deciduous plant; that is, it produces leaves on an annual basis, shedding them in the autumn. It is therefore too much to ask that a rose will

produce a perpetual screen of leaves similar to an evergreen hedge. However, because many varieties produce very thorny stems, it can be made to produce quite impenetrable barriers to both man and beast.

In wind Wind is very rarely a problem unless standard roses are planted on top of a hill where damage is inevitable. But modern roses hate draughts. This is quite different to wind and explains why roses are not happy in some modern conurbations.

A gap in a hedge or between two buildings is an invitation to disaster. The constant piercing wind is an anathema to a happy plant. In the country, similar conditions exist in gardens adjacent to woodlands where a cool draught of air, which may be welcome to the gardener, is disastrous to the plants.

In sun Roses are naturally sunseekers but can tolerate a considerable lack of sunlight for short periods of daylight, and can even give good results on sunless north-facing walls, if a modicum of reflected light is available. Dark sunless areas are hopeless. It is unfair to plant a rose underneath big broad-leaved trees. The problems of becoming established in dry soils with little light are insuperable.

In wet Roses do not like wet situations but will tolerate most soils (see soils on pp 24-25). They will withstand a considerable amount of flooding, but not if this is followed by a hard frost. Stagnant marshy conditions are death to the rose.

In drought Drought is a condition that the rose is curiously well adapted to tolerate. The majority of rose plants are budded on to a stock that has the potential to reach considerable depths.

The climate

Wild roses are well distributed in the northern hemisphere in temperate and Mediterranean zones, and modern varieties will naturally tolerate the same kind of weather. Extreme tropical heat is disastrous, as much as the extreme cold experienced in countries that have to contend with the vagaries of a continental climate. In the USA many plant catalogues and horticultural societies publish very useful charts giving plant hardiness zones for perennials. These are broadly accurate but do not take into account the vagaries of light and proximity to large stretches of water. Both of these factors can contribute to micro-climates. Even in a small island like the UK, the Gulf Stream can create softer growing conditions on the west coast of Scotland than in East Anglia.

Height is probably the greatest determining factor. On the Equator in East Africa it is possible to grow fabulous roses at 2500m (8–9000ft).

Roses in the garden

Roses are a very tolerant type of plant and will give great pleasure provided they are grown in a proper and sensible way. The range of varieties is so great these days that there is scarcely an area that will prove difficult to plant. What therefore is the potential for such a versatile genus?

Formal beds

There are relatively few types of bush rose that fail to look dramatic when planted *en masse* (Fig.2.1). Rose beds can give vivid stretches of colour, particularly when a single variety is used. Many public and private gardens can give testimony to this. However, the majority of roses are purchased by gardeners who do not aspire to such grandiose plans, although planning and design still requires much thought.

Although Hybrid Teas and Floribundas are the main constituents, quite dramatic effects have been created using Modern Shrubs, and at present large formal areas are being planted with modern recurrent-flowering ground covers. As in all walks of life, these days an element of practicality must intrude into the equation. There is a temptation to plant formal rose beds too wide. This may be pleasing to the designer but will be met with great opposition from the practical gardener. Attempting to cultivate or spray in plant widths of over two metres (six feet) is an unenviable chore.

Fig. 2.1 Bush roses will always give a stunning effect when planted in formal beds using one colour.

Borders

The purist would not countenance or conceive of planting roses in association with other plants some 60 years ago, but thankfully our attitudes have now changed and roses are to be found in the most unexpected places. They still require some consideration in placing to advantage and care must be taken to allow rose plants plenty of light, particularly early in the season. Groups of one variety planted in threes, fives or sevens can provide welcome splashes of colour. With some varieties the vivid deep copper and purple foliage can give an added dimension to a border. Shrub roses of all types and Floribundas are ideally suited to these positions (Fig. 2.2). An important factor to remember is that although much is made of preparing the beds (double-digging etc), for planting bush roses there appears to be a reluctance to remind gardeners that *all* situations where new rose plants are going to be sited need equally assiduous preparation.

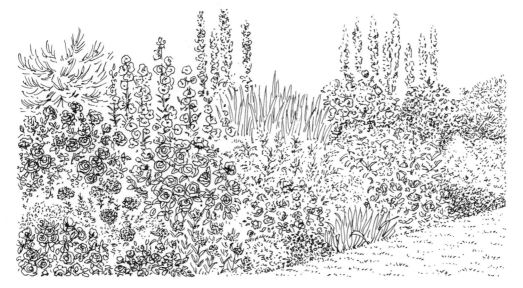

Fig. 2.2 Mixed borders can be given a lift with groups of roses.

Hedges

There is a reluctance to use alternatives to the rather drab laurels, loniceras or berberis as hedging material. The argument put forward is that the maintenance factor is of great concern. This is a fallacious argument. Some of the most dramatic effects can be achieved planting the rugosas which require no trimming at all (Fig. 2.3), or many of the myriad varieties of Shrub roses or Floribundas. In small formal gardens the very modern Patio rose is an ideal subject.

Fig. 2.3 (*Left*) A rose hedge can give colour for long periods.

Fig. 2.4 (*Right*) Specimen plants are ideal for formal lawns or conservation areas.

For the very spacious estates a large double hedge of the very vigorous ramblers will produce a most astonishing blaze of colour.

Specimen plants

Now that we are into the era of conservation, many gardens are devoting areas to the cultivation of wild flowers. This is a thoroughly commendable approach but unfortunately gives a colourless look after the euphoria of the spring flush. Specimen rose plants will extend the flowering period. Species roses can also contribute with their blaze of hips in the autumn (Fig.2.4). Some very formal lawns have been enhanced by the judicious planting of small groups of specimen roses.

A common fault is to allow grass to grow right up to the plants. Always give room for an annual mulch and fertilizer boost.

Pergolas, walls, pillars and trees

There are few gardens that cannot accommodate or in other circumstances require some form of camouflage in the form of climbing plants.

The Victorian concept of rose arbours has been revived recently, and can create a pleasing concept in many gardens (Fig. 2.5). Many garages which appear to intrude into gardens will certainly benefit from a touch of colour. Pillars of blooms can give much pleasure, although the presence of trees or tree trunks can present a challenge. Some of the fast-growing ramblers will give great value in this ambience.

Fig. 2.5 There are many gardens that can be given a romantic look with pergolas.

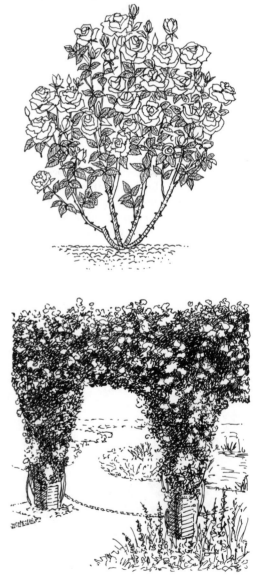

18

Like so much in the garden, it is a question of the right plant in the right place at the right time. The slower-growing recurrent flowering climbers are ideal for pillars or restricted walls; the more remontant climbers and ramblers for pergolas.

Hanging Baskets

The introduction of the more modest ground cover roses of the lax type has added a new dimension to the role of roses in the garden. Recently they have been used to enhance hanging baskets. As the rose by nature requires a good root run, this would appear to be an anomaly. Good results have however been obtained. Probably the best results can be obtained by using plants that have been propagated on their own roots. Whatever variety is used, the problem, as in all plants grown in stressful circumstances, is maintenance. They will require constant vigilance, good maintenance and plenty of water.

Planting distances

Formal rose beds require formal planning. The typical planting plan should acknowledge some basic measurements. The average bush (Hybrid Tea or Floribunda) will give a good reward planted about 60cm (2ft) apart from its neighbours. This is an average measurement which curiously requires little adjustment. Obviously the small-growing Floribundas and Patios can reduce these calculations to 45cm (1½ft), and the more vigorous types will go to 75cm (2½ft), but the basic measurement is extraordinarily accommodating for about 85% of varieties.

A vital measurement is the space allowed between the edge of the lawn and the plant (Fig. 2.6).

This is a grossly underestimated factor. The gardener must be mindful of maintaining a good clean edge and an adequate distance must be allowed – about 45cm (1½ft) is ideal. Torn clothing or branches damaged by the lawn mower are the result of sloppy planning with too small a space being allowed.

Planting in groups

With the liberalization of attitudes to plant uses and the introduction of the rose as a subject for informal planting, there is now ample scope with the newer introductions to plant in mixed borders. A great deal of harm has been caused by attempting to use

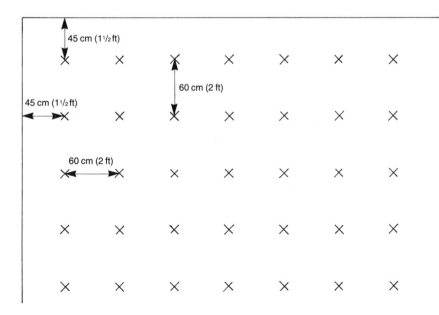

Fig. 2.6 Some basic measurements when planning a formal bed.

bush roses as single plants in these situations. A solitary Hybrid Tea can look completely lost and will probably lack the attention it should receive. Many of the more vigorous Floribundas can give the most astonishing displays of colour. A group of five 'Alexander' roses planted at the back of a border can give vibrance to any planting scheme. Similarly, groups of some of the Old Garden Roses can give beauty to a mixed border. Whichever types are used, due thought must be given to the relative height and stature. Group plants in clusters about 75cm (2¹/₂ft) plant to plant to obtain good results. It is as well to allow about 3sq m (10sq ft) for each variety. There will be the temptation to integrate other plant material, but this must be resisted as the roses will require as much light as possible, particularly early in the season.

Planting on walls and pergolas

Distance can sometimes be deceptive and planting climbers on walls is no stranger to this dilemma. The average well-grown recurrent climber is quite capable of maturing to occupy some 3m (10ft) of width, which may sound generous but in fact implies only 1¹/₂m (5ft) of growth each way. This in fact is not a great deal, but may appear very generous when the garden is marked out. Obviously something as mundane as a garage wall is very restrictive on space, and in a small area there will be the temptation to smother everything in sight.

In an ideal situation good coverage can be obtained by planting at a distance of 3–4m (12ft) climber to climber (Fig. 2.7a). The best support in these positions is wire string with the use of vine eyes (Fig. 2.7b) driven in to the wall. Wire strung 38–45 cm (15–18 in) apart and supported every 1.8m (6ft) is the ideal solution. Lattice-type support in the mode of wooden lathes or screens have become very popular but are not to be recommended. They may enhance an otherwise bare wall, but can quickly become impractical when a climbing rose begins to grow *behind* them, and an

Fig. 2.7
(*a*) Some basic measurements when planning and planting roses against a wall.
(*b*) Vine eye used to secure wire against wall.

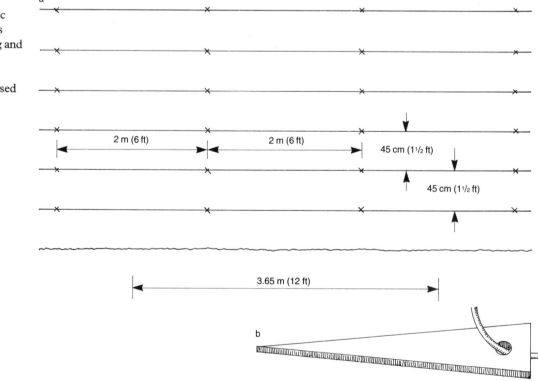

a

2 m (6 ft)   2 m (6 ft)   45 cm (1¹/₂ ft)

45 cm (1¹/₂ ft)

3.65 m (12 ft)

b

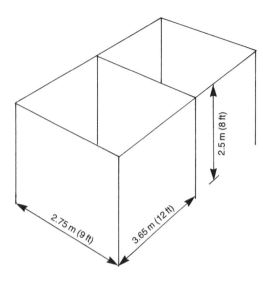

Fig. 2.8 Simple measurements to erect a pergola.

element of impracticality appears when pruning time comes round.

Pergolas must be planned to allow ramblers to grow freely without hindrance. The width is very much dependent on the general architecture of the garden, but a width of 1.8m (6ft) must be considered the norm, going to 3m (10ft) if space allows. Any distances less than this can only restrict the natural growth of the plant and the freedom of the visitor to move about. Useful measurements to consider for an extended rose pergola would be an avenue of 3m (10ft) wide with supports every 3.7m (12ft), with an overall height of 2.5m (8ft) (Fig. 2.8).

This type of construction, which can be a combination of bricks or wood, will prove eminently satisfactory. Another form is to construct a support of wires which will enable plants to be supported; the retaining posts being positioned at about 3m (10ft) apart. Thick ropes may be used but rose plants appear to dislike growing on them so they are not recommended.

On the Continent cast-iron supports have great appeal, but must be discouraged in the UK as the plants will not grow well against this cold inhospitable fabric in a damp climate. Poles may be architecturally and aesthetically acceptable but are not practical. A simple tripod form is easier to create and maintain (Fig. 2.9). Select good stout hardwood that has been well treated

with a wood preservative well before construction begins. Thin softwood may be cheap to purchase but can be very expensive to maintain.

Buying new plants

Although time and the opportunity to plant must be a determining factor in purchasing new plants, most good gardeners agree that autumn planting of bare-root material is probably best, and accordingly the nursery trade dispatches the majority of its production at this time. Bare-root plants will give the finest results, but they are not the easiest method of making readily available living material.

Pre-packed roses

This is probably the easiest form to purchase rose plants in small quantities. They

Fig. 2.9 A tripod will support many recurrent climbers.

are to all intents and purposes bare-roots which have the added protection of some material wrapped around the roots (to keep the plants alive) and are packed in some form of transparent material with an illustrated backing showing a colour picture of the variety, together with planting instructions. This mode of packing has made plants available to a wide range of outlets. In theory, this has extended the popularity of the rose! Unfortunately, in practice a considerable number of retailers, under pressure to sell many other seasonal lines, often have a lack of shelf space and consequently stocks plants much too early to enable ample room for Christmas trade goods. This in effect means that some pre-packs are offered for sale far too early in the autumn and the plants are therefore lifted before they have harvested off. Plants in pre-packs are ideal to purchase if they have been properly cared for. Overheated stores are not the ideal environment.

Containerized roses

These have now extended the planting season to virtually all the year round. Nevertheless the gardener must be aware of the constraints with this mode. Container roses are in effect bare-root plants that have been lifted by the nursery and potted on, usually in a rigid container (about 4 litres), in the winter months. They are grown on, pruned at the conventional time and generally offered for sale from the end of the bare-root season until mid-summer. It is unwise to purchase this type of plant after this time as the rose by its very nature is not an ideal subject to grow in a pot and so requires considerable maintenance to make it commercially presentable after this time. The purchaser is well advised to examine possible purchases for the quality of the plant, freedom from disease and proof that it has been adequately watered (Fig.2.10).

An additional hazard is that container roses must be constantly watered once replanted.

Where to choose roses

Prospective customers have a wide range of varieties to choose from and must therefore avail themselves of the opportunity to inspect possible purchases and their performance. There is ample opportunity to do this at flower shows, big national gardens and local enthusiasts who open their gardens for inspection with the added incentive of contributing to local charities. To the 'rose buff', the Chelsea Show in London, or the big national shows around the country, offer a chance to view the latest offerings from breeders. It is well to remember that at these functions, only the very best are on display.

The catalogues of the specialist nurseries are an education and can be quite persuasive. Beware of 'mail shots' late in the season with exceptional bargains.

The Royal National Rose Society garden at St. Albans in Hertfordshire, England, St. Annes Rose garden in Dublin, Dixon Park in Belfast, Zweibrucken and Mainau in Germany, Westbroekpark in The Hague, are but a few of a wide range of gardens that can give the prospective purchaser an idea of how the roses should grow. There are many smaller and less well known gardens that include specialist roses, such as Mottisfont in Hampshire, UK, where the Old

Fig. 2.10 A containerized rose plant that has been well maintained is essential.

Garden roses can be seen in profusion, but much can be gained by taking advantage of local gardens which are open at suitable times of the year.

Ordering from a specialist nursery

The discerning and emergent rose enthusiasts will quickly discover that the widest range of rose varieties is more easily available from specialist rose nurseries, where you will receive valuable information and be able to discuss rose problems with an expert. Which brings us to the moment when you order your roses for the autumn planting. If personal collection of an order is not possible, then careful note should be taken of the terms of sale and carriage charges. The novice gardener will discover that some varieties will quickly sell out, and therefore early ordering is advisable. This, in effect, means placing an order for specific varieties by late summer. The plants will not be delivered until the appropriate time in the autumn, but it is better to be safe than sorry. Most reputable suppliers will ask you to choose a substitute variety in the event of your chosen variety being sold out. Although suppliers should endeavour to supply the nearest alternative, you must be careful to nominate an alternative, or request that your order for the unavailable variety go forward to the following season.

Quality

Every plant purchased should be clearly labelled. The minimum information must be the name; some will give the colour and type and occasionally the supplier will give the information that the variety you have purchased is 'protected'.

The name is more than adequate, but do not be persuaded by the prefix Shrub/Fl/Cl/HT, as some growers will give a prefix that can be misleading. (It is easier to sell a variety as a Floribunda than as a Shrub.) No matter what it is called, the variety is still the same.

The colour description can sometimes be misleading but that is only caused by the limitations of space on a small label. If you know the variety you have ordered, you should know the colour to expect.

The information on protection is simply to warn you that if you have any pretentions to propagate the variety, then you will need a licence (see Chapter 7).

Plant guarantee
Most reputable nurseries and suppliers give a guarantee. Whilst nobody can absolutely promise that the plants you have purchased will perform miracles – after all, customers have been known to plant upside-down, not remove the plastic covering, and even to plant in pure chalk – the small print is worth examination. The basic conditions are that the instructions given in the catalogue are adhered to; usually this means care on arrival, heeling in if the situation demands, roots kept moist while planting and proper pruning.

Provided that the variety supplied is true to name, then do not complain on variations of colour as this can vary from one season to another with climatic changes. If the *quality* is suspect, there are guidelines to follow. Remember that the information on the label is necessarily brief. If the gardener is dissatisfied and a complaint is made, then the supplier will expect to have access to the plants and planting area should he request it. Fortunately complaints are very few and most reputable nurseries will send replacements without query the following season.

Containerized plants are never guaranteed.

What is a good plant?

We are in an era of the consumer watchdog and it might surprise purchasers to know that rose plants warrant considerable attention from the British Standards Institute and their European equivalents. The following criteria, it must be emphasized, are not mandatory but nevertheless are a move in the right direction. They are already demanded by big purchasers such as local authorities, but they are by their very nature flexible as to produce an overall measurement of, say, a bush is virtually impossible. As a simple comparison an Alsatian dog is hardly the same size as a Pekinese, but both can be of equal merit.

Basically, a first quality maiden bush rose should have three good stems each the thickness of a pencil emanating from the stock (Fig. 2.11). There should be no diseased or broken stems and an unpruned bush should have a minimum of 40cm (15in) of growth. The root system must be fibrous, free of broken and torn roots and suckers, and have a minimum length of 25cm (10in). The stems must be green and plump, not shrivelled, with no shot-out green growth and the roots should be in a moist condition. Climbers and ramblers must be in a similar condition with a minimum stem length of about 45cm (18in). Standards of first quality must have a minimum of two breaks (arms) and have good strong stems with, again, a fibrous root system that has not been subject to drying conditions (Fig. 2.12).

Fig. 2.11 The *minimum* criteria for a first-quality, bare-root plant.

Fig. 2.12 Minimum acceptable measurements for a standard rose tree.

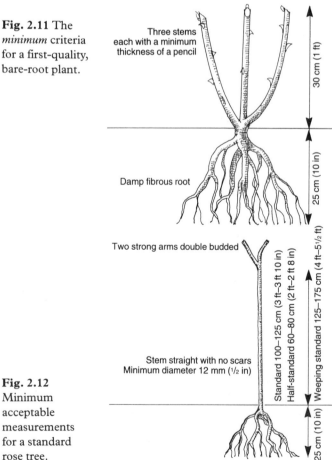

Three stems each with a minimum thickness of a pencil

30 cm (1 ft)

Damp fibrous root

25 cm (10 in)

Two strong arms double budded

Stem straight with no scars
Minimum diameter 12 mm (½ in)

Standard 100–125 cm (3 ft–3 ft 10 in)
Half-standard 60–80 cm (2 ft–2 ft 8 in)
Weeping standard 125–175 cm (4 ft–5½ ft)

25 cm (10 in)

Time to plant

Bare-root plants will give the most satisfactory results if planted in the autumn while the ground has still enough warmth to encourage a new root system. Good results can be obtained provided the soil is in a suitable condition and not waterlogged or in a frozen state. New plants can be handled at any time during the winter months provided that they are not in a frozen state. Pre-pack rose plants can be planted at much the same time.

Container-grown roses are available from early spring but are used to advantage in the late spring or early summer. Much disappointment can be caused by purchasing plants too early, before the root system has become established. The tremendous advantage to the gardener is that containerized roses have made it possible to plant virtually all the year round. This may not be to everybody's delight but if an unexpected fatality occurs, or if the soil is waterlogged or simply unmanageable during the conventional period, then all is not lost. It is however an expensive method of re-stocking the garden and this type of plant will demand a vigorous watering regime until well established.

Preparation of site

Preliminary planning, ordering and marking out of prospective planting positions would hopefully have been done some time previously to preparation of the site. Basic measurements have been discussed and the gardener has to face the fact that there are certain fundamental rituals to go through in order that all is ready when the plants do arrive. A new site will require thorough preparation.

Soils

To understand cultivation the gardener must understand the mode he is working with. Much is written describing the ideal soil for roses. Very simply one can divide soils into three textures, light, medium and heavy.

Light soils These have a high proportion of sand and/or alluvial sediment. They are easy to work and can be cultivated at most times of the year barring waterlogging and frost. Most plants will grow in them but because, particularly in the sands, they drain quickly, they cannot hold organic manure for very long and are what we call 'hungry'. This means that they appear to require more food. Nevertheless they will support roses well enough.

Medium loams These are an ideal mode to handle and rose plants do very well in them. Again though they will only produce as good a quality plant as the amount of plant food that is added.

Heavy sticky soils These are reputed to grow the best roses but require a good understanding. Young roots take some time to get established and a planting mixture is absolutely essential. Great damage can be caused to the structure of soils if they are handled in a wet, cold state. In practical terms this means that, particularly with heavy soils, preparation must be completed before the temperature drops and the autumn equinoxial storms commence. Where heavy soils make soil management difficult, great benefit can be gained by

early cultivation in time to allow the beneficial effects of deep frost to make a more friable medium to handle in the spring.

Double digging

Many cultivated areas can assume over the course of time a peculiar defect in the structure of the soil. This is the formation of a hard pan which occurs at about 30cm (12in) to 40cm (16in) below soil level. Agriculturists are familiar with this phenomena in some of their fields and use machines to break up this pan which is called sub-soiling. Gardeners preparing rose beds can emulate much the same activity by double digging – that is preparing the soil, integrating organic manure and breaking up the lower spit of soil with a fork at the same time. (Fig. 2.13).

The pH factor

Although the rose is a very tolerant genus, this cannot be said of every plant in the garden. The acidity of the soil or lack of it can influence the range of plants that can be grown. For instance rhododendrons like an acid soil. This factor is usually denoted by the pH reading and can be ascertained with a simple soil-testing kit obtainable from

Fig. 2.13
Principles of double digging.

Step 1

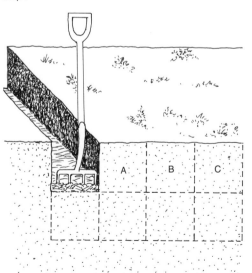

Step 2

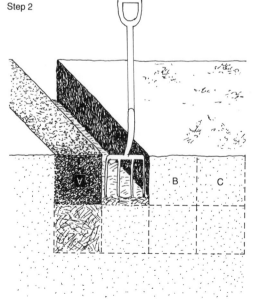

good garden shops. Roses are happiest in soil with a reading of 6.5. Neutral is 7. If the garden is in an area where limestone or chalk is in abundance, there is every chance that the soil is alkaline and the reading could well be 8 or 9. If azaleas and rhododendrons abound in your vicinity, then there is every reason to believe that the soil is acid.

Alkaline soils These can sometimes be neutralized with the addition of peat, but it is a difficult problem and the new gardener is advised to observe the plant performance in neighbouring gardens. Roses planted in these areas very often show symptoms of chlorosis, that is a yellowing of the leaves. There are foliar feeds, called sequestrenes, which come in spray form and will correct this condition, but they are very expensive and the concerned gardener could well find that there are other plants which are easier to grow in this soil.

Acid soils are relatively easy to correct if the condition is not too severe. Ground limestone must be applied some two months before planting at the rate of 85gm (3oz) to the sq m (yd) and lightly worked in.

The quality of composts

In the course of preparing a new rose bed or new planting site, the addition of a good quality compost is essential. To the countryman, farmyard manure is no problem, although even he would state a preference for well-rotted compost from store yard cattle to pig manure which is unpleasant to handle and very smelly.

To the city dweller, such a choice is not available, but there is great merit in making your own from domestic detritus. There is a selection of processing bins available, together with plenty of instructions. Any garden rubbish will break down, together with kitchen waste, but care must be taken never to use material that has been treated with weed killers. This applies to lawn cuttings in particular. There is a wide selection of garden composts available in garden shops.

Planting mixtures

A young rose plant has had a tortuous experience from life on a rose nursery to arrival in the garden, in preparation to planting in its permanent place. Not the least of its problems is the physical process of lifting, trimming, grading and packing. It will probably have been de-foliated; it will certainly have been trimmed back to a reasonable size and the roots will be shortened. All these processes will be expedited to present the customer with a standard product that, given reasonable care, will give great satisfaction for many years. The most important contribution the customer can make is to ensure that the plant has a good start in its permanent place. We have already discussed preparing the site; of equal importance is the environment the roses are actually planted in. Mention has already been made of the necessity to soften the blow to roots in a heavy soil but this is equally true in most other environments. In short it is essential when planting to ensure that the roots are actually planted in something 'comfortable'. This can best be described as a planting mixture. It must in no way be mistaken for compost introduced to the soil as manure. It can vary in composition from the simplest, which is a bucket full of damp peat with a handful of good quality bonemeal, to a complex mixture of equal parts (buckets) peat or peat substitute, sand, old leaf mould and good loamy soil, together with a handful of bonemeal. Either way, the important factor is to have this prepared before the plants arrive, allowing for about one large shovelful per plant.

On receiving new plants

In an ideal world bare-root plants will arrive in the morning and be planted in the afternoon. It seldom works that way. The gardener may not even be at home when the plants arrive. The important point to remember is that plants must not be handled in a frozen state. Therefore if the time of arrival is not propitious, bare-root roses must be stored in a frost free (but not warm) situation but only as a temporary measure. As soon as there is the opportunity, unpack the plants; if at all dry, dip (not soak) them in a bucket of cold water, and heel in immediately; that is, dig a trench sufficient in size to lay the plants in, with the roots well covered to prevent drying out. Standards and climbers are treated in the same way. If the plants are in big bundles cut the string and spread the plants out.

With pre-packed plants, again if it is not possible to plant immediately, these must be unpacked and heeled in, in a like manner.

Containerized plants are normally planted on arrival, but if there is any delay then they must be kept watered, at least three times a week.

Planting bare-root and pre-packed plants

Good preparation, that is, marking out, digging beds and having planting mixture to hand, will make the final part of the exercise a relatively simple matter. The final point is strategy. If the material to be planted is heeled in, do not lift too many at once. They will dry out. If they come straight from the package, keep them well covered until immediately before planting. In both instances dip them in a bucket of cold water immediately before planting.

Method

Dig the hole for a bush rose about 25 by 25cm (10in by 10in) and about 30cm (1ft) deep. If several are being planted, move the soil from the first prepared hole to the site of the final tree to be planted. The hole must be dug, leaving the marker stick in one corner. Place the plant against the stick, the soil level coming to the position where it was budded (the junction of the root stock and top growth). Cover the roots with a good spadeful of planting mixture and complete the planting by filling the hole with soil from the *second* plant position. (By adopting this method the soil is only moved once and much time is saved). As the operation proceeds, remember to firm in the soil by treading. If the ground is wet this may have to be postponed until drier conditions prevail.

The majority of bare roots are planted before the hard weather; because of the action of frost on freshly moved ground they will require re-treading again in the spring (Fig. 2.14).

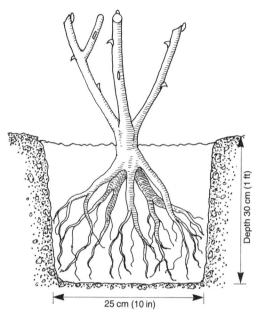

Depth 30 cm (1 ft)

25 cm (10 in)

Fig. 2.14 Planting a rose tree. Care must be taken when planting a rose tree to apply a good measure of planting mixture and firm well in.

Planting climbers and ramblers

There is little to add to the preceding instructions but mention must be made of planting against walls, tree stumps and similar erections. The soil in these situations is usually of poor quality, necessitating the complete replacement of at least $1/2$ cu m ($1/2$ cu yd) of soil. This must be made up by introducing a made-up compost or similar material that has not supported a rose for at least four years (Fig. 2.15).

Planting standards

Mention has already been made of the importance of placing standards so that they are not in an exposed position. The other important factor is making absolutely sure that they are well staked. Dig the hole as if for a bush, but slightly larger. Drive the supporting stake in far enough to allow it just to clear the standard head. This can be achieved by placing the standard against the stake before actually filling in the hole. Make sure that the standard's roots have been dipped in water, place in position, add

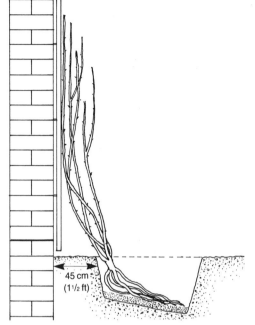

Fig. 2.15 Planting a climber against a wall giving ample distance from wall which is probably supported by deep footings.

Fig. 2.16 Planting a standard.

a large spadeful of planting mixture to envelop the roots and complete the operation by filling up with soil, treading in firmly and finally securing the standard to the stake with tree ties (Fig. 2.16).

How long will a rose tree live?

This is a debatable point which is determined as much by the climate and environment as it is by the variety. Generally speaking, the average life of a rose bush is about 15 years. It can be as short as three or four if it is struggling in a hostile soil or if a freak winter kills it. The commonest cause of fatality is erroneous or gross feeding. If a plant receives too much nitrogen late in the growing season, it will still be soft and sappy when the first frost comes along. This is a recipe for failure.

Moving an old plant

Occasionally there is the requirement to move a much-loved plant to a fresh position in the garden. This can be achieved with reasonable results but attention to a few simple details is important. To get the best results, move the plant in the autumn or early spring, which is the normal period to

move plants anyway. There is no reason, however, why rose plants cannot be moved at other times of the year. The secret of moving plants sucessfully is to reduce the stress caused by such a move. In the autumn or winter this means cutting the plant down to reasonable proportions as if you were pruning it. Never attempt to move an established rose plant without cutting it back first.

The problem can be a little more difficult if it is a climber or rambler. It is a waste of time attempting to move it unless something like 50% of the growth is removed. However, it must be remembered that climbing sports will revert to the bush forms if too much wood is removed and a well-established climbing variety of this type must never be cut down too hard – about 2m (6ft) of wood must be left.

Moving a plant in full growth (i.e. in summer)

This can sometimes be difficult but there is a reasonable chance of success if you follow the above rules. Never attempt to move the plant in its entirety. Cut it down well and,

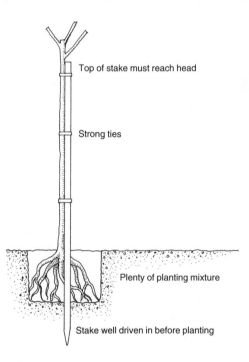

Top of stake must reach head

Strong ties

Plenty of planting mixture

Stake well driven in before planting

in addition, remove all the foliage to reduce the incidence of damage from de-hydration. Never attempt to remove the plant with a root ball as this is a waste of time – it is both time consuming and a clumsy exercise. A well-established plant will develop two types of root, a fibrous situation close to the surface and, as it ages, very coarse tap roots (they used to be called water roots). Inevitably when an old plant is dug up, these will have to be cut through. There is little merit in maintaining a long length of root. They will be torn on lifting and will require trimming with secateurs before re-planting. Some 30cm (1ft) of growth is more than adequate.

On replanting, the bigger trees will probably want staking for a season and of course climbers and ramblers will require tying back up.

Like all newly planted bushes or climbers, a planting mixture is essential and, dependent on the time of year, the replanted rose will require watering for the first month to six weeks – quite heavily in summer.

Rose-sick soil

The greatest problem facing the modern gardener with a limited area to cultivate is replacing tired or worn out soils. This can cause many problems and great expense if not recognized as the most important factor in this day and age.

Agriculturists discovered many years ago that a proper rotation of crops resulted in higher yields but did not know the reason why. Basically what happens is that if a particular genus is grown year after year on the same area, the soil becomes deprived of certain constituents relative to that type of plant. The soil, particularly where roses are concerned, can also work up antibodies which make the re-establishment of new plants very difficult. The irony of the situation is that this does not become apparent until old trees are removed, which may appear very healthy, and replacements are required.

No two experts will ever agree on the direct course of action. Suffice to say that the soil that has supported a rose plant for more than about three years can produce all the symptoms of rose-soil sickness; lack of vigour, an inability to become established etc. This can be solved in several ways. The simplest is on removing the plant(s) to give the soil a rest, which means either planting with another genus or putting down to fallow or grass for a period of about four to five years. This in many instances is completely impossible.

The alternative, therefore, is to replace the soil. Even in a small garden this is not impossible and simply means digging a hole for a new plant slightly bigger than would normally be the case and replacing with soil from another part of the garden that has not supported a rose plant in the last five years. Giving an extra helping of compost or manure will also ease the problem; it is the environment that the new roots are planted in which is the most important criterion. Bigger gardens have grander remedies. If a rose bed is in a prime site, a mechnical digger is the quick solution to remove about $\frac{1}{2}$m (18in) of soil and replace with a completely fresh compost (soil).

There are soil sterilants that can be used in much the same manner in the garden as in a greenhouse; however, they require professional attention and are becoming increasingly frowned upon, as there is some evidence that these chemicals can get into water courses.

Growing roses in association with other plants

Even the most avid rose fanatic must admit that a rosebed is not the most exciting attribute to the garden for long periods in the winter months. The problems are exacerbated by the fact that a well-maintained rose plant must allow ease of access and, of even greater importance, must have plenty of light, particularly in the early spring. However, if those criteria are accepted, then there is a wide variety of plants which will provide much needed colour and will give life to the dullest border.

Bulbs

Bulbs are probably the most natural solution, particularly daffodils. They have the merit of flowering early and with their narrow leaves can be grown with impunity. They are very successful planted in groups or clumps; nevertheless plant well away from the rose bushes. Broad-leaved tulips should not be encouraged as they tend to cut out the light at a critical time for the rose bushes.

Annuals

Annuals are a nuisance and will only be acceptable as edging plants. Bedding plants are a waste of time and are an admission that the rose is not doing its job.

Hedging

Modern garden designers are divided on the merits of low hedging in formal designs. There are two types that are commonly used; the box edging (*Buxus sempervirens* 'Suffructicosa') has been used for many years and the dwarf lavender *Lavandula* 'Munstead' Dwarf) which has many devotees. They are of equal merit and relatively easy to maintain; their use in the garden is very much a matter of personal taste. However, one factor that is consistently ignored is that this type of plant is the perfect shelter for many winged predators who use these accommodating plants to avoid the attention of various sprays. It is as well to give the plants adjacent to the roses the same prophylactic treatment.

Good garden practice with roses is to give a good summer mulch; this will of necessity preclude the use of many plants, particularly of a creeping nature.

Herbaceous borders

In the bigger and more informal planting schemes the rose, particularly as a spectacular shrub, can complement many other plants. Herbaceous borders are rarely planted today as they are considered too labour intensive and many cultivars in this category are difficult to control. They can be very invasive, which is self-defeating when consideration must be given to allowing rose plants plenty of light, particularly early in the growing season. If roses do predominate in this type of planting, consider-

ation must be given to providing bold splashes of colour during the winter months. This can be achieved by using many golden types of conifer, holly and the variegated elaeagnus. Interesting greens can be used with eucalyptus, mahonias, pittosporum and berberis. There are relatively few plants that can provide colour immediately after the first flush in early to midsummer, and the colour-conscious garden designer will do well to plant up varieties to fill this gap.

Clematis

Many of the more vigorous types of ramblers and climbers are natural candidates to support other climbing plants, and clematis must come top in this respect. It is wise to allow the host plants ample opportunity to become established before they are required to support some of the more vigorous types. Many critics of clematis argue that their use precludes good orderly pruning. This can very easily be avoided by selecting some of the late-flowering varieties, which are normally pruned at the same time as their rose counterparts.

Growing roses under glass

Many homes have an area that is particularly well lit and frost proof, such as a conservatory. The more fortunate may even have a greenhouse. The rose is a relatively easy plant under these conditions, provided you understand that heat or a frost-free environment is no substitute for light.

The object of growing roses under glass is to produce bloom out of season. This can be achieved without any expensive heating bills. Some polythene structures (tunnels) have the potential to produce good roses, but the lack of adequate ventilation can be frustrating and can lead to a multitude of disease problems.

Selection of varieties

The majority of modern Hybrid Teas and Floribundas can be grown with some success under glass. Those with a high petallage are generally more successful. Some of the early-flowering Hybrid Teas are best avoided as they will mature too quickly and are short lived. The beginner will be tempted to grow some of the cut-flower varieties more familar in the florist's shop. These may prove a disappointment as they have been bred to produce economic crops under very strict growing regimes.

Growing

The majority of successful rose enthusiasts who 'dabble' in growing a few plants under glass prefer to grow them in containers. Ample space must be given to allow these an adequate root run. Therefore it is advisable to plant them in large 20 l (5gal) containers. This must be done initially in the early autumn to allow the plant to become established.

Alternatively plant a season ahead and allow the plant to develop naturally outside a year before 'forcing', bringing the plants inside in late autumn preferably after an early frost. Prune in mid-winter, slightly harder than is the normal practice. Allow them to grow naturally but slowly in a frost-free environment from this time.

Unless extreme weather conditions prevail do not force; rather keep them as relatively cool as possible and they will produce bloom of the most amazing quality, usually some weeks earlier than is normally expected. Once the early flush of flower is enjoyed, the containers may be put outside to give space for more economic plants. Alternatively, if space allows, plants can be grown *in situ* with much the same culture, but it will of course commit the greenhouse to a one-crop mode which is a terrible waste of facilities.

Whichever method is used, hygiene is of primary importance. Particular care must be taken to scrub out the growing area thoroughly every season and a strict spraying regime must be adhered to, which is discussed in Chapter 8.

CHAPTER 3

Maintenance

A healthy plant is a happy plant. Not a particularly profound statement but remarkably accurate. Even the most unenlightened visitor to a garden will recognize a plant that is not doing well; it will look unhealthy, almost anaemic. Many soils that appear to have difficulty in supporting good plants can, with a modicum of assistance, produce astonishing results. We shall therefore first examine the environment that the rose is growing in and the help we can give to it.

Mulches

A mulch is described as an organic preparation that is used to cover the ground: a rather bland fact which describes an integral part of one of the most important elements of good husbandry. If the earth is allowed to settle down for the season it will naturally slightly open up and establish air holes which will allow a rapid de-hydration of the soil. Many arable farmers, particularly in arid areas, are very conscious of this phenomenon and in the most primitive cultivations will go to extraordinary lengths just to maintain a dust mulch on their crops. To achieve this they will constantly hoe or move the top few inches of soil with horse-drawn implements or hand tools. In extreme situations this simple practice can be used on rose beds.

The constant movement of the soil breaks the surface and maintains the moisture content. In addition to helping the soil in this way, it also helps to maintain a weed-free environment. If something of greater nutritional value can be used, then naturally the plants will benefit to a far greater extent. The bonus of applying a valuable organic cover or mulch is therefore three-fold: the soil is helped to retain moisture, extra food can be made available to the plants, and a weed-free environment is maintained.

Mulches are available in several forms.

Peat

Peat was at one time considered the ideal, but mistakenly so, and is a tremendous waste of the earth's meagre resources. An additional fact is that, contrary to previous assumptions, there is no food value in peat whatsoever, although it is a superb soil conditioner.

Well-rotted manure

The ideal mulch for a rose bed is very well-rotted farmyard manure. Stacked for two or three seasons, it will break down into valuable friable material, and if stacked and turned once or twice will make a very successful medium to spread over the rose bed to a depth of about two or three inches. The one handicap is that if it is not prepared properly it may be full of weed seed and therefore becomes labour intensive to the garden.

Although a good dressing of well-rotted manure (Fig.3.1) applied in late winter or early spring can be called a mulch, it is in fact part of the normal feeding programme of the rose. This can be very helpful and

Fig. 3.1. Most mulches can be applied quite generously but only 5cm (2in) deep for grass cuttings.

beneficial but care must be taken to apply this very early, and will need to be compensated with a balanced fertilizer or else the extra nitrogen will encourage very soft growth, which will invite disease.

Although in theory any old manure obtained in the country should be helpful, in fact there are several sources which must be avoided. Pig manure is very smelly, which makes it unpleasant to handle, and will attract flies with its pestiforous odour. The other medium which will actually damage the young growth is poultry manure. The odours from this material are obnoxious and have much the same effect as fresh pig manure; the fumes given off from the manure burn the lower leaves of the plant. There is little point in having a lovely rose garden which is an attraction to flies and becomes a vast manure heap.

Chopped bark
Very finely chopped bark from timber mills is an excellent substitute. It is absolutely sterile and will eventually break down and contribute to the organic composition of the soil. However, this is also its handicap. Unless the mulch has been properly prepared and partially broken down, the process will be completed on the rose bed, drawing in the available nitrogen in the soil, although eventually food will become available. The strategy, therefore, is to produce processed bark mulch, which has added nutrients, to prevent any initial starvation of the plant. There is always a good selection at most garden centres.

Lawn-mowing cuttings
Gardens with a plentiful supply of lawn-mowing cuttings have a ready-made mulch available, but it must be applied relatively thinly, only about 5cm (2in) deep, and must be fresh. Rotting lawn mowings can be unpleasant and smelly, and they can also be full of weed seed. Another obstacle which is very often overlooked is that there is a danger that weed killer has been used on the lawns and to use this type of material is inviting disaster.

Practitioners of the application of fresh lawn mowing cuttings claim that there is strong evidence to support the theory that the control of black spot can be maintained with this medium.

Alternative mulches are well-rotted leaf mould, garden composts or similar compounds.

Applying mulches
There are very strict criteria for the application of mulches. They must be applied only after the surface of the soil has been cleared of any weed and, probably of greater importance, never apply any mulches if the surface of the soil is dry.

In an an ideal world, a timetable for applying mulches would read something like this:

Late winter – apply well-rotted manure together with an application of sulphate of potash at a rate of 60g per sq m (2oz per sq yd).

Mid-spring – give the rose beds their annual feed of a well-balanced rose fertilizer.

Late spring – thoroughly hoe the surface of the rose beds, removing any weeds, and apply the designated mulch. If lawn mowing cuttings are going to be used, commence this operation now, but be frugal with the amounts and never apply more than 5cm (2in) in depth, at a time.

Never apply mulches after mid-summer. There is bound to be some food value left in this material and the last thing that any gardener wants to do is encourage late growth in the roses, resulting in the production of soft plants to face the winter.

Fertilizers
There are three principal constituents that comprise food for the plant: nitrogen, phosphates and potash. There are also a considerable number of minor chemicals, usually called trace elements, which include iron, magnesium, sulphur and very tiny amounts of manganese, copper, zinc, molybdenum and chlorine. Lime is also an essential ingredient of any good soil, but this is discussed in Chapter 2 (see page 26) and is really a matter to be considered when preparing the rose bed.

Nitrogen

This is always considered the most essential element, but its excessive application is also the most abused process in the garden. Nitrogen must be available to encourage growth in the plant; lack of this vitally important ingredient results in pale, unhealthy looking leaves. An excess results in very dark foliage and very, very soft growth. There are many ways which can be used to apply nitrogen but it is of greater benefit applied in a compound fertilizer.

Phosphorus

Phosphorus helps towards the general promotion of the plant and in fact encourages early growth and conversely helps to produce hard wood to prepare the plant for the rigours of a hard winter. Its most popular form of specialist application is bone meal, which is the ideal mixture to use around the roots of new plants. This, thoroughly mixed with a planting mixture, will encourage rapid root growth and can be obtained at any good garden centre. Care must be taken to use a good quality product which is sold as 'steamed' bone meal. Cheap forms can do a lot of damage to plant life and can spread anthrax. Always use gloves when handling any garden chemical or fertilizer.

Potash

The third constituent which is essential to a plant, but most particularly to the rose, is potash. This will produce a hard plant and counteract the excesses of nitrogen. The wise rose grower will apply this very early in the season to promote general hardiness in the plant.

These three constituents can be applied advantageously as a compound mixture. The ideal proportions for a general *rose* fertilizer are one part of nitrogen, one part of phosphorus and two parts of potash as active ingredients. The trace elements are usually included in a high quality product. The great danger is obtaining these chemicals in some form not specifically for roses. Apart from bone meal in the planting mixture and potash as a late winter feed, never attempt to apply them in any other form than as a compound *rose* fertilizer. A good fertilizer programme, giving a well balanced feed, should be planned meticulously and will give great rewards to the gardener and promote a healthy, disease-resistant plant (Fig. 3.2).

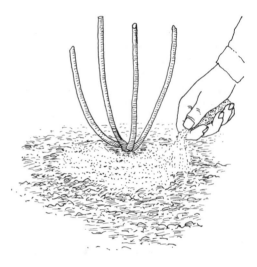

Fig. 3.2 Care must be taken when spreading fertilizer to avoid the crown of the plant.

Feeding timetable

Late winter – apply sulphate of potash.

Mid-spring – give a good general compound rose fertilizer and lightly hoe in before applying a mulch (if it is going to be used).

Early to mid-summer – immediately after the first flush of flower, apply a second dressing of the fertilizer used earlier in the year.

After mid-summer – never apply any plant food.

Weed control

There is an old country saying which says that any garden that does not have weeds will never grow anything else much either. This is perfectly true, but at the same time it must be said that the presence of weeds in a garden is both distracting to the eye and is a great detriment to the plants one wishes to cultivate. We are all well versed in the phrase that 'a weed is a plant in a wrong position'.

The rose is extremely tolerant of competition but nevertheless cannot be expected to give of its best if surrounded by invasive material, whether it be an intrusive neighbouring plant which cuts out the sun or a hungry weed which is depriving the cultivar of the available plant food.

Weeds can be divided into two main groups relative to their method of regeneration.

Perennial weeds

The new owner of a garden, particularly a neglected garden, will want time to identify the weed problem and establish a course of action. Perennial weeds are the most difficult to deal with and eliminating the problem is easier if the rose bed is cleaned before planting commences. In extreme circumstances a *total* weed-killer may have to be applied, but remember that this method of eradication will only have a curative effect if applied when the weed is in full leaf. This means that the operative season is in spring or early autumn, when weeds of any kind are at their most vulnerable.

On open ground the application is a relatively simple process which presents no problems. Policy and fashion changes so quickly in the world of horticulture that it would be a pointless exercise to specify particular chemicals to use. On open ground nevertheless the choice is quite broad and the operative description is 'complete or total weedkiller'. The description on the package or bottle must be quite specific, identifying the particular type of weed which it will eliminate. There are sprays that will kill off just the growth above ground; this may be satisfactory from a cosmetic point of view but is rather a waste of time if roots and rhizomes are the objective.

The particular weeds of a perennial nature which can prove the most difficult to eliminate are the rhizomes (roots) of the perennial grasses. This is the root system which spreads with alarming rapidity and can quite quickly choke a choice plant. Each and every county or country has their own colloquial name – couch grass, scutch and creeping grass are just a sample. The other types of perennial weed which can cause problems are the intrusive nettles, convolvulus, thistles, willow herb and ground elder. These types of plant, like the grass family, are difficult to elimi-nate from an established rose bed and are much easier to dispose of *before* any planting commences.

Care must be taken when applying weed killers, to confine the application to specific areas and to apply accurately with the recommended proportions. Never to spray on windy days and particularly with total weed killers, not to walk on choice lawns with traces of the spray on your boots. The result can be some embarrassing and ugly footprints.

Annual weeds

This type of weed can in many ways be rather more intrusive but much easier to cope with. Before the age of weed killers farmers would control this problem by summer fallowing. This in effect means leaving the fields empty of crops for the summer to allow a germination of the more obtrusive annual weeds. Some form of cultivation was practised during the growing season to kill and exhaust the soil of its unwelcome harvest. This method of giving the ground a 'rest' is now considered wasteful, but was at the time a very good and important part of agricultural husbandry. Apart from the purely physical exercise of hoeing the weeds, other methods can be used to prevent the more intrusive invaders.

The chemical used is what we call a 'pre-emergent' weed killer. The application of the spray on the soil surface prevents the production of a weed crop. The spray is applied very evenly to the soil which has recently been cultivated (hoed), and the active chemical prevents germination by being absorbed in the first 5-8cm (2-3in) and thereby producing a tier of treated soil which the weeds cannot germinate in. Because its effectiveness is caused by killing any germinating seeds, and because this chemical is only absorbed by the top layer of soil, any active ingredient cannot possibly affect established plants i.e. roses or, for that matter, perennial weeds.

This may all appear an ideal solution in an ideal world. Unfortunately the application of pre-emergent weed killers has produced a problem that was inconceivable when they were first used. This is the development of weed killer-resistant strains of various garden invaders. They are principally members of the wild pansy, the annual chickweed and fat-hen families. This is a somewhat tedious phenomenon which can only be corrected by using newer and more modern types of chemical.

There are two seasons in the year when the application of pre-emergent weed killers can be at their most effective. The first is early spring, which will give the best results. Having cleaned up the rose beds after pruning but *before* the application of a mulch, apply evenly when the soil conditions are appropriate – that is, when the soil is damp but clear of weeds. The second season is autumn, when a further application may be made after the rose bed has been tidied up for the winter. This will prevent any early winter germination.

It is important to remember that the principle of this type of weed control is that the soil absorbs the chemical to produce a sterile non-productive barrier to small germinating plants. Once applied therefore, the surface of the soil must not be disturbed or else this barrier is broken and it will all be a waste of time.

Types of weed killer

Some weed killers work through the action of the chemical in the soil and therefore may have to be watered in. The problem here is that it is not uncommon for a considerable time to elapse before further cultivation can be proceeded with. Contact weed killers are therefore a better solution, but if applied to the wrong plant can be very demoralizing.

Problems do occur when perennial weeds have become intrusive in an established rose bed. This is a nightmare and very difficult to rectify. The only really practical solution is to prepare a solution of a selected weed killer and apply on each individual weed with a paint brush or similar piece of equipment. Never attempt to spray individual weeds in an established bed, as the risk of drift is much too great. The process of painting on a weed killer may sound laborious but can be very effec-

tive. Thistles and the *Convolvulus* genus, which are difficult to eliminate, can easily be controlled by this method.

Applying weed killer

It cannot be stressed too strongly that at all times care must be taken to apply any garden spray accurately and evenly; it therefore pays handsomely to practise the application using plain water on an open surface, preferably on a strip of concrete where results can be observed quite graphically. It is surprising to learn how spreading 4 l (1gal) of water evenly over 10sq m (10sq yd) of soil can be such an exacting exercise (Fig. 3.3).

Finally, it is a sad reflection on gardeners that the majority of damage done in the garden is caused by absent-mindedness. Always thoroughly wash out all watering cans and spraying equipment which have been used to apply weed killer. A solution of hot soda water is quite the best, and never use weed killer equipment for any other purpose in the garden (Fig. 3.4).

Hoeing

Understandably some gardeners are reluctant to apply any form of chemical to the soil and even the most avid weed killer practitioner will admit that occasionally the the excessive use of some of these chemicals has resulted in the adulteration of

Fig. 3.3 This lance (boom) will fit the majority of watering cans to enable an even distribution of a soluble weed killer.

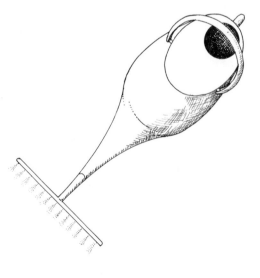

that was commonly used was the dog rose (*R. canina*), which gave a first quality plant but unfortunately in the wild has the tendency to propagate itself, producing underground stems or more colloquially 'runners' or suckers. This may be satisfactory to produce an effective hedge, but when this same variety is domesticated and used as a stock, it can be a positive menace. The production of this subterranean growth, which is what it is, can occur with alarming rapidity and will be a positive nuisance to the rose it is intended to support.

Apart from weed control and disease prevention, the elimination of this unwanted growth is the main problem in the rose garden. This occurs on rose bushes that have been propagated on a stock in two forms. The roots will produce long lateral growths and appear sometimes some distance away from the main plant. At other times, seemingly wild roses appear growing up through the middle of the cultivar and appear to come from the centre of the plant.

The first problem, therefore, is the identification of these suckers. It was once generally assumed that all you had to do was count the number of leaflets on a suspect growth; if there were seven it was a sucker, if only five it was the cultivar. Unfortunately, this is a somewhat misleading assumption because many of the older ramblers and climbers (and shrubs) have seven leaflets, and so too do many modern Ground Cover and Patio roses. The conclusion can fairly be made that all suckers do have seven leaves and it is a reasonable observation to say that they are probably thornier, spindlier and the colour of the leaves is much paler. However, there are spindly, pale-coloured, seven-leaved rose varieties and so to the less experienced gardener the only really certain way of identifying a sucker is to look at the part of the stock from which it grows, relative to the rest of the plant. A sucker can only grow from below the position where the plant was propagated. Any new growth from above this budding point must be the cultivar; any growth from below this point has got to be a sucker (Fig.3.5).

Fig. 3.4 Weedkiller damage can be caused by wind drift of agricultural sprays or wind drift of lawn weedkiller spray.

water courses. Hoeing is the only non-chemical method effective for controlling weeds. This can be a simple and therapeutic exercise if the weeds are controlled at a very early stage when they are at their most vulnerable. The light Dutch hoe is quite the most suitable tool for this purpose. This can only of course be really effective to control annual weeds, and has little effect on perennials; indeed it may even persuade them to grow stronger. The only remedy here is to fork out the offending invader. If this is the only solution always remember that loosened soil, particularly if it is close to rose plants, must be firmly trodden again. As we shall discuss in the next section, loose soil encourages suckers.

Suckers and suckering

As explained later in Chapter 6, the majority of roses grown today are in effect two quite distinct rose types; the root system is an appropriate stock that has the potential to give, supply and support the other half of the plant, the cultivar, which with the development of the modern rose has lost its ability to make its own root system in a satisfactory manner. Originally the root stock

Fig. 3.5
A graphic
illustration of a
typical sucker.

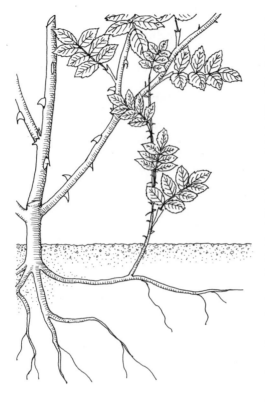

Controlling suckers

If the offending sucker is allowed to become established, it will in time become so strong that the cultivar will deteriorate to the point where it will eventually die. The elimination of this unwanted growth is therefore paramount.

The type of sucker which appears some distance from the plant is probably the easiest to control. Simply ease the ground with a fork and gently pull up the sucker; this may well travel back some distance to the root where it started out life. If the stem is traced back successfully, then a good strong tug will remove the unwanted extraneous growth, but also remove the position from which it grew. This may be a somewhat alarming process to describe but it is certainly the most satisfactory. Never cut a sucker off at ground level, as this will simply remove the top growth and encourage proliferation of more branches below ground level.

The more difficult situation to deal with is the sucker that appears growing up through the middle of the plant. This may mean removing some of the soil to reveal the position from which it is growing. The remedy here is to gouge out the unwanted growth, which may mean removing a portion of the plant along with it. Tearing it out in this instance is not advised as there is the likelihood that some of the fabric may be left to encourage further invasive and unwanted material.

There are certain precautions that can be taken to prevent the incidence of suckers. Loose planting is probably the cause of the majority of suckers occurring. Therefore tread in all newly planted material very firmly. The other precaution to take is never to loosen an established plant by the insidious practice that some gardeners have of forking or pricking the rose bed over in the spring to present a beautiful appearance – very effective cosmetically but a disaster to the plants. Not only does it loosen the root system, which again encourages suckers, but there is also a great danger that the roots very close to the surface, the fibrous roots on which a plant relies to absorb plant food, will be destroyed. A vigorous hoeing is all that is required.

Stocks that do not produce suckers

The preceding paragraphs have dealt quite explicitly with the very real problems that occur with rose suckers. Very fortunately, in recent years much research has gone into testing various types of stock that do not share the proclivity of *R. canina* to 'do its own thing'.

The greatest advance has been made with the widespread adoption by the rose nurseries of the stock *R. laxa*. Of somewhat obscure origin, there is no doubt that rose bushes budded on this stock are not so prone to the problems of suckers. There are other factors to consider, such as that *R. laxa* has to be budded very early in the season and there is a considerable incidence of rust. But the fact remains that roses grown on *R. laxa* are almost free of suckers and the plant produced is of a very high quality.

There are other stocks that are being tested and some are in production. Unfortunately the majority have frailties which cannot usefully produce a trouble-free plant; for instance some will only grow on light soil; others are unsatisfactory with certain colour types.

Roses grown on their own roots

There is now a realization within the close association of professional breeders that the very best new roses will only be successful if they can be grown on their roots. Towards this goal it is significant that the newest Patio roses and Ground Covers have this potential, which will inevitably lead to the demise of rose-stock growers. It must be remembered that there are many plants that naturally produce suckers if purchased as 'grown on their own roots', particularly some of the Old Garden Roses and the rugosas. If the fortunate customers can obtain this type of plant, then they must remember that 'suckers' from these are in fact the true cultivar.

Suckers on standards

Very few rosarians will admit that a standard stem is by origin a sucker, or the result of a cutting which can produce suckers. The control of this extra growth has to be controlled in two respects. The suckers that grow from the root system which has already been discussed, and the lateral growth that appears on the stem itself. Although controlled on the nursery, they can proliferate in the garden. They appear as side shoots and can be identified by growing straight from the stem or barrel of the standard. The secret of controlling these nuisances is to remove them in the very young bud stage when they are easily rubbed off (Fig. 3.6). If they are allowed to grow too big, a very sharp knife or secateurs have to be used. Do not tear or pull them off, it will only lead to a fatal skinning of the bark and an advantageous point of entry for cankers.

Dead heading

Once a stem has produced a flower its existence on the plant becomes superfluous, unless of course it is being grown on for its value to produce a hip which will enhance the garden in the autumn. This extraneous material must therefore be eliminated and the problem arises, as to how much or what length of stem must be removed. It is also important to remember that by judicious dead heading, the plant can be persuaded to produce further flushes of bloom during the season and well on into the autumn.

The simple exercise of dead heading does give us the opportunity to discuss the functions of the plant. The root, which we are conversant with, will provide sustenance for the continuous growth of the tree. Likewise the leaf is important as it provides the mechanism to convert the energy forces of the sun, through the exercise of photosynthesis, to provide energy for the plant to survive. A defoliated (leafless) plant will soon deteriorate and die. The bloom, which is the end product from the gardener's point of view, is the means whereby the plant will perpetuate itself by the simple expediency of producing a seed head. The energy of the plant is then devoted to producing growth to sustain flower production and a harvest of hips. If, after the first flush of flower, the plant can

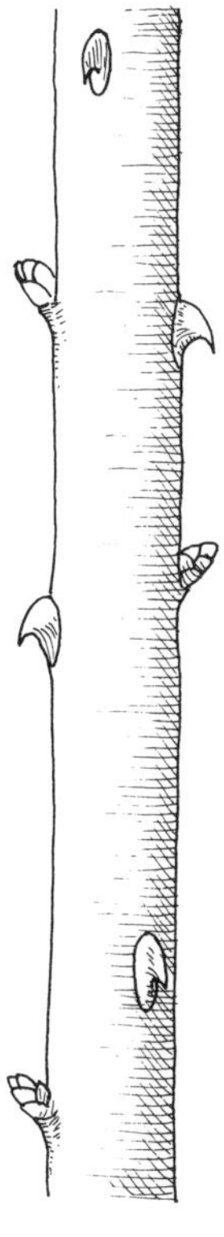

Fig. 3.6 Suckers on a standard stem are easily rubbed off.

be persuaded to produce further flower, then the garden and the gardener receives a bonus. The object of dead heading is to dissuade the plant from developing a seed head which absorbs much of the plant's energy. For the busy gardener the simplest method is to literally snap off the head – an exercise that is not too demanding. Care must be taken to collect the broken heads littering up the garden which, apart from looking untidy, will encourage disease. With the more dedicated rose lover, a thorough dead heading is mandatory.

The flowering stem of most roses is composed of a series of healthy leaves with growth buds culminating in a flower head. Serious dead heading means removing the old flower together with, and this is most important, the first three or four leaves (eyes) (Fig. 3.7). This is because the eyes immediately below the flower head are rarely productive or capable of producing good quality bloom. A good pair of light secateurs is most important. Again, when this extraneous growth is removed, have a container handy to collect the detritus and avoid the build up of garden debris.

It cannot be stressed too strongly that a variety that is in the garden for its display of hips must never be dead headed.

In certain circumstances there may be a call to remove more of the stem than just the topmost substandard eyes. This is fully discussed under the separate subject of summer pruning (see page 52).

Other important areas of maintenance

The rose plant, as the gardener will appreciate, is an extremely tough individual which with a modicum of attention will give great pleasure. There are one or two further ways we can help to make a better display, including giving it adequate support. Climbers and ramblers will require support, which is discussed elsewhere, but this must be maintained. The most useful material to tie up loose branches is soft string. This may have a relatively short life span but is kinder to the plant than strips of wire or plastic. Both are very abrasive to the plant and may well cut into the stems; the first warning of this is a supposedly strong branch which has snapped off in an autumn gale. On inspection the offending piece of plastic tie has bitten into the stem and weakened it. Soft string is inexpensive and kinder to the fabric of the plant.

Staking

Supporting a standard is vitally important and calls for some research into the best material to use. The strongest is without a doubt a steel bar or pipe, but unfortunately neither of these is visually attractive. However there is no doubt that it is the best material to use. Rose stems do not however appreciate being tied to cold metal. This can be avoided by using a substantial tree tie to distance the plant from the metal (Fig.3.8). This does mean using plastic and therefore it will be of benefit to wrap some hessian strip round the stem before wrapping the tie to the plant.

An alternative method of staking is to use a wooden stake. Many garden centres stock totally inadequate sized pieces of timber produced from soft wood and very thin. The ideal stake to support a good standard

Fig. 3.7
Deadheading. Remove an old flowering stem with a minimum of three leaves.

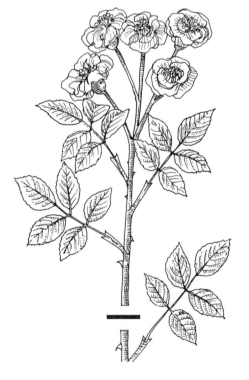

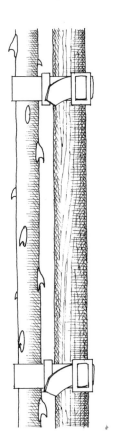

by which the plant can absorb the benefits of manure and fertilizers; and tap roots, a rather misleading expression, or water roots which is the old country expression. Either way the fibrous system finds the food and the stronger roots the water. The danger with watering is that the fine balance between these two root systems can easily be disturbed. Modern practice suggests that there are very good reasons in a dry spring to water newly planted rose stocks, particularly when using *R. laxa* which has to be budded so early. It is vital to obtain a good-sized plant as quickly as possible.

The frequent use of water in an established rose bed is quite a different matter and is to be avoided. There is every reason, however, to support the practice of irrigating freshly planted containerized roses; indeed it is vital. Any plant that has led an existence for any length of time in a pot or container, with adequate food and water, must have a terrible shock to be planted into the alien environment of a rose bed in the late spring or early summer. Heavy watering in these circumstances is absolutely essential. Bare-root trees that have been planted conventionally in the autumn with the added benefit of a good planting mixture, rarely require any help unless the spring has been very dry, when some short term watering may be necessary.

There is another occasion when watering is essential. Sometimes a newly planted climbing or rambling rose will remain inordinately long in a seemingly moribund condition. The fabric of the tree appears healthy but there is no apparent movement or show of fresh growth. If this condition persists it can be 'woken up'. This means, in effect, giving it copious amounts of water in heavy doses. Three or four bucketfuls, or a lengthy period with the hose pipe, will have an immediate and beneficial result. Do not persist with this treatment; two or three times at ten-day intervals will be more than adequate. Established plants, if heavily watered for a lengthy period during the summer months, will put on gross soft growth which will not harden up enough to face the rigours of a severe winter.

head should be teak or a similar hard wood which is straight grained (no knots) and approximately 4cm × 4cm (1½ × 1½ins) square. The stakes must be well treated with a wood preservative; as many of these treatments are quite toxic to plant life they should be given time to be absorbed before the stake is used. This may mean preparing material well in advance and it is always wise to have one or two stakes in reserve.

Watering

The root system of the rose is quite extensive but easily disrupted if interfered with. The roots can in a short space of time (two years) penetrate to a depth of 1.8m (6ft), provided of course that there is an amenable environment to grow into.

The fabric of the roots can easily be identified by their size and divided into two types: a fibrous root system which is relatively close to the surface and is the channel

Fig. 3.9 An old plastic bag filled with dry wood shavings – a method of protecting rose-plants in severe climates.

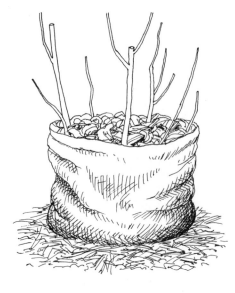

Preparing for winter

A simple exercise in late autumn is to check the rose garden in an attempt to forestall needless damage in the winter weather. Some modern varieties have an annoying habit of producing very large shoots quite late on. Any late show of bloom is most welcome but it might be at the expense of the stability of the plant. It is therefore wise to trim extraneous material and reduce the size of plants in order to reduce the windage; there is also the satisfaction of having a trimmed and tidy rose bed to face the winter months. Do not, particularly in areas that have a relatively mild winter, cut down the plant too much and throw it into growth that will inevitably be cut off in the spring. Although Chapter 4 covers the care and maintenance of climbers, it is well to remember here that young strong canes of this type of plant must at all times be secured as they progress. Many gardeners are unable to spare much time in the autumn, but it is wise nevertheless to secure these long branches in order to avoid damage during the winter storms. This will ensure that there is plenty of young wood for the spring pruning and maintenance.

Protection from frost

Many gardeners who live in areas where the climate is hostile to roses will go to some considerable lengths to protect their plants from the damage caused by extreme cold. The simplest method is to grow a very hard plant and never feed it after mid-summer; there is also ample evidence to suggest that excessive nitrogen can make a plant more vulnerable.

Plants can also be protected from the ravages of winter by covering them with some form of material. The simplest way is to cut plants down to about 45cm (1ft 6in) and cover them with large upturned plant pots or containers which have been lightly stuffed with loose straw or coarse wood shavings. An alternative is to produce a cage around each plant (fine wire and old fertilizer bags have been used) and fill again with straw or wood shavings (Fig. 3.9). At the end of the winter the whole edifice is demolished, removed, and normally pruning and cultivation commences.

Standards which are more vulnerable, can be protected by wrapping the head in a 'dolly' of straw (Fig. 3.10). A more common practice is to gently bend them over to ground level (the soil may have to be removed to one side to do this) and the plant is then completely covered with straw and hessian.

Protecting climbers and ramblers is virtually impossible.

Fig. 3.10 A method of covering a standard for protection against frost damage.

Maintenance timetable

The climate in many parts of the world is extremely predictable but elsewhere can be frustrating. However much gardeners would like to think otherwise, the following operations are very much determined by the prevailing weather conditions and although seasonal advice can be given, it must be accepted that latitude must be allowed according to the vagaries of nature. This timetable is suggested with the advice that early winter is assumed to be December in the northern hemisphere and mid-summer is July. Similarly June is early winter in the southern hemisphere and mid-summer is January (a full conversion chart is given at the front of this book).

Early winter – In colder climes, plants that require protection must be wrapped up by now. Planting can still proceed provided the soil is not waterlogged.

Mid-winter – Check garden tools and order rose fertilizer for the spring and summer. Standard ties and stakes may want checking, renewing or strengthening.

Late winter – Apply sulphate of potash, check spray equipment. Head back budded stocks. In the greenhouse the final pruning must be completed and a minimum temperature of 5°C (40°F) must be established.

Early spring – Take delivery of farmyard manure to stack for autumn planting. Commence pruning bush roses. Finish spring planting of bare-root roses. Clean up beds, apply pre-emergent weed killer and treat with a good organic mulch. Plant stocks for budding. Greenhouse temperature should be a minimum of 10°C (50°F).

Mid-spring – The first application of a comprehensive rose fertilizer is appropriate now.

Late spring – Keep a watchful eye for aphids and other winged invaders. Spray if necessary. Weeds may now make their unwelcome appearance. A light hoe is very efficient, pleasant to work with and very effective on warm dry days.

Early summer – Blind shoots may appear, caused by late spring frosts. Cut them down by about half their length. Species (wild) roses are beginning to flower. Visit gardens when they should look at their best. Start budding. Clean out greenhouse.

Mid-summer – The fruits of your endeavours are there to be enjoyed. Watch for further invasion of aphids. Visit gardens and flower shows to see the newest introductions. This is the latest time to apply a boost of fertilizer to encourage an autumn flush of flower. Budding should be completed by now.

Late summer – Carefully survey the garden to mark out positions and plans for autumn planting and order new plants from specialist rose nurseries. Mark out and prepare new rose beds. Remove any older fading plants now.

Early autumn – Many climbers and ramblers are still in full production making much new growth. Gently tie these shoots up to prevent damage in the wind. Scrub out, disinfect and sterilize the greenhouse.

Mid-autumn – Commence planting new purchases and move any established plants to their new positions. Cut back established bush roses by a third to reduce wind damage. If possible prune ramblers and climbers now.

Late autumn – Complete planting and protect plants from frost in cold climates.

CHAPTER 4

Pruning

The cultivation of the rose is a relatively simple operation with which most enthusiasts are very conversant and quite lucid until they are asked to discuss the merits of various methods of pruning. At this point, explanations become either involved to the point of obscurity, or simplistic leading to neglect. Pruning is defined as the cutting away of surplus branches to encourage a regeneration of new growth. Why then is there so much confusion, particularly in instructions to new gardeners on the merits of pruning? To understand the situation, one must understand the development of the modern rose.

It can generally be assumed that wild (species) roses do not require pruning in the true sense of the word as they are the product of the natural selection of nature's bountiful production of plants. As the genus *Rosa* became more and more sophisticated through artificial selection and cultivation, a cult became established that any animal or plant could be manipulated to improve its productivity. The rose became an object to prize, as one would a piece of garden furniture, for supplying colour and plant form to enhance the garden. Little heed was taken of the necessity to employ a skill to obtain this object, and in modern phraseology it became 'labour intensive'. The demand for bigger and better blooms on a more vigorous plant had a higher priority than the ease of cultivation. A modern Hybrid Tea must be pruned annually, even if it is just hacking it down by half in order that it will give a good return the following season. Significantly, many modern types of rose that are being bred as landscaping material, particularly the Ground covers and Shrubs, require very little maintenance and 'thrive on neglect'.

The problems of pruning occur only in climates where the weather is sufficiently mild enough to allow overwintering wood to survive. Very cold climates totally eliminate this problem. Frost cuts the plant down to ground level or snow level and the spring operation is reduced to cutting off the damaged wood. The result, provided the remainder of the plant is alive, is the most astonishing and uninhibited growth, producing bloom in an extraordinarily short space of time.

Tools

The one and only criterion that any pruning tool can be assessed by is as an efficient instrument capable of producing a quality cut. This is paramount.

Secateurs

Today secateurs are a precision tool that obtain a degree of excellence unheard of 50 years ago. Until recently it was considered that a strong sharp pruning knife was the only instrument which could confidently be expected to give good service. The modern secateur, sometimes called two-bladed or side-by-side secateurs (Fig. 4.1*a*), will give a good clean cut, very close to the quality of the knife. Usually made of a high grade steel, they can be obtained in a number of sizes to fit any person, to accommodate left or right-handed users, and have a robustness suited to the use that they can be expected to render. The best quality also have self-locking devices to ensure ease of movement, and replaceable blades. Such is the perfection that has been produced that even professionals can expect a good pair to last for many seasons. They must be well cared for, and scrubbed clean regularly to prevent the spread of virus diseases through the sap. Small carborundum stones will keep a good edge to the blade, and a frequent oiling will keep the action and the spring in good working order.

One word of warning: old dead wood,

the sort that will accumulate on big neglected stumps and branches, will very quickly destroy the edge of a finely honed blade. It is therefore advisable to keep an old pair of secateurs or a good small saw handy to remove this sort of material. There are other models available, principally the one-bladed type (Fig. 4.1*b*) that possesses one cutting blade which cuts down on to a flat anvil. The subsequent wound on the plant is a sad sight, with much bruised fabric and torn tissue.

Saws

First thoughts would suggest that a saw cannot possibly be necessary in the rose garden. However, some big branches and old stumps have to be removed occasionally and, as we have already discussed, secateurs are not appropriate in this instance. There are pruning saws available, varying in size from the smallest with a 15cm (6in) retractable blade, to the very largest which have a close affinity to a Gurkha *kukri* (Fig. 4.2*b*). There is a wide selection in most garden shops, suitable for every size of operation. The one you choose must be of good quality, sharp, and possess a thinnish blade to make it useful in confined spaces.

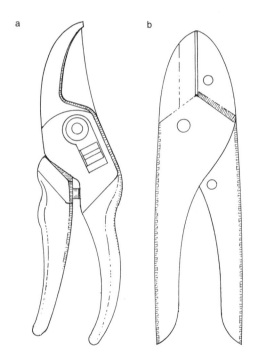

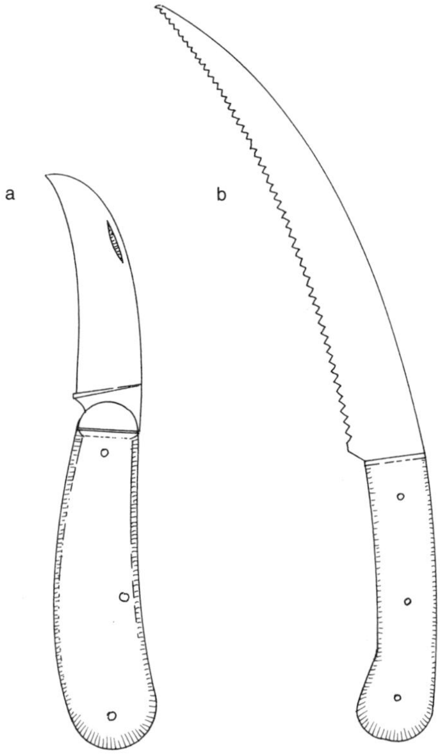

Fig. 4.1 Secateurs (*Left*). (*a*) Two bladed or side-by-side. (*b*) One bladed or anvil.

Knives

There are many types of knife and a true rose grower will always feel undressed if he does not have some form of cutting implement in his pocket. For pruning purposes, a heavy type is recommended with a broad 8cm (3in) blade. A wood handle that is comfortable to hold is essential (Fig. 4.2*a*) Considerable skill is required to use one of these knives, which is the reason why there was a myth established that an expert had to be called in to do the pruning. Fortunately the modern type of side by side secateurs has solved that problem.

Fig. 4.2 (*Right*). (*a*) A good pruning knife. (*b*) Pruning saw.

Long-handled pruners

Many gardeners prefer to remove bigger branches with a powerful cutting tool, variously called long arms or duck-bills. They are in effect a simple pair of secateurs with long arms. Some are very light and ineffectual, others robust to the point that a big human frame and strong limbs are a necessity (Fig.4.3*a*). Their advantage is that the removal of the bigger branches does not require quite so much dexterity and your back does not come under so much stress.

Gloves

Good strong gloves are essential to handle prunings. There is a tremendous choice available and generally the better quality productions using top quality hides are preferable to cheap rubber or plastic (Fig. 4.3*b*). Some operatives prefer to use tools without gloves, finding that they can handle implements more efficiently. A word of warning however; it is advisable, particularly in some areas where tetanus is prevalent, to wear gloves at all times, and have the necessary injections to prevent complications.

Fig. 4.3 (*Left*).
(*a*) Long
handled pruners.
(*b*) Gloves.

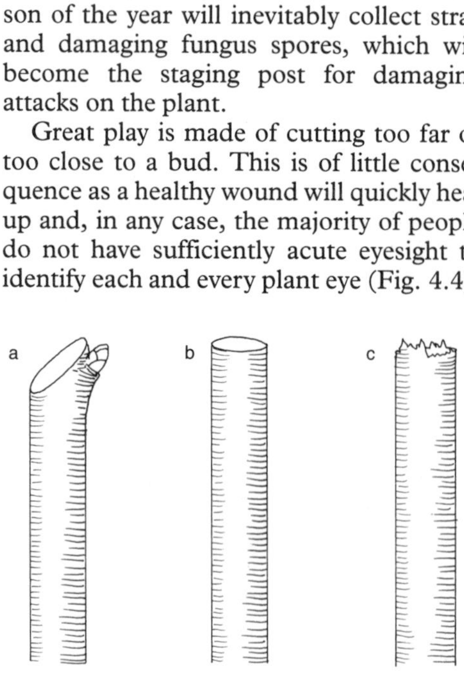

**Fig. 4.4 Pruning
cuts** (*Right*).
(*a*) Perfect
– on the slant.
(*b*) Straight across
– a host to fungus
spores.
(*c*) Jagged –
an invitation to
die back.

Extras

Two other pieces of equipment will help: small *carborundum stones* to touch up or sharpen cutting edges, and *kneeling pads* which can help if branches have to be dealt with at ground level. Finally always have a plentiful supply of *soft string* to tie up branches.

Quality of cut

Most articles and books on pruning have the statutory illustration showing the good, the bad and the indifferent method of cutting, but very rarely the reason. Obviously a good clean cut is absolutely essential if for no other reason than that there is a certain satisfaction in a job well done. A rough cut will leave damaged fabric which is an open invitation to invasive spores that will eventually cause die-back.

The cut should always be at a slant to the stem. There are three reasons for this. First, the growth cells on a woody stem are longitudinal and can be cut with greater ease on their length than straight across; secondly, an elongated cut will always heal up far more satisfactorily; and thirdly, if the cut is slanted it is not prone to the collection of droplets of water which in the season of the year will inevitably collect stray and damaging fungus spores, which will become the staging post for damaging attacks on the plant.

Great play is made of cutting too far or too close to a bud. This is of little consequence as a healthy wound will quickly heal up and, in any case, the majority of people do not have sufficiently acute eyesight to identify each and every plant eye (Fig. 4.4).

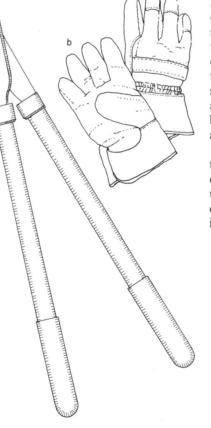

When to prune

The correct time to prune is a matter of some complexity to many gardeners which can cause more trouble to the rose lover than the rose. Rule one is never cut rose material when it is in a frozen state. This will lead to bruised and damaged wood. This does not mean that roses cannot be pruned in frosty weather, far from it. Provided the fabric of the plant is not in a frozen condition, it can be cut at any time. This means in effect waiting for the plant to thaw and not worrying about the cold weather the following night.

As to the season, this can vary relative to the area where the roses are grown. Generally, pruning of bush roses should be done in early spring, just as the sap starts to run and the stem buds start to swell. Height above sea level has probably a greater control over this matter than latitude. Sometimes, even in relatively warm areas, some cold valleys can be identified and it is wise to be prudent. Great damage can be caused by pruning too early. This may cause young important growth to start too early, which in some areas will become a hostage to fortune when late spring frosts will burn up very susceptible growth. Autumn pruning is advised in some areas but this is only possible if there is no danger of warm winter spells. Conversely, in an area which does not usually expect cold winters, there can be a proliferation of young growth far too early in a conventional season and there is a reluctance to remove this growth which will give cause to very light pruning. This is a mistake. This very early green growth in all probability has suffered from several relatively cold nights and will produce blind shoots.

Methods of pruning

There are currently three schools of thought on pruning methods, which bear some relation to what the gardener expects from a plant.

The avidly keen exhibitor will concentrate on the production of high quality bloom to the exclusion of any other criteria. Plants are vigorously cut down very hard; only the strongest and healthiest stems are allowed to develop and the result is eminently satisfactory on the show bench.

The decorative or amenity horticulturist will concentrate on two things: a highly productive plant which can be maintained as disease free as the plant will allow, and will give flower production which will be as continuous as possible.

Finally, there is the home gardener who manages to produce fabulous results with only very casual pruning methods. Such is the prodigious resilience of the rose that each and every method has its adherents and in most circumstances the results are successful (Fig. 4.5).

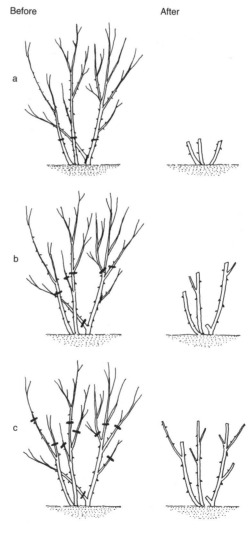

Before   After

a

b

c

Fig. 4.5 Types of pruning.
(*a*) *Hard* for the production of exhibitions blooms.
(*b*) *Moderate* for a display in the ordinary garden.
(*c*) *Light* for vigorous bush varieties and modern recurrent flowering shrubs.

The principles of pruning a modern rose bush

As a bush rose matures, it will accumulate a quantity of wood on an annual basis. The majority of this wood is there to produce flower and once it has fulfilled this function becomes obsolete. The simple purpose of pruning is to remove this redundant wood in order that the plant can concentrate on producing further flushes of flower. A plant, however, must be allowed to develop, extending its root system and accumulating a structure to support bigger and better blooms. The priority then is to reduce the spent flowering stems in the summer, thereby preventing the development of seed heads; this is called dead heading. In the following spring the plant is further reduced, more of the old flowering wood is removed, and the plant is able to go into flower production again.

As the bush ages it will accumulate a considerable fabric that is non-productive in the form of twiggy material, old stumps and a certain amount of dead wood (Fig. 4.6a). The dead wood usually occurs as a result of the fabric not maturing before the rigours of the winter set in. In the simplest terms, therefore, pruning a bush rose can be separated into two readily identifiable actions. Firstly, remove the unwanted twigs and stumps (Fig. 4.6b); in many respects this is of greater importance than deciding how much of the remainder to cut out. Once the plant has been cleaned up there remains the removal of the remaining growth (Fig. 4.6c).

The question most frequently asked is 'how far down should this type of growth be removed'? Probably the most constructive method of establishing this is to divide the total plant into three parts. The first third is normally removed in the autumn to reduce the windage on the fabric of the tree (see page 42); the remaining portion of the plant is then pruned by half in the early spring. These are relatively rough proportions, ignoring the number of eyes on a stem which many commentators have a fixation on counting, but it does allow for a reasonable size plant to develop over the years. This advice is given irrespective of the variety or height of the plant and is equally appropriate when discussing a Hybrid Tea or a Floribunda. The breeding of these two types is so close that the old adage that Floribundas were always pruned much longer than their large-flowered cousins is totally ignored.

Fig. 4.6 Pruning an established bush.
(*a*) A five-year old bush (Hybrid Tea or Floribunda) full of dead and scrubby wood. (*b*) The same plant cleaned up. The most important stage in pruning. (*c*) The properly pruned plant.

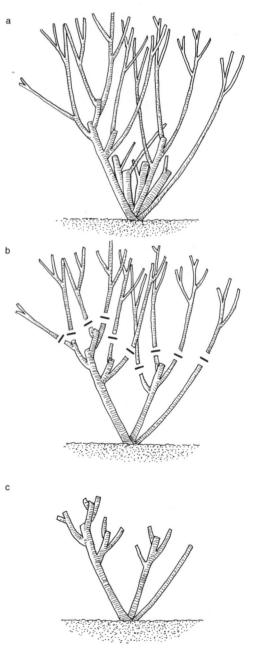

The Royal
National Rose
Society's Gardens
at St. Albans are a
mecca for every
lover of roses and
display a riot of
colour in the
summer months.

The rose garden at Mottisfont Abbey in Hampshire is a feast of old garden roses which are imaginatively planted in a tranquil ambience.

A typical rose nursery scene in mid-summer. Visitors are always welcome to walk round the rose fields at this time of the year.

Rose borders can provide colour for a long period with a back drop of topiary at the RNRS, St. Albans gardens.

'Rosa Glauca' (*R. rubrifolia*) has the most astonishing deep purple foliage and stems with a multitude of bright scarlet hips in the autumn.

'Canary Bird' is one of the earliest species (wild) roses to flower and will mature into a perfect shrub with bright yellow flowers and fern-like foliage.

R. moyesii 'Geranium' is the most prolific member of this fecund family with an abundance of flask-shaped scarlet hips.

'Ferdinand Pichard', a Hybrid Perpetual with the stripes that are an occasional feature with certain lines of breeding.

'Mme. Isaac Pereire' has the heaviest fragrance of the Old Garden roses with a profusion of large blooms and a long flowering period.

'Roger Lambelin' is pure Victoriana. The novelty value of this variety is well worth the extra effort to grow it.

'Charles de Mills' has the most fascinating flower form of all the Gallicas and epitomizes the legendary beauty of the Old Garden forms.

Pruning a newly planted rose (bare root)

The most neglected rose plant in the garden is the newly planted bush rose. Everybody assumes that because it arrives in a somewhat abbreviated condition, once planted it will require no further attention for at least one season. This is quite wrong. In general terms a new bush rose tree will be reduced to about 40cm (15in) before despatch. These plants must be pruned in their first spring to about 15cm (6in) (Fig. 4.7). This is imperative and does not relate to the eventual height of the plant in

Many gardeners are unable to plant bare-root trees until the spring because of inhospitable soil conditions; if they are received unpruned at this time of the year, there is no reason why they should not be pruned *before* they are planted (Fig. 4.9*a,b*) – a simple exercise which is much kinder to the back.

Containerized roses should be pruned well before delivery is taken of them and therefore do not present a problem.

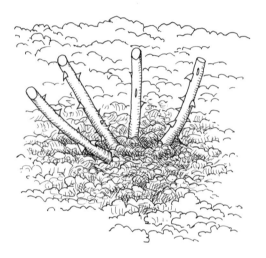

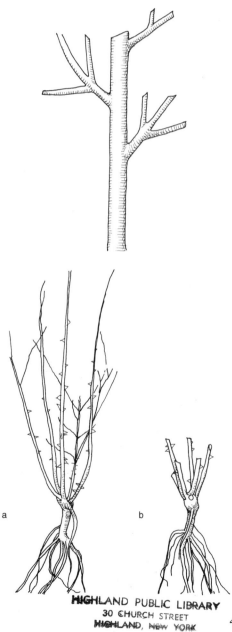

later life. Every opportunity must be given to a freshly planted bush to establish a root system and this can be achieved by reducing the top growth as it attempts to become established.

As with all freshly planted additions to the garden, particularly if they have experienced a frosty winter, the soil will need retreading. New Patios and Miniatures must receive the same treatment in proportion. Shrubs, Climbers and Ramblers, and Ground covers will arrive already cut down much harder, relatively speaking, than bushes, and will require no additional attention for at least the first season, apart from removing any little bits of die-back. Maiden standard bush roses will require pruning back by about two thirds, but shrub and weeping standards are better left alone (Fig. 4.8).

Fig. 4.7 (*Left*) A maiden rose bush pruned in its first spring in the garden.

Fig. 4.8 (*Right*) A maiden standard pruned in its first spring.

a   b

Fig. 4.9 Pruning a young plant in the spring before planting. This of course only relates to bush roses (Hybrid Teas, Floribundas, Patio and Miniature roses).

**Fig. 4.10
Pruning a
recurrent
climber,
'Golden
Showers'.**
(*a*) Before
pruning.
(*b*) After.
(*c*) The following
summer.

Pruning recurrent-flowering climbers and ramblers

As explained in other chapters, the modern climber or rambler has the potential to produce flower throughout the summer and autumn. In essence this means that it is not dependent on only the previous year's growth but on new wood as it is produced. The aim of pruning this type of plant is to preserve as much wood as possible and therefore there is not the necessity to differentiate between the various types or functions of the tree's fabric. The emphasis therefore is on simply dead heading the plant and possibly re-positioning new branches that have evolved in the previous twelve months (Fig. 4.10*a,b,c*). Eventually the plant will accumulate big ugly unproductive lengths or stumps, and these will have to be eliminated but not very frequently.

Pruning summer-flowering climbers and ramblers

This type of plant has the potential to grow to quite astonishing heights and breadths and if trained properly has the capability to produce an abundant display of flower, but sadly for only the high summer season. It is completely dependent on the amount of young growth that it is capable of producing and supporting. The finest quality bloom will always be produced on the wood made during the previous growing season. It is imperative that all new wood must be carefully secured as it grows. For the best results, contrary to the advice given on spring pruning for bush roses, most climbers and ramblers will give a better show when pruned and repositioned in the autumn. Apart from the end result, there is also the advantage that old wood is easier to identify at that time of year and furthermore, if the plant is re-tied before the winter storms, it should stand a better chance of survival.

Quite the best way to tackle these big plants is the bold approach. Cut all the strings supporting the growth and gently allow the plant to fall back from its supports. Having freed all the plant material, check and if necessary renew any wires,

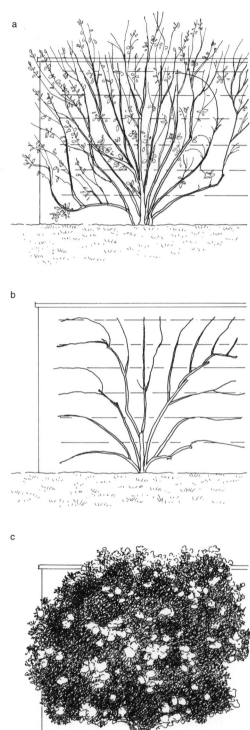

a

b

c

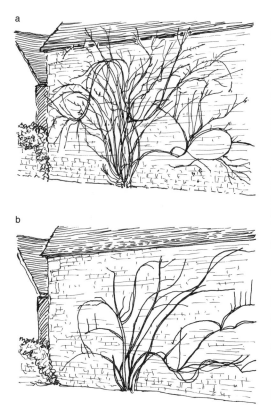

vine eyes, poles and any other supports. Then proceed carefully to thin out the growth of the plant, preserving any new stems in their entirety and trimming back older stems. This means, in effect, cutting back the flowering wood, easily identified on most varieties by short lengths of stems with exhausted flower heads, to about 8cm (3in). Once the thinning has been completed, proceed to tie the canes back up one at a time to get a good spread. Vigorous ramblers require most of the old wood to be removed (Fig. 4.11*a,b*). Many of the fast-growing climbers can receive much the same treatment.

As a climber or rambler ages, it will get the annoying habit of only producing flower at the end of the branches. This in effect means out of reach, usually under the eaves of the house, where it has an adverse affect on guttering. Cutting off this growth at that point will only aggravate the situation and encourage further destruction of the property. There is a simple solution to

this problem. Even the longest and oldest branches can be induced to produce bloom farther down the stem by putting stress on the erring stems. Simply bend them over in the fashion of an arc (Fig. 4.12*a,b*). This can be done with as many branches as are available and induces not only an astonishing show of flower, but new growth from the base of the plant.

Inevitably there are vigorous varieties whose existence in the garden is dependent on their ability to climb or ramble through trees. These are best encouraged by ample feeding and allowed to grow naturally. They may benefit from dead-heading if this can be achieved.

Finally there are a few climbers that will only produce flower if an accumulation of wood is encouraged. The Banksian rose and 'Kiftsgate' come into this category. On no account cut these plants about; it will only result in an increased production of coarse non-flowering wood.

Fig. 4.11 Pruning a neglected rambler. (*a*) Before pruning. (*b*) After.

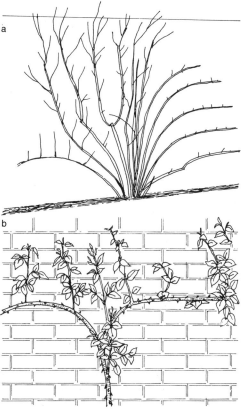

Fig. 4.12 Principles of pruning climbers and ramblers. (*a*) Method of bending branches to encourage flowering breaks. (*b*) New growth occurring where stress has been made on branches.

Fig. 4.13 Pruning a Modern Shrub rose.

Pruning Old Garden Roses (summer flowering)

These plants, as the definition infers, flower on the wood produced the previous year. This in effect means that if they are cut about, their flower production will be considerably reduced. The moral of this story is therefore to shape the plant if absolutely necessary, dead head if feasible, and leave well alone. Extra growth can, however, be encouraged by the simple expedient of *summer pruning*. Once the shrubs have finished flowering in mid-summer simply cut out about half of the flowering branches in their entirety. This will throw the plant into a new surge of young growth, particularly if a little extra rose food is given. The new canes will sometimes appear upright, but will bend over beautifully with the weight of flower the following season.

Pruning recurrent-flowering shrub roses

These are a mixed bunch, including the Bourbons, Hybrid Musks and the stronger-growing Hybrid Perpetuals. The method here is to treat them as overgrown Floribundas. Heavily dead head them during the summer months to encourage a good shape to the plant, and in the following spring do much the same with the remaining branches and cut out the occasional worn out stem (Fig. 4.13*a,b*).

Pruning Miniatures and Patios

These are all treated in much the same way as the shorter-growing bushes. This means a Miniature usually expected to flower at about 23–30cm (9–12in) should be cut down to 10cm (4in). This type of plant will collect a tremendous amount of rubbish in the base, which must be removed (a tedious business).

Patios and short-growing Floribundas are treated in a similar method, allowing more wood to remain. A Patio usually expected to grow to 45cm (18in) should be reduced to 15cm (6in).

Roses that should never be pruned

The zest for pruning can become compul-

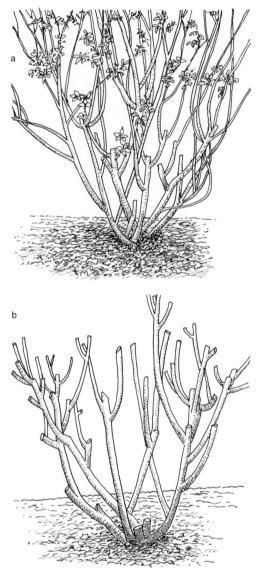

a

b

sive and much damage is done wielding the secateurs in a thoughtless manner on a considerable number of varieties that require little or no attention at all. These are principally the wild roses (species) which must be allowed to grow in a perfectly natural manner or they will lose their individuality and charm. The young growths, in particular, must never be shortened. If this happens the result will be an ugly and stunted plant. If the species appears to be getting too big or out of hand the correct approach is to thin by cutting out some of the older stems close to the base of the plant. The *rugosa* family, equally, are much happier when allowed to grow naturally, to make a reasonably shaped shrub (see *rugosas* A-Z on page 109). The concept of the newest Ground covers is a plant that is trouble-free and makes little demand on maintenance costs. The newer and more vigorous types should never be cut about. The tidy gardener may feel that dead heading is in order but this is probably a mistake. Many of them are producing some fine displays of autumnal foliage and hips.

Pruning standards

As a general rule it can be safely assumed that Hybrid Tea and Floribunda varieties grown on standards should be treated in much the same manner as their bush counterparts. The shape of these, however, is of prime consideration and care must be taken to present a rounded appearance to the pruned head (Fig. 4.14*a,b,c*). This may mean cutting the leading upright shoots down slightly harder than the side growths. Patio and Miniature standards must be pruned hard. Weeping standards are prob-

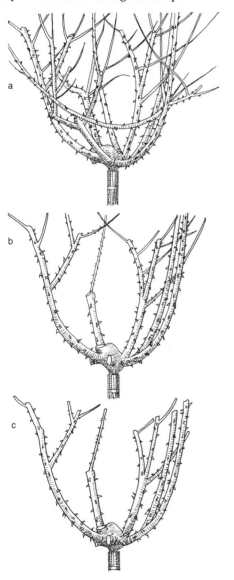

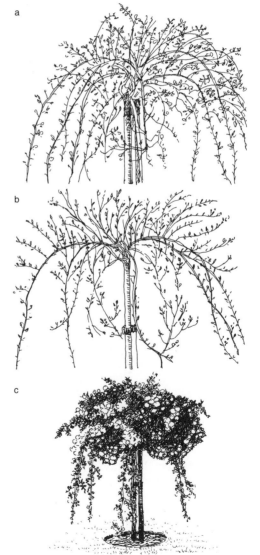

Fig. 4.14 Pruning an established bush standard (*Left*). (*a*) Before pruning check the stake and ties. (*b*) Thin out old twiggy wood and very old branches. (*c*) Cut back on to strong healthy wood.

Fig. 4.15 Pruning a weeping standard, 'Dorothy Perkins' (*Right*). (*a*) A full head in the autumn. (*b*) Pruned. Note no shoots have been shortened, just thinned. (*c*) In full flower the following summer.

Fig. 4.16
Pruning a shrub standard, 'The Fairy'.
(*a*) Before pruning. Note no dead heading has been done.
(*b*) Thinned.
(*c*) Cut back.
NB This particular plant has been cut back very hard.
(*d*) The following summer.

ably better for being left strictly alone, apart from cutting out some of the ageing flower shoots (Fig. 4.15*a,b,c*). Shrub standards, of whatever mode, must be allowed to grow naturally and require little treatment other than dead heading. They will sometimes accumulate scrubby growth in the head which must be removed (Fig. 4.16*a,b,c,d*).

Pruning in very hot climates

Some roses, particularly the modern Hybrid Teas and Floribundas, can enjoy considerable differences in temperature, but where it is constantly warm the growth can only be limited by watering, or the lack of it. Probably the biggest shock to rose lovers who attempt to grow their favourite flower in warmer regions is to discover that conventional pruning is probably best forgotten. Plants grown in these conditions do not like being cut about and are far better left to their own devices and occasionally dead headed. This will inevitably result in some plants growing to an astonishing size, but so be it. Never attempt to cut down any plants in very hot periods but rather wait until the commencement of cooler wet seasons. Apart from the Chinas, very few of the Old roses will grow in heat unless they receive the benefit of a good winter rest.

Pruning in the greenhouse

Most plants grown for pleasure in the greenhouse receive the benefit of a rest outside during the summer and autumn and are brought back in during the mid-autumn period. Apart from being tidied up and re-potted if necessary, they must not be pruned immediately. They are far better left to acclimatize to the changed environment. Calculating the time from pruning to flower production can be done with remarkable accuracy and is more dependent on the amount of sunlight they will receive. As a general rule, using little or no heat an early-flowering Hybrid Tea will take about 12 weeks from time of pruning to flowering. Some late developers can however progress much more slowly and 14-16 weeks is not uncommon. When pruning bush varieties, only the very best

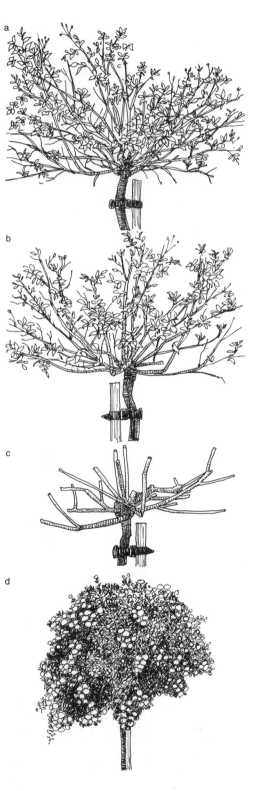

a

b

c

d

and strongest shoots should remain but, generally speaking, apart from freshly potted-up varieties, they will be better for good lengths left on the tree, up to about 1m (3ft).

Continental pruning

Recently experiments have been conducted to encourage many modern cultivars to develop as shrubs and some remarkable results have been achieved. Basically these have been very successful in countries or provinces that have the benefit of reasonably cold winters, short springs and hot summers. The plants have been very lightly pruned or trimmed to allow them to develop as shrubs. The results have been very pleasing and are beginning to make hybridists aware that the rose was originally a shrub and can be cultivated as such. The experiments have centred very much on old ramblers and climbers, Old Garden roses, modern Floribundas and Ground covers. Because of the necessity to build up plants by this style of cultivation, they will accumulate a considerable quantity of old growth. A rigid spraying programme therefore is essential.

Pruning experiments in the UK

A series of demonstrations is currently being conducted at the Royal National Rose Society's gardens at St. Albans in Hertfordshire. The theory is that, provided the plant is reduced by about half, literally chopped off with hedge clippers or other similar implements, the plant should be garden worthy. The initial results have been quite staggering, with a higher flower rate than could normally be expected, in contrast with the plants alongside that have been conventionally pruned. There is evidence to support the theory that old wood left on the plant, provided it is not moribund, can contribute and has some potential to provide extra impetus to the plant. These demonstrations are at an early stage and are relevant to a few selected varieties. In previous experiments with this method of pruning in other parts of the country the results were very similar for a few years, but eventually the plants broke down under the burden of the old wood they were carrying. The present series of experiments are at this moment very salutory and suggest that some very modern varieties are tougher and more adaptable than their forebears.

CHAPTER 5

Diseases and Predators

It is in the way of nature that all flora and fauna are bedevilled by enemies which appear to preclude a quiet and orderly existence. Sometimes these enemies play a great part in the balance of nature, but on occasions they are an impediment we can all do without. Garden plants are no strangers to this phenomenon and the rose is not unique in having various enemies, the majority of which can be controlled. It must be realized that garden roses, particularly modern varieties, are grown in an alien environment where diseases are prevalent and predators are positively encouraged. Creating a garden where all plants lead a carefree and trouble-free existence is the ideal.

Diseases

The range of diseases that effect the genus *Rosa*, with the exception of the viruses, have a fungal origin. Apart from some of the rusts they are not instantly fatal and with a certain amount of good husbandry all can be contained. However, before discussing the ailments of the rose, it would be appropriate to discuss the conditions under which they are encouraged. The rapid explosion of new varieties has certainly widened the choice of colour and habit of growth, unfortunately not always selected for their resistance to disease. The situation has been exacerbated by the use of varieties derived from *Rosa foetida*. The introduction of this line of breeding certainly widened the colour range, with the deep yellows and bi-colours. Unfortunately, these parents are pre-disposed to black spot. Similarly the Bourbons, and more particularly one of their parents, the Gallicas, introduced a propensity to mildew.

Rose breeders, although conscious of these frailties, were so keen to use the new found breeding lines to produce new colours, that they accepted these unfortunate handicaps. There is now a great deal of time and money being invested to rid the rose of some of these problems, but in the meantime we have to accept that some of even the most popular varieties are prone to black spot and mildew.

This is also aggravated by some of the older roses preferring different types of soil. In short an inappropriate disease-prone variety grown in a hostile soil can quickly deteriorate, whereas the same cultivar in happier conditions can excel. This is the reason why older catalogues would describe a variety as 'prone to such and such a disease' in a heavy (or light) soil. With some varieties this had little effect on sales and could in certain circumstances attract customers.

Disease-prone varieties

It is almost impossible to determine breeding lines that can bequeath a resistance to disease. Suffice to say that modern rose trials are extremely stringent and the majority of award-winning varieties would never have been successful if they did not have a good health record.

Environments which encourage disease

Fungus diseases are usually spread in environments which suffer from extremes of temperature, humidity and drought: they can also find host plants where the fertilizer regimes have been abused. Thus some varieties appear to be prone to mildew if the roots are subject to drought; conversely, mildew appears to be rife when there are warm moist atmospheres and cold nights. Black spot appears to be more prevalent if plants have received too much nitrogenous fertilizer or an unbalanced diet. All things being equal, therefore, a healthy, well fed plant has a greater chance to resist the attentions of aggressive disease spores.

56

Fresh new soils, a high degree of cultivation and proper maintenance are a great advantage. The rose appreciates and can offer greater resistance if there is ample available potash applied at the rate of 60g to the square metre (2oz to to the square yard). The application of a good balanced *rose* fertilizer, which always has a slightly higher proportion of potash than ordinary garden fertilizers, is an absolute must. Never plant any variety where there is a suspicion of disease without the benefit of plenty of air between the plants. Finally, it is flying in the face of fate to expect plants to remain healthy if planted close to notorious disease-prone cultivars. A classic example of this is an old rambler like 'Dorothy Perkins', which appears to attract mildew from the day it is planted. Some varieties appear to be prone to black spot in certain soils; only experience will determine these frail varieties, but if discovered they are best removed before creating too much damage to the rest of the rose garden.

Garden designs can determine the health of many plants. With roses, a draught created by badly situated hedges or rather unfortunate gaps can wreak havoc.

Precautions

On the principle that prevention is better than cure, we can recommend some fundamental precautions to reduce the incidence of disease in the garden. Establish that the soil has been properly prepared (see Chapter 2) with a good application of organic compost, or a basic garden fertilizer if this is unobtainable. It might be as well to check on the pH of the soil (see Chapter 2); the ideal is 6.5 as roses prefer an acid rather than an alkaline soil. Endeavour to give your established rose plants a basic application of potash in late winter and always use a fertilizer recommended for roses in the spring and summer. Do not pick up from a 'farmer friend' some cheap agricultural fertilizer which is almost certain to contain too much nitrogen.

Always keep rose beds clean of garden rubbish and reduce the old and dead wood on plants to a minimum – they are a perfect haven for every fungus spore to overwinter

and be released at the most propitious time in the summer.

Do not be a hostage to fortune and grow varieties which are notoriously prone to disease. In conclusion, remember that the average very modern rose variety has been subjected to extremely vigorous trials and, compared to its very recent ancestors (some 50 years ago), is a remarkably resilient plant. However it is totally unfair to expect miracles from plants immediately adjacent to an 'accident prone' variety.

Common rose diseases

Black spot (*Diplocarpon rosae*)

Big black spots appearing on leaves in the summer and autumn are the most obvious symptom of this pernicious ailment. They are usually round but can sometimes appear jagged (Fig. 5.1). As the leaves age they will sometimes turn yellow and fall off.

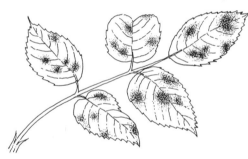

Fig. 5.1
Blackspot.

The persistent defoliation is the root cause of all the problems associated with this disease. No rose plant can survive and be productive if it is constantly losing its leaves, which are the source of much sustenance and essential to its existence.

Apart from spraying, which at best can only be a prevention not a cure, there are certain fundamental precautions to observe. Primarily the health of the rose must be maintained by balanced feeding; secondly, as with mildew, keep old and dead wood to a minimum which must be removed and burnt.

Some gardeners have their own patent precautions ranging from applying local nostrums to mulching with fresh lawn mowings, which was very fashionable many years ago but fell out of favour after one or two fatal results using weed-killer-treated material. There is no reason to discourage this practice, provided that a pure product can be obtained and a mulch is applied to a maximum depth of 5cm (2in).

Modern thinking suggests that a good spray with a systemic fungicide immediately pruning has been completed, is very effective. The important point to remember is that the spray must cover the whole plant and the surface of the soil immediately round the plant. As a postscript, it is worth mentioning that spots can appear on early leaf growth; this must not be confused with black spot and is more often than not a symptom of mineral deficiencies (see end of chapter).

Cankers

There are various cankers which can attack a rose plant. Their origin is usually damaged rose tissue caused by broken stems, or wounds resulting from the heavy-handed use of garden tools. The infected tissue assumes a swollen appearance and eventually rotting will spread around the stem and the plant collapses. Fortunately this is not a very common occurrence and can be controlled by the application of grafting wax or a similar product on the wound at the time of the accident. Material that has been damaged by canker must be burnt and not shredded or composted (Fig. 5.2).

Fig. 5.2 Canker.

Downy or Black mildew (Peronospora sparsa)

This is an insidious disease that has only recently become prevalent in Europe, although antipodean rose growers have been familiar with it for years. The symptoms are irregular brown or purplish spots on the surface of the leaves and (under a microscope) the appearance of small white fungal tufts on the underside. To the inexperienced gardener, the first symptoms are a slight leaf curl and a rapid defoliation. This has become prevalent in greenhouse crops, particularly in polythene tunnels. There is mounting evidence that plants that have been propagated by tissue culture (micro-propagation) are the source of these infestations.

Although conscientious spraying with a good systemic has some control, complete wetting of the foliage underneath as well as on top is essential. The defoliation of the plant, which is usually the first symptom that is apparent to most gardeners, cannot be prevented. The greatest control is achieved by growing in a well ventilated environment and if in a greenhouse, to grow plants which have been propagated by more conventional methods.

Powdery mildew (Sphaerotheca pannosa var. rosae)

This appears as a blue-grey mould on young rose leaves from the middle of the spring onwards, with a preference for late summer and early autumn. Lush tender growth is most vulnerable, which implies that plants that have received too much nitrogen are at the greatest risk. Removal or destruction of infected material is a rather pointless exercise. Some varieties can be infected at the neck of a flower bud which can deter its development and one or two varieties can suffer from infection in the bloom. There is evidence to suppose that 'balling', that is the rotting of emerging flower buds, is accelerated by the presence of mildew in the plant.

The one consolation with this particular type of mildew is that it does not impair the performance of the plant and, if controlled by judicious spraying, will not deter the future productivity of the plant (Fig. 5.3).

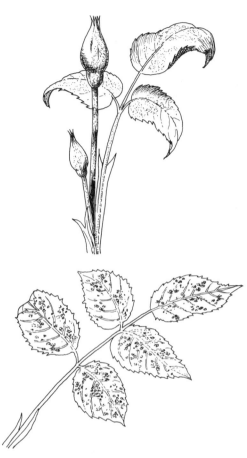

Rose Rust (Phragmidium mucronatum)
A destructive disease which can in some areas kill a plant *in situ* in a short space of time (a few weeks). The symptoms can easily be identified by the appearance of tiny orange red pustules which turn black as the season progresses (Fig. 5.4). The leaves look sickly and turn yellow, eventually falling off. Rust, which was endemic to the West Country of the UK has now become common to many other areas as a direct result of the Clean Air Act. There is much confusion with this disease as there is a presumption that it can spread from other genera. This is totally erroneous, indeed impossible. To add to the confusion there is a presumption that it will spread from the stock that the majority of roses are grown on, *R. laxa*. This again is totally wrong. The *laxa* rust is quite a different strain. There was an assumption that the only remedy

was to remove the affected plants or at the very least cut them back hard. Fortunately this rather drastic remedy has now been discarded although it would be wise to remove any badly diseased plants if they appear prone year after year. A very new spray, curiously enough developed to contain rust on economic crops, has proved very efficacious.

Viruses
There are three forms of virus which can be identified and which work to the detriment of the plant. They have one characteristic in common: they are spread through infected sap.

Rose mosaic
The symptoms are easy to identify; yellow and white spots start at the centre of a leaf and spread outwards but can also appear as bright yellow veins or wavy lines (Fig. 5.5*a*).

Yellow mosaic
Similar in appearance to the previous malady, but the spots and patches of yellow are bigger and brighter (Fig. 5.5*b*).

Fig. 5.3 Mildew.

Fig. 5.4 Rust.

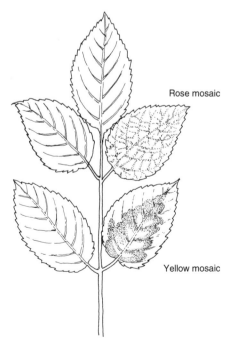

Rose mosaic

Yellow mosaic

Fig. 5.5 Viruses.

Rose wilt

Identified by malformation and bending of very young rose stems, discolouration of leaves and the foliage dying back. Dirty budding knives and secateurs are the obvious carriers, although unwashed hands can be a source and instances have occurred through the attention of insects that exist on rose sap such as aphids. The remedies are both precautionary and prophylactic. Always clean knives and secateurs regularly, and certainly after handling possibly infected material.

Virus-infected leaves can look very pretty and in some genera is considered an attraction. This is not so with roses. However, misleading symptoms can appear in mid-spring in situations where pre-emergent weed killers have been applied too enthusiastically; this can induce veining of the leaves with a yellow pattern. It is therefore wise to allow this phenomenon to disappear before the plant health officer inspects the plants.

Remedies

Surgical spirit is quite the most successful detergent. A good propagator will clean down his tools and hands regularly, and certainly between handling varieties. Cleaning secateurs when any rose material is handled should be a matter of habit. Experiments have proved that infected varieties can be cleaned up by subjecting them to heat in a greenhouse, thereby producing healthy propagating material. Viruses, although producing unsightly leaves, rarely affect plants although there can be a deterioration of vigour over a long period. Infected crops can be disbarred by plant inspectors who will not grant export licences to the suspect varieties.

Chemical sprays

There is a whole range of chemicals which are now recommended to control the attacks of fungus diseases. They can be conveniently divided into two groups relating to their function. There are the sprays that are a simple form of protection and will kill invading spores. These, if applied, are only efficient while they remain on the

plant. Thus a heavy thunderstorm will remove this form of protection and a respray will be necessary.

The more modern sprays are what we call systemics: that means that, when applied, they are absorbed by the plant and give resistance to invading spores. They are very efficient but on some varieties have a short life span of active resistance. They can also become addictive to a plant and a cessation of a spray programme can invite even heavier infestations. The remedy is to alternate formulations and prevent this peculiar phenomenon.

Application of sprays

The majority of modern sprays can only be efficient if properly applied and a complete wetting of the entire leaf structure is achieved. Care must be taken to mix chemicals very precisely, paying strict attention to the maker's instructions on the bottle or package. Never transfer chemicals to an unmarked container and never keep any prepared and used sprays overnight. The wise gardener will always wear rubber gloves when handling concentrates, and also wear a rudimentary face mask. Before mixing sprays always thoroughly clean the containers; hot soapy soda water is quite the best. Repeat after use in exactly the same way.

Sprayers

There are a multitude of appliances and the choice is very much a personal one. Small

Fig. 5.6 Spraying appliances. There are many types of sprayers of varying capacities and thoroughness of action.

Ready-to-use trigger sprayer

Refillable trigger sprayer

Compression sprayer

Hose-end dilutor

Recommended chemicals against pests and diseases

There are a great many chemicals available to control pests and diseases. Some formulations, although having the same basic contents, are distributed under a variety of trade names which can be very confusing. This list therefore suggests active ingredients which are published on all containers and does not attempt to differentiate between one constituent and another.

The control of cankers and viruses is mentioned in the text.

There are now available a range of sprays that are in effect cocktails. These can be very efficient and avoid endless mixing. The majority are mixtures of compatible fungicides and aphicides, together with a bonus of a good foliar feed.

Black spot	Benomyl	*Powdery mildew*	Benomyl
	Bupirimate		Cycloheximide
	Carbendazim		Dodemorph
	Chlorothalonil		Thiophanate-Methyl
	Fenarimol		Triforine
	Mancozeb	*Rust*	Mancozeb
	Maneb		Myclobutanil
	Theophanate-Methyl		Oxycarboxin
	Triforine		Propiconazole
Downy mildew	Mancozeb		Triforine

numbers can be dealt with using hand sprays, but bigger quantities will require knap-sack applicators and some form of mechanical equipment (Fig. 5.6). Efficient spraying is only achieved if the correct proportions of recommended chemicals are applied. This means calibrating the equipment. Practise using plain water; this is time well spent. Where instructions insist on quantities per sq m/yd/hectare/acre, again practise. An efficient operative will rehearse even the most familiar equipment at the beginning of each season and if wise will repeat at some convenient time later on. Never use weed control equipment to apply fungicides or *vice versa*.

Mineral Deficiencies

Although technically this particular problem should not appear here, many symptoms are mistakenly interpreted as diseases. In effect what occurs is that a rose is dependent on a balanced food regime; if this for any reason is not available to the plant, apart from obvious lack of vigour the leaves assume discolourations relevant to the mineral that is missing. This can occur in one of two ways; either an essential ingredient is completely absent or alternatively the presence of a dominant mineral can 'lock up' the availability of essential nutrients.

Iron deficiency

This is perhaps a slightly misleading title, as very few soils are in fact deficient in iron. However, the presence of limestone or chalk in the soil can lock up the availability of iron which, although is only required as a trace element, is essential to the wellbeing of the rose. In extreme cases, the leaves assume a chlorotic appearance; that is the young leaves have a bleached or yellow colour (Fig. 5.7a).

There are many suggested remedies, involving the application of very expensive foliar feeds known as chelates or sequestrates. The manufacturer's instructions must be strictly adhered to but in very severe malfunctions the import of a more balanced soil may be necessary. Alternatively, with the benefit of neighbours' experiences, grow only the varieties which appear to thrive in your immediate neighbourhood.

Fig. 5.7 Mineral deficiencies.

(*a*) *Iron shortage.* Leaves with large yellow areas. Young leaves are worst affected, turning almost entirely yellow.

(*b*) *Manganese shortage.* Leaves with yellow bands between veins. Oldest leaves are worse affected.

(*c*) *Nitrogen shortage.* Young leaves small and pale green. Red spots sometimes develop and leaf fall is early. Stems are stunted and weak.

(*d*) *Phosphate shortage.* Young leaves small and dark green, with purplish tints on underside. Leaf fall is early and stems stunted and weak.

(*e*) *Potash shortage.* Young leaves reddish, mature leaves green with brown, brittle margins. Flowers are small. This is common on sandy soils.

(*f*) *Magnesium shortage.* Leaves pale at centre, with dead areas close to midrib. Oldest leaves are worst affected and leaf fall is early.

Manganese deficiency

The symptoms are yellow bands appearing between the veins of leaves and can occur in much the same environment as iron deficiency, but also on highly organic soils (peats) and marshy ground.

The remedy is similar, using sequestrates. Although widespread, it does not have anything like the same devastating effect (Fig. 5.7*b*).

Nitrogen deficiency

A not-uncommon complaint, particularly on 'hungry' soils (that is, very light sandy soils which have not been given any fertilizers, particularly of an organic nature). The plants appear stunted, lacking vigour, and red spots sometimes appear.

The remedy is very simple, involving copious applications of manure or garden compost in late winter and/or a balanced rose fertilizer in the early spring (Fig. 5.7*c*).

Phosphate deficiency

The syptoms of this shortage can look very pretty, with the young leaves becoming blue-green with dull purple tints, and the plant can appear stunted.

A well-balanced fertilizer will very quickly remedy the situation (Fig. 5.7*d*).

Potash deficiency

The young leaves assume a reddish tinge and the edges turn brittle and brown, a phenomenon that can sometimes appear on plants grown in very light soils.

As potash is an essential component of good rose fertilizers, there should be no problem with its application (Fig. 5.7*e*).

Magnesium deficiency

The leaves appear pale at the centre with dead areas and is prevalent in older foliage. Not a very great nuisance and a light application of ground limestone can solve the problem for the following season (Fig. 5.7*f*).

Predators

It is a waste of time to complain about the voracious appetites of a wide variety of creatures who consider that a succulent rose has been specifically planted to provide them with ample nutrition during the summer months. Unfortunately breeders have not been successful in producing aphid-free or rabbit-proof roses. Notwithstanding this, there are some elementary precautions which can be taken to reduce the incidence of visits.

The greatest control the gardener has is to reduce possible overnight or seasonal lodgings for predators. In practice this means restricting such cover very close to rose beds. Small lavender hedges and garden features of a similar nature should be kept to a minimum. The alternative is very simple – in the course of seasonal spraying allow time and material to give these garden extras a good drenching. The number of pests which can attack a rose is quite extensive, but because the major damage is caused by only a handful of miscreants we shall deal with them first.

Common rose pests

Rose aphids
The greenfly/blackfly populations are determined by climatic conditions and the availability of plant material to feed on. In the rose world their main diet is the sap on very young green shoots and buds, and heavy infestations can cause great damage in early summer (Fig. 5.8). Very little can be done to deter their invasions, although some authorities suggest that too much nitrogen can encourage very soft growth and give these aphids a mean advantage. There is now ample evidence to suggest that aphids, together with other predators who exist on plant sap, are instrumental in the spread of virus diseases. Control with modern systemic sprays is very effective and makes life much easier in the garden. Nevertheless there are still many old-fashioned remedies to this problem, ranging from a good drench of soapy water to the efficacy of praying for a good thunderstorm, which appears to clean up plants rapidly.

Most gardeners have little spare time and the quickest solution to the aphid problem is to spray with a cocktail of recommended chemicals, the principle being that advantage should be taken when spraying of coping with all problems. Aphid control is at its most effective if applied in early summer, which is an appropriate time to give the first fungicide of the season. There are now rose spray mixtures which contain both an aphicide, a fungicide and a foliar feed, and these are very efficient.

Aphids

Fig. 5.8 Aphids (greenfly).

It is worth taking note of the fact that greenfly have a slightly peculiar sex life; without going into too much detail, it means that females can produce young indefinitely, without the attention of males; furthermore, some aphicides will kill pregnant females but not their young. In effect this means that, except when using some of the very modern sprays, an application twice within 10 days is essential.

Sundry beetles
Much can be said about the myriads of beetles, wasps and flies which inhabit a garden and regard rose leaves as convenient food and lodgings. Their visits are infrequent and are more of a nuisance than a positive menace to the rose plants. The Japanese beetle in North America can be especially intrusive.

Physical control can be exercised and in the worst cases control with an insecticide will give good results.

Sundry caterpillars

There are whole hosts of caterpillars, apart from those already discussed, which regard young rose leaves as a succulent repast. In the majority of cases they are not particularly invasive, but can be intrusive if allowed to take hold. Many gardeners take delight in picking off the offending creatures and disposing of them; however, if an invasion occurs, spraying may become a necessity. Care must be taken to use a specific which will kill caterpillars. Many aphicides do not have these properties.

Leaf-rolling sawfly

This particular pest can only be controlled if its peculiar life cycle is understood. The symptoms are quite dramatic, almost surreal. In early summer rose leaves assume an extraordinary pinnate shape, rolling up tight in a perpendicular mode (Fig. 5.9). The leaves will eventually turn yellow and fall off. Fortunately the apparent damage has no lasting effect.

The fly emerges from the rose bed in a hot late spring day and crawls up to the soft foliage of the chosen plant, where it eventually deposits its eggs. In the process the fly apparently injects the leaf with a chemical which causes the rolling effect, thereby protecting the maturing larvae. The cycle is completed with the larvae returning to the soil where it pupates and waits for the next season. The fly is occasionally spread by the wind but normally occurs in old rose gardens where there is better opportunity for a population to build up.

In theory the control is manifested by the removal of the curled leaves, but in fact the caterpillars have usually already emerged before the malformed leaf becomes apparent – rather like shutting the stable door after the horse has bolted. The answer is to trap the offending insect somewhere on its journey. Quite the most efficient method is to spray the plant and the soil before the fly emerges. Alternatively, remove the rolled leaves in the hope that some caterpillars have not emerged and spray the plant thoroughly with a specific for caterpillars.

Red spider mite

Although this pest is usually associated with the greenhouse, it can become insidious outside. An infestation becomes visible when the leaves appear to lack colour and eventually fall off. The mites, which are very, very small, appear on the underside of the leaves and are reddish brown. This is very rare outside and only occurs in the early summer in very dry conditions. It is very difficult to control, but the most important point to remember is that a very fine nozzle must be used on the sprayer and the plant must be completely wetted.

Good results have been obtained by using a winter wash of tar oil, a remedy which fruit growers are more familiar with, but which appears to have efficacious results against a variety of pests during the winter months. Apparently this spray can kill eggs etc in the ground.

Rose slug sawfly

This fly shares a similar life cycle to the roller fly but the damage is more obvious. The larvae feed on the foliage, leaving a skeleton structure (Fig. 5.10). The spray used for the leaf roller will control this pest.

Thrips

From the human point of view these are probably the most irritating insects. They appear in swarms in early summer, particularly in hot moist atmospheres and consequently have been called thunder flies.

Fig. 5.9 Leaf rolling sawfly.

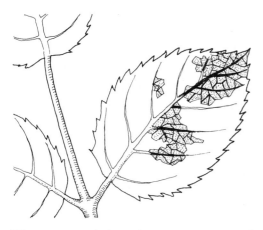

Fig. 5.10 Rose slug sawfly.

absolutely essential. In this respect great emphasis must be placed on hygiene. Before the beginning of each growing season the complete building must be thoroughly washed down using a general purpose disinfectant. This applies equally to any structure in the greenhouse and the floor where a sterilant may be necessary. The time spent doing this is amply repaid and must not be neglected. As a general rule, allow at least six weeks before putting in new plants after cleansing.

Because of the high humidity, the greatest problem is mildew; black spot and rust are very rare. Ample ventilation is essential, as is regular spraying. The modern systemic sprays are adequate. Red spider mite can be a problem and local advice may have

They can reach into the most unexpected crevices (human and vegetable) and are very difficult to deter. They have a penchant for light-coloured rose varieties and appear just as the bud is opening, creating unsightly dark edges to the petals and stains inside (Fig. 5.11). They disappear as quickly as they appear, but nevertheless have to be deterred, and heavy overhead watering can be effective. Most gardeners pray for cold wet weather at these times and accept that a visit from thrips is the price to pay for growing pale pink roses.

Fig. 5.11 Thrips.

Control of pests and diseases in the greenhouse

The environment in a greenhouse is so conducive to diseases and pests that control is

Recommended chemicals against pests Like the fungicides there are innumerable formulations sold under a variety of		trade names. These are the active constituents:	
Beetles	As for caterpillars	*Rose aphids*	Dimethoate Malathion Pirimiphos-Methyl Fenitrothion
Caterpillars	Fenitrothion Gamma H.C.H. Permethrin Pirimiphos-Methyl	*Saw flies*	Fenitrothion Pirimiphos-Methyl
Red spider	An insecticide can be recommended but cold water sprays are cheaper and more effective	*Thrips*	As for aphids

to be obtained from a horticultural adviser. There are sprays which may be effective and biological control with predators is available in some areas.

Rabbits and hares
The shock of walking round the garden in early summer and finding young rose shoots chewed off some 10cm (4in) from the ground is a traumatic experience. Rabbits are quite capable of causing a tremendous amount of damage to young rose shoots in the spring, and fending them off can be an expensive business. A distinct feature of the depredations from this animal is that no matter where they breed in temperate regions, they will always have a preference for one variety, the Floribunda 'Iceberg', followed in pecking order by 'Super Star' and 'Mr Lincoln'. Therefore, if it is suspected that rabbits are causing damage and these varieties are growing in the garden, it is a very reliable sign if they appear to be damaged.

Hares do not appear to have the same fastidious palates, and will literally nibble their way through gardens to provide easy access from one point to another.

Many solutions have been proposed to combat the depredations of the rabbit, including obnoxious sprays as a deterrent, a machine that produces subsonic sound waves which are claimed to disorientate them (very successful in open areas), and more recently electric fences. However a rabbit-proof fence about 1m (3ft) high would appear to be the most reliable solution to date (Fig. 5.12).

Deer
Damage to rose plants by deer has become a major problem in many places, even in built-up areas which have previously been unaffected, as the animals are becoming much bolder. It is generally agreed that deer-proof fencing with a minimum height of 1.8m (6ft) is the only really practical solution.

Fig. 5.12
Rabbit-proof wire.
1. Minimum height above ground 1m (3ft).
2. At least 15cm (6in) below ground.
3. Poles 2m (6ft apart).
4. Fine mesh strong chicken wire.
5. Posts strong enough to strain wire on.

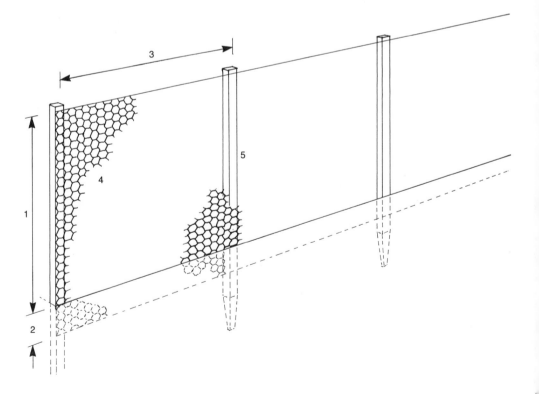

CHAPTER 6

Propagation

The development of the rose has been well chronicled. There is, however, little documentation concerning the history of the easy and rapid multiplication of the genus, probably the greatest impediment to increasing the popularity of any garden plant. As roses became more widely grown it was no trouble to filch from the garden of the 'big house' a 'slip' of a coveted variety. This was very satisfactory until the advent of the truly modern rose, when it was apparent that notwithstanding the novelty value, there appeared to be a diminution of vigour. Briefly, as rose breeders were producing more and more sophisticated plants and flower forms, the genus lost the ability to make its own root system and a more vigorous root system had to be found. This caused the introduction into rose growing of the technique we now call 'budding'.

Budding

The technique of budding has been known for centuries but the application to rose growing is relatively recent. (There still remains the ability of some varieties to be propagated by cuttings, which will be discussed later in this chapter.)

Every plant requires a strong and vigorous root system, and given that a modern rose bush has lost the ability to produce its own root system, a means has to be found to provide this. Budding is the name given to this process. The bud concerned is the dormant eye lying within the leaf axil of the stem of the rose. This is transferred to a root stock which will give the required vigour.

The principle of budding can only be achieved if a fundamental botanical fact is understood. The active or growing part of the plant is the line of cells immediately below the bark, botanically known as the cambium but more commonly called the sapwood. Two facts emerge from this: budding cannot be successful unless the cambium of both plants is accessible, that is the sap is flowing; and, secondly, the operation can only be completed satisfactorily if the cambium of both plants is joined. Therefore budding can only be achieved with the genus *Rosa* from early to late summer.

Although, in theory, any variety of rose can be budded on to another, this in practice is vastly reduced by the ability of the putative root stock to accept a scion and secondly the availability of the root stock in sufficient quantity to be a viable proposition.

Words used in budding

In discussing the process of propagation, there are a number of words that must be defined: the *stock* is the simplest and refers to the entire plant which is used to provide the root system (Fig. 6.1) – it can be sometimes be called the root stock. The *scion* is the correct name for the portion of the plant which will be implanted in the stock.

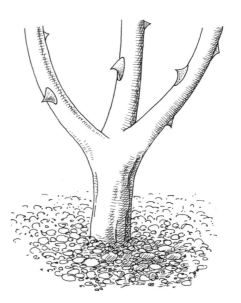

Fig. 6.1 Stock prepared to take bud in early summer.

Scion incompatability occurs when a scion will not weld on to the stock.

Although commercially a high success rate can be expected when budding is practised, a 95% success rate is normal; a poor crop is described as a poor 'take'. As has already been explained, successful budding can only be achieved if the sap is running. If for any reason this is not so, both the stock and buds are described as 'dry'.

Seedling stocks are plants that have been raised from seed; this is an extremely skilled exercise which has been perfected by a few specialist nurserymen in various parts of the world.

Seedling root stocks

Rosa canina Probably the most natural and easiest stock to work. The sap runs for an extraordinary length of season from late spring to early autumn. There are many selected clones, the majority of which are unfortunately only compatible with the areas where they have been identified. The greatest impediment to using this type is its tendency to throw suckers; that is, the root stock growing independently of the cultivar and eventually causing it to fail.

Rosa canina inermis A selection of a relatively thornless variety which is very winter hardy but has the added bonus of adaptability for use as a stock for forcing varieties (cut flower). Has proved successful in northern Europe.

Rosa corymbifera laxa Probably the most popular stock, producing a consistently heavy crop of plants. Must be budded early as it dries up by mid-summer and can be devastated by rust.

Rosa multiflora An extremely fast-growing plant which is used in many parts of the world but can prove difficult with certain types of bush.

Cuttings as root stocks

When it was discovered that the emerging rose varieties produced a better class of plant and bloom on a root stock, cuttings were initially used of these species.

Rosa manetti Still widely used in very hot climates, although was originally successful with the old Hybrid Perpetuals.

Rosa multiflora Quite the easiest plant to produce cuttings. In some hot countries it is possible to take a cutting, root it, bud and produce a saleable plant within six months. Not favoured in very cold climates where a combination of scion incompatability and susceptibility to frost damage occurs.

Standard Stems

Rosa canina (the dog rose) was used for many years. Dug out of the hedges from good sources, but now a rarity that has almost become extinct with the advent of mechanical hedging equipment.

Rosa rugosa rugosa There are many selected forms of this species which for many years after the demise of *Rosa canina* were used to the exclusion of any other pretender. Very easy to cultivate, producing high quality plants, but the stem was never robust and necessitated rigorous staking. Prone to damage if the roots are allowed to dry out, and incompatible with some types.

There are forms of selected *R.canina* but they are only compatible with certain cultivars. Recently much research has been done on a replacement for *R.rugosa*. There is great promise from two British sources, 'Rocket' (Harwhippet) and 'Chessum's Choice' (Chestock).

Planting the stock

In this age of specialization, each facet of horticultural production has produced its own gurus. Raising root stocks is no stranger to this; indeed it is a skill that was probably developed earlier than many other nursery practices. The seedling stocks are lifted in the autumn (a stock is graded by its diameter, 3–5mm ($1/8$–$3/16$in), 5–8mm ($3/16$–$5/16$in) and 8–12mm ($5/16$–$1/2$in), and correspondingly priced), and dispatched during the winter. A standard stem is graded by its height. On receipt of the stocks they are usually heeled in. Great attention must be paid to the soil they will eventually be planted in: good clean ground, well cultivated but not too heavily manured, and completely free from perennial weeds.

The stocks always arrive untrimmed; it is a matter of choice as to whether or not they should be cut down before planting, but for ease of handling, a plant with 18cm (7in) of root and a 14cm (6in) top is adequate. A 5–8mm (3/16–5/16in) diameter plant is the most popular but the smaller size is favoured in early maturing areas with light soil and the heavy big stock is planted in cold areas where early budding is demanded.

The stocks in a small garden are planted with the aid of a dibber, the same implement that is used to plant cabbages etc, usually in early to mid-spring depending on the soil conditions. Spaced approximately 18–20cm (7–8in) apart and, if a quantity are planted, the rows are about 90cm (3ft) apart. Commercially this is done by a tractor-mounted machine not unlike a cabbage planter. About 40,000 stocks can be planted per working day at 52,000 per hectare (22,500 per acre.) The stock is planted to a depth that will lightly cover the 'collar', that is the part of the plant which will be worked on just below the point that the top growth emanates from the collar. Apart from keeping it weed free, there is no other attention required until budding. In a dry spring they may require watering to obtain rapid establishment.

When to bud

Given an equable growing period, the stock will grow very quickly and the barrel will be big enough to take a bud when it is about 12–18mm (1/2–3/4in) in size. This is generally from early summer onwards. The operative time to bud is usually determined by the availability of the *bud wood*.

Collecting bud wood

This is usually collected immediately before budding, it must be ripe but not dry. This in reality on a bush rose is immediately after the stem has produced a bloom. The wood will have matured sufficiently and the bark bearing the bud will be hard

enough to be manipulated. Bud wood is collected from the selected variety, cutting a whole stem and removing the two or three top eyes which are usually barren, and the foliage, to leave a stem with a modest leaf stock about 1cm (3/8in) long (Fig. 6.2). Care must be taken to keep the bud stick moist. This is usually achieved by wrapping it in damp newspaper or moss. Do not, unless absolutely necessary stand it in water. An extra precaution can be taken by adding at the usual rate a fungicide to the water that will soak the newspaper.

Bud wood can be stored like this for quite long periods and is the usual method of dispatching a new variety to a distant garden (nursery). The bud wood is usually spined or thorned immediately before budding.

Preparing for budding

Two essential pieces of equipment are required to complete the operation. A budding knife shaped rather like the old-fashioned pen-knife (Fig. 6.3), which is

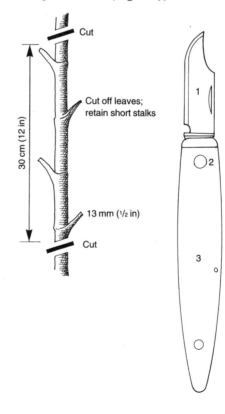

Fig. 6.2 Stick of buds (*Left*). Select a strong shoot of the chosen variety which has just finished flowering.

Fig. 6.3 A typical budding knife (*Right*).
1. Surgical steel blade.
2. Strong tight shoulder.
3. Good bone handle, shaped to open stock.

Fig. 6.4 Cutting (preparing) a bud (*Left*).
(*a*) Taking bud off stick.
(*b*) Bud completely free.
(*c*) Taking sliver of wood from back.
(*d*) Prepared bud.

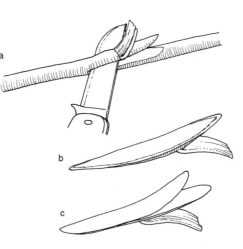

reversed, any wood being removed, and the bud trimmed ready to insert into the stock (Fig. 6.4*a*–*d*). The stock is prepared by cutting into the barrel as lightly as possible, initially with a horizontal cut followed by a vertical T shape. A slight easing of the bark with the reverse end of the budding knife will reveal the cambium (Fig. 6.5*a*–*d*). The bud is inserted into the stock and the natural elasticity of the bark will secure the bud. The operation is completed by tying in with the raffia or budding patch (Fig. 6.6*a*–*d*). The whole operation, if successful, will heal up very quickly and the ties will naturally rot away as the stock continues to grow. Sometimes if budded early, the bud will begin to grow immediately (shot out) but this is not to be encouraged. The bud will normally lie dormant until the following spring.

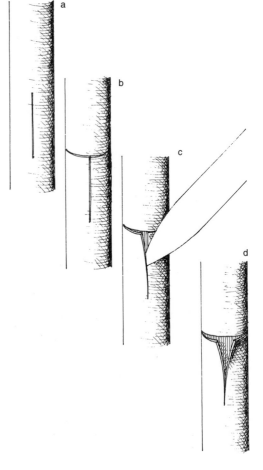

comfortable to the operator, with a blade of high quality steel and a handle, usually made of bone, possessing a pointed sharp butt which can be used to ease open the cut stock. Raffia will also be required to 'tie in' the bud; of good quality, pliable and ideally cut in lengths of about 40cm (15in). The alternative to raffia is strips of perishable rubber or patches fixed with a small staple (obtainable from a friendly nursery). The stock is cleaned of surplus soil to reveal the neck (barrel), which can be wiped clean with a piece of rag.

Fig. 6.5 Opening stock (*Right*).
(*a*) First cut.
(*b*) Second cut.
(*c*) Easing open bark with bone of budding knife handle.
(*d*) Stock ready to take bud.

Budding

Budding commences by simply cutting the stick to remove a portion of the stem, the eye and the leaf stock. This is done by taking care to cut only a sliver of the wood, together with the bud which is then

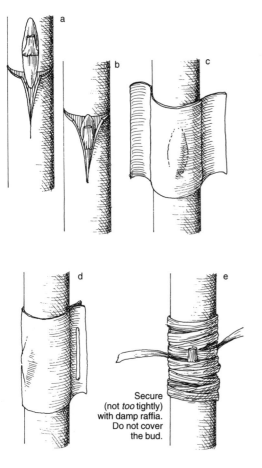

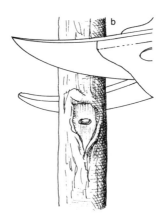

Grafting

Although budding roses is the conventional method of propagating garden roses it is not the only means of producing a rose plant. Many millions of plants are produced annually by bench grafting, which is usually done in the winter or early spring. This is a method that is basically similar to budding in that the principle of the cambium of both stock and scion are joined. The fundamental difference is that whereas only a small portion of the bark carrying the eye is utilized in budding, in grafting the wood carrying the eye *and* the bark is used.

Method

Selected root-stocks are placed in a greenhouse, given bottom heat and within two or three weeks are lifted and the top growth removed. A cut is made at the top, rather

Fig. 6.6 Stock receiving bud – tying-in.
(*a*) Pushing bud in. Bud *in situ*.
(*c*) Putting on rubber tie.
(*d*) Rubber tie.
(*e*) Raffia tie.

Fig. 6.6 Stock receiving bud – tying-in.
(*a*) Pushing bud in. Bud *in situ*.
(*c*) Putting on rubber tie.
(*d*) Rubber tie.
(*e*) Raffia tie.

Secure (not *too* tightly) with damp raffia. Do not cover the bud.

Standard stems are budded in exactly the same way, usually straight into the stem. The height that this is done from ground level determines its type, half-standards 0.5–0.75m (18in to 2ft), and full standards 1m (3¼ft).

Heading back

The following spring the top of the stock is removed with a good strong pair of secateurs (or long-arms) immediately above the T cut (Fig. 6.7*a–d*), the top growth being removed and burnt. As the sap starts to rise the dormant eye will swell, develop, and as the season progresses, will grow very rapidly to produce flower (on a bush plant) by the middle of the summer. The growth will mature by early autumn and the young maiden plant is fit to be lifted, graded and dispatched to its eventual permanent planting position.

Fig. 6.7 Budding continued – cutting back and growing on.
(*a*) Overwintering.
(*b*) Snagging back.
(*c*) Stock in early spring.
(*d*) Young buds in late spring.

like budding, and a piece of stem sliced diagonally about 2.5–7.5cm (1–3in) long, carrying one or two eyes, is slipped inside and bound up (Fig. 6.8*a–c*). The completed graft is then placed in a heated frame which binds together and heals very quickly. After weaning (being progressively introduced into at more equable temperature), the completed plant is then grown on and will produce new wood very rapidly. This method is used principally in the production of plants for forcing for the cut-flower trade. Many Miniature roses were also produced in this way and it is a favourite method of building up stock plants of garden varieties for the supply of budding wood very quickly.

Roses from cuttings

The propagation of plants from cuttings has been known to man since prehistoric times and was the principal method of

Fig. 6.8 Grafting. (*a*) Stock prepared to take graft. (*b*) Graft cut from mother plant. (*c*) Stock receiving grafts.

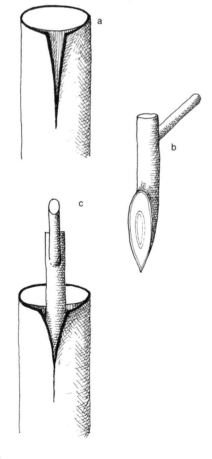

increasing hardy plant populations. Modern day techniques have produced more sophisticated methods and it is convenient to discuss these by the origin of the materials used.

Hardwood cuttings

The majority of species, Old Garden roses, old Climbers and Ramblers and some of the very modern Ground covers are very easily propagated by this method. With big wooded plants, cut good hardwood in late summer or early autumn. Divide into lengths of about 20–25cm (8–10in). The base of the cutting must cut across an eye or bud which is slightly gouged out. The next two eyes are trimmed back hard leaving one or two complete buds at the top of the stem which may or may not still carry leaves (Fig. 6.9). The prepared stem is then dipped in a hardwood rooting compound and planted in a cold frame or protected area.

A high proportion of plants can be obtained by this method, provided the cuttings are well buried, that is, only the two top eyes are above soil level and they are planted in a shaded area. Some gardeners will actually cover the cuttings in the initial stages with black polythene. Successfully rooted plants can be moved into their permanent positions in a matter of six months but with some of the Old Garden roses this may take a year. The great advantage with cuttings is that they cannot produce suckers. Nevertheless most modern Hybrid Teas and Floribundas will never produce quality bloom if produced by this method.

Softwood cuttings

This method of propagation has become very fashionable recently and is the method used to propagate many of the modern Ground covers, Pot roses and various other cultivars that have proved difficult until now by other methods.

Basically the technique requires soft green wood, preferably grown inside a heated propagating unit. The wood is gathered from very young green growth, most successfully in spring and early summer. The stems are cut into very short 3cm (1in)

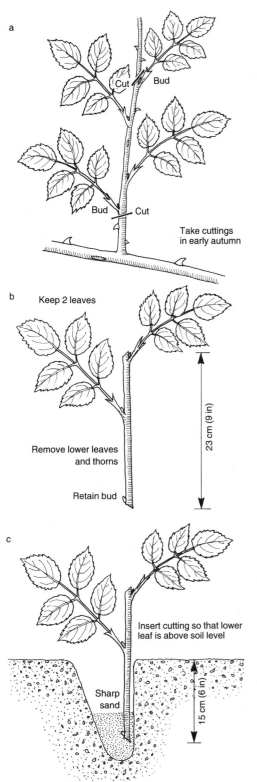

a

Cut Bud

Bud Cut

Take cuttings
in early autumn

b

Keep 2 leaves

Remove lower leaves
and thorns

Retain bud

23 cm (9 in)

c

Insert cutting so that lower
leaf is above soil level

Sharp
sand

15 cm (6 in)

pieces, carrying one or two buds, and retaining the leaves. After dipping in mild fungicide to control botrytis, they are then treated with *soft wood* rooting compound and planted into seed trays with pure sand (Fig. 6.10). They then progress to a mist unit with a constant temperature of about 24°C (80°F).

The cuttings will strike roots rapidly. The leaves have an alarming habit of falling off which is no problem, but they must be cleared up quickly to prevent botrytis, and with gradual weaning the cuttings can be potted up in a matter of weeks.

The majority of Pot roses sold in supermarkets are produced by this method.

Micropropagation – tissue culture

This method of multiplying stocks became very fashionable some 20 years ago. It is a system of using the fast-growing plant tip grown on in a culture under very strict laboratory conditions.

A micro-propagating unit is an expensive investment in specialist equipment which can be extremely successful if managed well and the appropriate genera are identified to profit from this method of propagation. The rose has been used with mixed results and there is still a lot of work to be completed to make it a reliable commercial proposition.

Fig. 6.9 Taking a hardwood cutting.
(*a*) Choose a ripe (thorns break off cleanly) and young shoot (this year's growth). It should be about the thickness of a pencil.
(*b*) Dip the bottom of the cutting into a rooting hormone.
(*c*) Dig a trench with one vertical wall at a site in the garden which gets some shade. Place the cuttings about 15cm (6in) apart, firm the sand around the stems and then replace the soil. Tread it down firmly and water thoroughly.

Firm the soil after heavy winter frosts. In spring and summer keep the cuttings watered during prolonged dry weather – remove any flower buds which may form. By late autumn the cuttings should be well-rooted and ready for planting.

Fig. 6.10 Soft-wood cuttings, showing soft-wood in a propagating bag. The bag must be kept in a humid atmosphere.

CHAPTER 7

Breeding Roses

Much has been written earlier in this book on the history and development of the rose from its origin in the wild to the modern sophisticated plant that we are familiar with today. The reader will naturally come to the conclusion therefore that, because of this evolution, the genes of the modern plant are a combination of many lines of breeding. Because of this 'mixture' and the physical nature of the rose it is impossible to breed true from seed. That is, if a ripe seed of 'Peace' is sown and successfully germinated, it will not produce replicas of the mother plant. This is why vegetative propagation was discussed in a separate chapter.

To breed a new rose entails the selection of parents, the fertilization of the female part of the flower, raising the seed and selecting possible contenders to market. The first part of this exercise, the pollination procedure, is called *hybridizing* and can be qualified today by the modern expression 'planned parenthood'.

Although the knowledge that plants are grown from seed is as old as mankind itself, only relatively recently (1691) did botanists discover that plants possess a sex life – that is, that all plants have male and female parts. In some they are in separate plants, for instance some holly varieties are either male or female (the female bearing the berries). In others the plants are hermaphrodite, that is they bear both male and female parts. The rose is of this type.

However, devotees of the rose were conspicuously slow in taking advantage of this discovery and new varieties were normally introduced by chance seedlings, mutations or, and this was the commonest, natural selection of superior clones and their stabilization by vegetative propagation. The first production of a new rose cultivar by deliberate hybridizing did not occur until the first half of the nineteenth century, probably about 1820, in France.

Finally, we must establish an anomaly in the nomenclature of this operation. To the purist a *hybrid* is the result of a cross between two species and therefore *hybridization* should be the description given to this simple operation, only in fact it is now accepted that the verb is used to cover any cross breeding, whatever the origin of the parents.

Producing seedlings is a relatively simple exercise which can give immense satisfaction to the raiser if a successful and unique plant is the final result. However, to the beginner, it can be very frustrating if certain criteria are not acknowledged.

Scent

Because a modern rose is the end result of a protracted and confused breeding programme, it may sometimes be very difficult to identify putative parents that will produce progeny with specific characteristics. Scent is probably the most elusive and is usually considered a bonus in any breeding programme. There is, however, great merit in the theory that as rose breeding progresses, scent will not be such an elusive feature. This is attributed to the fact that the scent factor appeared to be at its nadir when hybridists, driven by the search for new flower forms and colours, used parents where these factors, colour and type, dominate. There was therefore grounds for the somewhat petulant comment that Modern roses had lost their scent. There is now ample evidence to suggest that the wheel has now turned full circle. Indeed it is now virtually impossible to gain any major award for a new variety unless it possesses this essential ingredient. Nevertheless, to select a parent that will bequeath this quality is still a very difficult problem.

Disease resistance

There is no doubt that there was good reason to suppose that scent and mildew were a common factor in the genetic composition of new varieties a quarter of a century ago. By skilful and accurate research, this has been virtually eliminated. A tendency to black spot and a weakness towards rust is usually identified during the hybridist's selection and has short shrift if it appears in rose trials. The offending variety is quickly despatched. There are, however, some breeding lines that have a remarkable history of healthiness and have been identified by breeders. They usually use the 'blood' from these varieties to build up a breeding stock to back cross with others which have other selected attributes.

Type of plant

In the population explosion of varieties since the conception of the Floribunda rose, it was very easy to predict the type of rose one was breeding. In the last 20 years, however, it has become apparent that the blood of the two distinct types, large flowered and cluster flowered, has become so inextricably mixed that it is very difficult to define certain types – so much so that seedlings on trial at many gardens are entered as Floribunda/Hybrid Tea or *vice versa*. The alternative is the increasing usage of the description Grandiflora, common in the States but much deprecated in Europe and Asia.

Colour

This factor in breeding can be extremely elusive and is usually associated with a dominant parent. This can sometimes be extremely irritating, particularly as in the history of the rose pink appears as the all pervasive tint, which leads to the comment that all seedling roses are pink. An interesting factor is that historically it has been determined that although there are probably about 150 species sufficiently unique to be identified as separate entities, only the blood of about 15 to 20 have ever been used in modern rose breeding. This has been demonstrated by Harkness when using *Rosa hulthemosa* and McGredy when he produced the famous strain of hand-painted roses. However, in both of these

instances, particularly McGredy, the novelty of different colour variations was quite startling but was not easily accepted by the buying public.

The lesson to the young hybridist is therefore to go forth. There are a great many possibilities but remember that, although a unique colour or flower form is tremendously exciting, customer acceptability is a great leveller.

The mechanics of hybridizing

The novice hybridist must first of all become familiar and conversant with the relevant parts of the flower of the rose, as this is the operative part that he must concern himself with. Fig. 7.1 is explicit and demonstrates the pertinent parts. All rose blooms possess these essential elements, though they may vary in their shape, size, colour and multiplicity of petals, stamens etc. The identification of the male and female constituents is of primary consideration.

Flower parts

As a bloom develops the *sepals* are the green outside protective covering that becomes apparent first. These will curl back to reveal the *petals*. At this stage the *receptacle* that will eventually develop into a hip is small and immature. This encompasses the *ovary*, containing the putative seed. The petals will open to reveal the *anthers* bearing

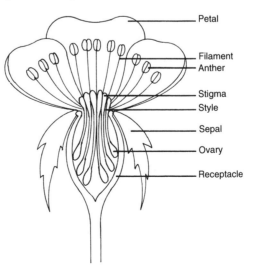

Fig. 7.1 Parts of rose flower.

pollen. These are the male part of the flower. The anthers are supported by stems called *filaments*. The centre of the flower, the *stigma*, is the female part of the flower which will receive the pollen. The consummation of *pollination* is completed when the pollen adheres to the stigma, travels down the *style* to the *ovary* and fertilizes the ovules which will then develop into seed.

Preparation of the flower

If the flower is allowed to develop naturally, the pollen will ripen and unless transported elsewhere, either by mechanical means or by insect, bird or wind, will perform its function by pollinating its own stigma. This is called self-pollination. The first purpose of the hybridizer is to prevent this happening. The operation is called emasculation. The flower is deprived of the male part by removing the pollen. This is a simple exercise but must be done with care. As the flower develops, the sepals will fold back revealing the petals which have to be removed to give access to the anthers and stigma. In most Hybrid Teas and Floribundas, this is best done immediately the petals begin to fold back. Because the pollen on some types of multiflora develops very quickly, removal of the petals may have to be hastened and it is a tedious operation removing very immature petals. Suffice to say that the petals are usually removed (Fig. 7.2) by a sharp twist to reveal the

immature anthers (Fig. 7.3*a*). These must be removed by cutting the filaments and picking out the anthers, usually with a pair of tweezers. Occasionally the anthers are inextricably entwined in the stigma and care must be taken to delicately remove these to produce a completely female flower (Fig. 7.3*b*).

The process of using pollen from another flower is called cross-pollination. When the immature anthers have been removed, they may be stored in a dry atmosphere to be used to pollinate another flower or alternatively disposed of. Small petrie dishes are ideal for this purpose. The stigma is considered ready to receive pollen when it appears to turn sticky, about 24 hours after emasculation. The pollen is ready to use when it appears floury.

Application of pollen

In a commercial breeding house the hydridizer will normally 'strip' or prepare rose heads one day, carefully marking the prepared hip, and pollinate and complete the operation the following day. This is a good practice to follow. Great care must be taken to apply the pollen with a camel hair brush which must be sterilized between varieties if there is a change of pollen. A single light stroke with a loaded brush is quite adequate (Fig. 7.3*c*). The embryo hip is then labelled and record of the parents entered in a seedling book. Some operators

Fig. 7.2
Preparing bloom for pollination (*Left*). Sharply remove petals by twisting off.

Fig. 7.3
Pollination (*Right*).
(*a*) Stamen standing proud.
(*b*) Stamens removed.
(*c*) Pollination.

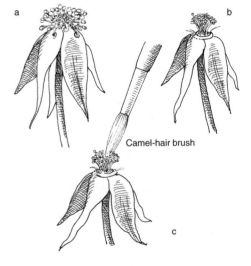

Camel-hair brush

dust the head with a fungicide to control botrytis. This may not become apparent until well on into the summer when the hybridizer is devastated to see seemingly ripening heads begin to rot. There is little one can do to stem this catastrophe other than to keep a very clean greenhouse and maintain a dry atmosphere, with irrigation kept to a minimum (Fig. 7.4).

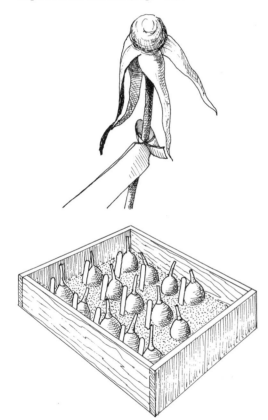

Successful harvesting of the hips should commence in late autumn. The procedure is to carefully pick off the hips, together with the label (Fig. 7.5). The seeds are picked out of the hip and meticulously placed by variety in small cartons and enveloped in a moist medium, usually vermiculite or damp fine sand, and stored at a temperature of about 16°C (60°F) for about six weeks. This process is called *stratification* and is the method of breaking down the outside husk of the seed and encouraging successful germination. The operation is completed by exposing the seeds immediately before sowing to a short sharp refrigeration for about 10 days. At all times care must be taken to prevent mice eating the seeds, which they consider a delicacy.

Sowing the seed

The seed beds should be prepared using a high quality seed compost (John Innes Seed Compost or the equivalent). A good depth of about 15cm (6in) is adequate and must never be allowed to dry out. The seed carefully removed from the vermiculite is sown in rows about 4cm (1½in) apart and 2½cm (1in) seed to seed (Fig. 7.6a). About 1cm (3/8in) of soil is placed over and the surface topped with a fine sharp sand (Fig. 7.6b).

Germination

Night heat is required to encourage germination and plenty of light is paramount. The first seedlings may appear within two weeks but it can take as long as two months (instances have been known of seedlings appearing after two years). The rate of germination can be very unpredictable and

Fig. 7.4 Pollination – labelled rose hip (*Left top*). Hip developing in the autumn, with label giving details of the cross.

Fig. 7.5 Seeds stratified (*Left centre*). Hips when harvested must never be allowed to dry out. These will be opened up and the seeds stratified in vermiculite.

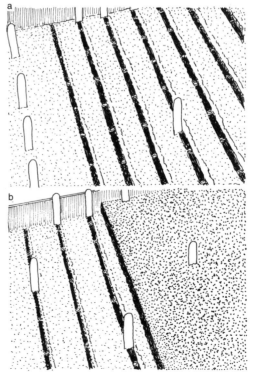

Fig. 7.6 (*Right*) (a) Sowing seed. (b) Covering with sharp sand to keep beds healthy.

Fig. 7.7 An even germination.

will vary from variety to variety. Some Floribundas will give amazing results, whereas some Hybrid Teas can be extremely disappointing (Fig. 7.7).

The seedlings

Given good growing conditions, remembering that any excessive heat is detrimental. Seedlings will usually flower about 8 to 10 weeks after germinating. This is the time when the skill is required to select possible varieties to bud on. Little can be learnt at this stage other than the colour. A tremendous number will be revolting shades of pale pink and red and are rarely worth taking notice of. A good plant will grow about 25cm (10in) high and it will be possible to obtain about four buds to propagate. Alternatively, at the end of the summer, they can be planted out to grow on their own roots, but there is little merit in this.

Fig. 7.8 Field of budded seedlings.

Selecting seedlings

Having successfully budded possible 'winners' (Fig. 7.8), the hybridist will have to wait until the following summer when the fruits of his endeavours will be in full show. The process of selecting viable varieties to proceed to the next step, sending them to rose trials, can take three or four seasons. Apart from working up a stock, much trial and tribulation will occur when selecting a possible 'world beater', only to discover that it does not like the wet, fades in the sun, is prone to disease, and so it goes on. The odds on breeding a really good variety are quite commonly quoted as 60,000 to 1.

Planning a breeding programme

The casual gardener with a greenhouse will experience great pleasure from simply breeding a new rose. The more serious hybridist will want to formulate a breeding programme. This will entail selecting possible parents with characteristics which it is desired to use or develop to give to its progeny. In practice a greater harvest of viable seeds is easier to obtain from Floribundas. Look at the varieties that have characteristics which you want to emulate: colour, foliage, growth, flower form and/or disease resistance. There is a common assumption that an amateur breeder works to a short programme, whereas a professional has a greater and longer perspective and will breed to produce seedlings with dominant characteristics which will be used to produce several generations before satisfactory results can be expected. This is the reason why published parents will very often just be stated as seedling × seedling.

Preparing parent plants

As has already been mentioned, successful breeding can only be fully accomplished with the benefit of a greenhouse. The plants selected must be planted up early in the autumn in adequately prepared containers. The present method is to use big plastic or metal drums, usually with a capacity of 25 l (5–6gal) and good quality potting compost (John Innes No 3). The

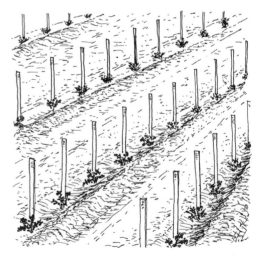

plants are pruned in early winter and grown on in a frost-free environment. Heat is only used if intensive cold conditions prevail. A good parent plant will develop in the course of one or two seasons to produce a bountiful harvest of flowers and hips. The greenhouse must be well sterilized annually and, apart from the initial watering, irrigation using some form of a spaghetti system is adequate.

Once hybridization is complete, the minimum amount of watering is all that is required and any extraneous growth discouraged or eliminated.

Testing new seedling roses

If a new rose is to be successfully commercialized, it will have to be adequately tested. There are many experienced rose nurserymen who will be pleased to provide this facility. They will bud possible contenders probably alongside other varieties undergoing a similar procedure. It is a sobering experience to see one's variety fighting it out with the rest. The prudent hybridizer will receive some form of acknowledgement that his variety has been accepted with the undertaking that there is no contractual obligation to proceed with its subsequent development. The nurseryman will also exercise the right to destroy any varieties that are disease prone. Testings may well prove that a variety is a viable commercial proposition.

National and International Trials

The next logical step is to propagate sufficient plants to distribute to well established trials both at home and abroad. The majority of countries that have rose societies also conduct trials for new varieties, and in some countries there are possibly two or three venues. Probably the most famous are held in The Hague, Holland; Dortmund, Germany; Paris, France; Rome, Italy; Madrid, Spain; Geneva, Switzerland and Dublin, Eire. The Hague Rose Trials are extremely comprehensive and include seedlings where six plants have to be supplied for a two-year trial; if these results are outstanding, a further 25 plants of the same variety are entered for a further seven years.

The trials of the Royal National Rose Society at St. Albans in Hertfordshire, are usually described as the most vigorous. Plants are tested over a three-year period. The rose trials in Belfast, at the Sir Thomas and Lady Dixon Park, are a little different. The criterion for entry there is roses that have already been marketed usually for a minimum of two years. They are planted in beds of 25 bushes and are judged over a period of two years. The trials, which started in the 1960s, are part of a large rose garden forming one of the best displays in Europe. The USA has similar schemes, as do Australia and New Zealand.

Development of a new rose

A good new rose will be recognized very quickly and in the hands of an efficient agent will be taken up by many nurserymen at home and abroad. The first step is to obtain legal protection for it. Some people will call it patenting, but it is a term that is not popular and the general phrase is to 'apply for protection'. In effect this means applying to the Agricultural Department in the country concerned. In the UK, this is the Plant Varieties Rights Office, who administer schemes for decorative varieties of roses, chrysanthemums, shrubs etc. and for economic plants, wheat, oilseed rape, potatoes etc. In effect this means proving the unique qualities of the subject applied for. If successful, the variety is given a grant, which in effect entitles the owner of the plant or his agent to charge a royalty for every unit that is propagated. This facility will normally be applicable for 21 years.

Naming a Rose

There are two stages to the naming of a rose. All protected varieties receive what is called a *denomination*, that is a recognizable series of letters that are identified with that variety and are used throughout the world. This must be prefaced by the breeder's name. Thus the rose distributed in the UK as 'Simba' is catalogued 'Simba' (Korbelma). The denomination Korbelma denotes that the breeder is Kordes (KOR) and the remaining letters make a recognizable name usually written with in-house inferences. The name Korbelma is used to obtain protection wherever there is this facility around the world. The name 'Simba' is used in the UK and is called the *fancy* name. This fancy name may be different in other parts of the world. In Germany, for example, it is called 'Helmut Schmidt' – hardly the name to sell a rose elsewhere!

There are also other reasons to use a different name, mainly to do with local regional demands and the pitfalls of literal translations. Descriptive ('Scented Air'), commercial ('St. Bruno'), historic ('Christopher Columbus'), T.V. personality ('Sue Lawley'). Unique in the UK is that a rose can be named for a fee, which can be very expensive if it is a good variety with high awards.

There is an increasing practice for breeders to introduce new varieties simply under a denomination and only give a fancy name when a sure market has become established. This is not so confusing as it may appear. Good names are very hard to come by and there is a reluctance to waste good opportunities. This should not be confused with the fable that old varieties are sometimes re-named to give an impetus to flagging sales. Such a practice would be very hard to implement and would be stopped if it were ever to happen.

Plant breeding organizations

There are many organizations, both of a national and international character, who work on behalf of breeders. BARB (The British Association Representing Breeders) is the organization that administers schemes for the collection of royalties on behalf of rose breeders in the UK for plants grown in this country; it also represents their cause in legislative matters. CIOPORA (The International Community of Breeders of Asexually Reproduced Ornamentals and Fruit Tree Varieties) is the international association which protects breeders' interests worldwide, and UPOV (International Union for the Protection of New Varieties of Plants) is the organization which comprises government bodies who recognize plant breeders' rights.

The unique feature of all these organizations is the proper administration and protection of breeders' interests with the sole intention of giving the breeder a fair reward for his efforts, and finance for the further development of bigger and better new roses and other plants.

Alternative methods of breeding

Historically, before the discovery of the mechanics of rose breeding, new roses were produced by one of two methods, random harvesting of hips or mutations. This was very successful with some of the species and is still practised with some of the primitive forms of Miniature roses. For reasons that were given earlier in this chapter, the practice is not reliable and is rarely used today. The selection of new varieties by observing and stabilizing mutations or sports was very common and is occasionally used today. Sometimes a well-known variety will produce a distinct colour break, a not unusual occurrence with certain types, particularly dwarf *R. polyantha* Pompoms. If bud wood is taken from this material it can be stabilized and propagated. There are, however, very few garden varieties that are commercially viable using this method.

Occasionally a bush can develop or throw a climbing branch. This can again be budded on and is called a climbing sport. Some very famous climbers have originated in this way, for example 'Cécile Brunner, Climbing'. There is a danger that some of the climbing sports, albeit very vigorous, are reluctant to produce much flower, and in the majority of varieties are only summer flowering.

There are in existence certain growth regulators that can produce colour mutations. Although producing some interesting results, they are rarely of any commercial significance.

Simply selecting improved forms of specific varieties is a method that appears to have been abandoned but is still worthy of consideration. It was practised with considerable success some years ago in selecting mother plants for the production of seeds in forestry. There is ample evidence to support the theory that renewed vigour can be

'Graham Thomas' is the most successful of the 'English' roses and is a great asset to shrub borders when lightly pruned.

'Marguerite Hilling' the flushed sport of 'Nevada', both of which make up into well-shaped shrubs with masses of colour.

'Miss Pam Ayres', a modern Shrub with strong upright stems producing a wealth of bloom throughout the summer.

Modern roses
can give an extra
dimension to a
perennial border
but must be given
plenty of light.

'R. glauca' (R. rubrifolia) with its unique coloured foliage can give extra colour to a border which is important in all gardens.

'Brown Velvet' is a fascinating Floribunda which introduces a new colour variation into the rose world.

'Arcadian' has the most perfect flower form and refutes the notion that all Floribundas are flat and single.

'Amber Queen', a fragrant Floribunda which is very popular particularly in the United States and will make a handsome medium-sized bush.

'Freedom', probably the most underrated modern Hybrid Tea which deserves greater recognition and is very free flowering.

'Savoy Hotel'.
New Hybrid Teas
are scarce, this
perfectly formed
pale pink is proof
that there is still
ample scope for
the rose breeder.

encouraged by taking bud wood from outstanding individual plants and, probably of greater importance, the relative position of the buds to the plant.

Genetic engineering

This is widely discussed as the breakthrough that plant breeders are looking for, and was given prominence with the possible discovery of the gene to produce the colour blue in roses, a factor that is impossible at the moment because of the absence of the chemical delphinidin. This raises interesting factors of both a moral and practical relevance. If the technique is to be used to cover the ills of disease, it will be money well invested; if used to introduce new colours it is of doubtful benefit as the rose buying public are strangely conservative.

Rose breeders and the development of the Modern rose

In any review of the history and development of the rose, it is worthy of note that one simple factor shines through; it is the skill of a mere handful of hybridists who, contrary to public belief, have not relied on freak occurrences but on their ability to observe, record and research the occasional breakthrough in breeding, coupled with a profound knowledge of the Modern rose, that has resulted in successful breeding programmes.

Pernet Ducher

The French breeder Pernet Ducher probably made the first great advance at the turn of the century when after years of patient and painstaking work he was able to introduce a true yellow into bush roses by crossing primitive Hybrid Teas of that time with the species rose *Rosa lutea* (Persian Yellow), thereby introducing a truly vivid selection of yellows and bi-colours to the world of roses. This development, which was slow to start, gave a new meaning to the phrase that the rose is the world's most popular garden plant. It was unfortunate that scent was of secondary importance and a susceptibility to black spot was

another handicap. Some 100 years have elapsed since Pernet Ducher's breakthrough, and it has taken that length of time to breed out both of these inherited faults.

McGredy and Dickson

The famous breeding establishments of McGredy and Dickson, both from Northern Ireland, produced a prodigious number of new varieties between 1900 and 1950, concentrating on Hybrid Tea bush roses, with a high proportion of exhibition varieties. Legend has it that these two nurseries introduced more new roses at that time than the combined production of the rest of the world.

Since those days, Sam McGredy, now living in New Zealand, has produced a wide range of recurrent-flowering Climbers, many Floribundas and Hybrid Teas, and quite dramatically introduced a new colour form into Floribundas with the 'hand-painted' (Picasso) strain. This is a remarkable breakthrough which is slowly becoming apparent in some of his newer Hybrid Teas.

The Dickson family (who actually started breeding roses some 50 years earlier than McGredy), having produced some very successful Floribundas recently, have created a new dimension with red Hybrid Teas which have become the benchmark for any aspiring breeder seeking new varieties in this colour. The family are currently in the forefront of breeding new forms of patio roses.

Kordes

Kordes in Germany, currently the biggest breeder in the world of garden and cut flower roses, have produced a whole range of varieties. Their biggest contribution was the quest to produce recurrent-flowering Climbers (*R. kordesii*) which were very successful, and the breeding line that produced the brilliant 'day-glow' scarlets. They are currently producing healthy lines of the new Ground cover roses and are engaged in the long-term development of Shrub roses with Hybrid Tea quality blooms.

The Poulsens

The Poulsen family in Denmark will always be associated with the beginning of the era of the Floribunda. 'Poulsen' roses as they were called; latterly, Hybrid Polyanthas came to prominence in the 1930s. Named after various ladies of this famous family, they became legendary in their own life times. Lately, the younger generation have been very successful breeding new Ground cover roses and Miniature roses for the 'pot rose' trade.

The Meillands

The Meilland family (in Antibes, France) will always be remembered for breeding probably the most famous rose of all time, 'Peace'. This rose, with its remarkable vigour and disease resistance, probably gave a greater impetus to the extraordinary growth in the rose trade which occurred in the 1950s and 1960s than any other variety. As is not uncommon in the history of rose breeding, it was never very successful in directly breeding new varieties, although there are few Modern bush roses that do not have 'Peace' blood somewhere in their ancestry. This south of France firm is currently breeding a successful line of Shrub and Ground cover roses which are apparently suited to the warmer areas of Europe and the States.

Peter Ilsink

In Holland the most exciting rose breeder is Peter Ilsink who, having produced some very healthy Shrub and Ground cover varieties, is obtaining great results using completely new breeding lines.

Cockers and Harkness

Two British firms have come into prominence in recent years. Cockers of Aberdeen and Harkness of Hitchin, who both started breeding roses some 30 years ago, have duly combined their research talents and have produced some remarkable breaks. Alec Cocker's variety 'Silver Jubilee' is a free-flowering pink Hybrid Tea with colourful undertones, which has quickly become successful in the UK and is a very dominant parent.

Jack Harkness, although producing a wide range of varieties, including 'Alexander', which could be called the ultimate in vermilion roses, has produced some original research using a little known species *R. hulthemosa*. This has unique colouring in the flower. The line of breeding has a long way to go yet but there is a promise of new forms of flower and Shrub roses using this blood line. Their biggest success to date, apart from this experiment, is the beautiful and highly scented Climber 'Compassion'.

Gene Boerner and other New World breeders

In the USA the rose world owes a great debt to a famous hybridist Gene Boerner, whose startling Floribunda 'Masquerade' caused many a head to turn. A yellow that turns red as it ages, it was the first of a whole line of multi-coloured varieties.

To many newcomers, it is a shock to discover that the Queen Elizabeth rose is American by origin. The Armstrong nurseries in California, where it originated, have sadly disappeared. Ralph Moore, a slightly eccentric American breeder of Miniature roses completes the complement of New World breeders.

The future

And so to join the new generation of Dicksons, Tantau and Kordes, who is to follow? To predict with any accuracy the direction of rose breeding into the next century is a difficult proposition. There are new names on the horizon: Noack in Germany is becoming quite successful; in the UK Fryer is producing some good Patios and Warner has shown originality with his Miniature Climbers. Austin is producing an exciting line of New English roses, which unfortunately require some protection from disease.

There may be a future in genetic engineering, but laboratory technicians will have to learn that the history of rose breeding will only remain successful if a proper appreciation is taken of the principle that new advances can only be achieved with accurate observation and a fundamental understanding of the development of the rose.

Some popular misconceptions about the rose

Inevitably the history and development of such a popular garden plant as the rose has given rise to a whole series of popular fallacies.

The rose is not mentioned in the New Testament. Much research has gone into this astonishing fact but there is no reason to doubt it.

The modern rose does not possess the scent of its ancestors

There is no doubt that some 50 years ago roses had reached the nadir of their olfactory potential. The reason was quite simple: when roses of European descent, which were heavily scented, were crossed with the China varieties, flower, form and colour became the dominant characteristics, together with remontancy. This has now been more than compensated for to the extent that very few new triallists would gain any recognition if they were completely scentless, and many can compete quite successfully with their ancestors.

The description Tea was given to roses in the nineteenth century because they had a pleasing fragrance associated with tea

Quite wrong. It originated in the collective description given to the new imports from the East which were brought back to Europe in tea chests – the only available means of transport which could be used to keep plants alive on what was a long and arduous journey.

Roses will only grow on clay soils

This was a popular belief for many years, but appears to have fallen out of favour recently. Although there was some truth in this statement, it was actively supported by the fact that many rose nurseries some 100 years ago were on heavy soils. Few rosarians would subscribe to this theory today.

The dog rose (R. canina) *is a native of the UK*

It was imported by the Romans some 2,000 years ago. Like so many plants that were introduced as empires expanded at that time, it arrived on these shores for use as a medicinal herb. Both its leaf and hip were assumed to have prophylactic attributes.

Blue roses

As in many other walks of life, fashion and colour have a considerable influence on the varieties produced. There have always been deep purples and 'bluey' reds, but it is totally impossible at the present time to breed a true blue rose, due to the absence of the chemical delphinidin.

A rose can revert

There is a presumption that as a rose plant ages, it will revert to the wild type. This is totally erroneous. Sometimes through age and neglect a plant will appear to lose its vigour; it may even in certain circumstances lose some of its colour. It cannot, however, turn back into a dog rose. What can sometimes happen is that the stock that the cultivar is budded on (see chapter on propagating) can throw suckers, that is, 'do its own thing'. If the stock is sufficiently strong enough the cultivar will eventually deteriorate into oblivion and the stock will take over.

A named rose can appear in a variety of colours

If a gardener plants a 'Silver Jubilee', it will always be a pink, it cannot be a red 'Silver Jubilee' or a yellow. There may be mutations but they are usually named to show the origin, but little else. The multicoloured form of 'Peace' is 'Chicago Peace', another form 'Kronenbourg'. There is 'Pink Peace', but it is an entirely different variety which owes little to its namesake.

CHAPTER 8

Showing Roses

The rose is essentially a garden plant which very fortunately can be cut, and thereby is a most suitable subject to enhance the dinner table, decorate with a feast of colour many situations indoors, be proffered as a token of love and affection, and on sadder occasions a tribute to loved ones. After the introduction of the China blood, it very quickly became popular for exhibition purposes at flower shows. Indeed the formation of the oldest rose society in the world, the National Rose Society (now the *Royal National Rose Society*) can trace its history back to certain enthusiasts who joined together to hold the first National Rose Show in 1858, although the Society itself was not formed until 1876. Historically there had been flower shows in the UK since about 1640, but the rose did not come into prominence for another 200 years.

With the introduction of large, almost grotesque, blooms of the Hybrid perpetuals, the rose very quickly attracted exhibitors who vied with each other to grow the biggest and the best. They were called box blooms (Fig. 8.1) and cutting for a show in those early days called for tremendous attention to the refinements of gauging the potential of specimen blooms. Classes in these categories ranged from a modest entry of six blooms to the epitome of excellence in the professionals classes of 72 blooms with no duplications. This was in the good (or bad?) old days when co-ordinating train times was of equal importance as assessing the strength of the opposition. There was very little in the way of weather forecasting and a strict reading of the cricket scores was as valuable as any other intelligence in the general weather patterns. Nevertheless it was not uncommon for professionals or amateurs to travel extraordinary distances and exhibit in as many as 30 shows in a season.

The Modern rose is a much more decorative plant and there is not the same emphasis on size. Rose classes at most flower shows are now divided into speci-

Fig. 8.1
Memories of a bygone age. Box of 24 distinct varieties.

men blooms, a rapidly dying category, and decorative arrangements. In commercial exhibits, even a display of cut flower is a relative novelty at the bigger functions, and greater emphasis is made of the complete plant grown specially for exhibition purposes.

Commercial exhibits

The introduction of the 'new' Floribundas spelt the death knell of the rigid type of nurseryman's competitions where size of bloom was paramount. There are today three basic modes when staging nursery groups. *The bowl*, usually with a diameter of about 35cm (12in), with a grid to allow a good displacement of bloom; (this has been superseded by blocks of oasis). Something in excess of 40 blooms will fill a bowl well, with 35–40cm (15–20in) length stems. A well-cut variety, either Floribunda or Hybrid Tea, suitably conditioned, will endure the rigours of a flower show for four days. *Tall vases* with wide necks will accommodate much the same number of blooms, as will *troughs*, both again using oasis to stabilize the stems. The number of varieties cut is dependent on the size of the stand, but an island group 6m (20ft) by 12m (40ft) will normally require about 80 bowls. A nursery field of about 100,000 maiden plants should be more than adequate to find these numbers. It is interesting to take note of a strong pertinent fact: if a nursery is not 'on cut' (that is, for any reason whatever, a variety or varieties is not in full flush, the number to cut from is totally irrelevant. Commercial stands are normally judged on the versatility of varieties, the quality of the bloom, the standard of arrangement and the freedom from disease.

The Amateur Exhibitor

The truly great horticultural societies of this world can trace their origins to rivalry on the amateur show bench. Rose competitions have fostered tremendous interest in the cultivation of the genus *Rosa* and there are many historical comparisons. The development of the modern car has been motivated by the quest for excellence on the race track; the weekend sailor benefits greatly from lessons learnt in the Fastnet Race; and on the agricultural front, higher yields of economic crops were encouraged by competitions at shows.

There are, of course, excesses and the deliberate pursuit of the perfect gigantic bloom has on occasion been carried to extremes, resulting in lack of plant vigour and resistance to disease. However, we now live in a more egalitarian society where the customer has a greater influence on the merits of a product than the 'medal chaser', with the direct result of the arrival of the keen exhibitor endeavouring to produce the best from varieties 'on the shelf'. This has virtually spelt out the demise of the exhibition varieties whose popularity almost caused disaster for the rose trade when naive gardeners attempted to grow for their enjoyment varieties whose names were gleaned from the lists of prize winners at national shows.

Selecting varieties to show

The preceding comments may discourage potential exhibitors from engaging in competing at their local flower shows which would be a sad loss to societies and even more to themselves. The saving grace is that the majority of modern varieties of bush rose are of such a high standard and so prolific both in flower power and quality, that it can be argued that it is probably easier today to grow and enjoy roses and be equally successful on the show bench than at any time in the history of the rose.

There are, of course, some varieties which consistently gain award after award, but which are notoriously devoid of any contribution to the garden. The novice exhibitor is, however, advised to avoid growing these in his garden.

Growing for exhibition purposes

Good cultivation and the attention to basic principles is the foundation of any good garden practice. Some growers can be persuaded that the biggest and best blooms can only be achieved with excessive use of organic compost, a liberal application of fertilizer and copious watering to produce the correct results. There is some merit in this comment but it must be qualified by good husbandry. The finest blooms are obtained by a combination of these criteria with the fine point that only a hard well-grown plant will produce the best results. Excessive nitrogen will lead to strong soft growth that is a hostage to climatic variations and an encouragement to damage from mildew and blackspot.

Rule one therefore is the liberal application of sulphate of potash very early on in the growing season, usually about 60–70g (2–2¹/₂oz) per sq m (yd). This must be the foundation of all good rose cultivation. The normal application of a top mulch of well-rotted farmyard manure and a generous contribution of a *rose* fertilizer in late spring is essential. Provided these basic principles are adhered to, the putative exhibitor can give the plant an extra push with dried blood or a similar compound in early summer to improve the quality of the bloom.

There is some merit in using foliar feeds, as a boost applied some four weeks before cutting for a show. This is very dependent on the soil and the tonic used. Probably the best is dried sheep droppings steeped in water, and the resulting 'brew' sprayed on to the plants.

Each gardener has their own favourite prescription. What is absolutely certain is that many of these formulas may be successful but they will only improve a good plant and never revive a poor one. The single greatest aid that a possible bloom or blooms can be given is to direct the plant to grow only the strongest shoots. In short, make the plant concentrate its mind on the object of the exercise, to produce prize-winning blooms. This can be done from the earliest growth through to bud formation.

Strong shoots can easily be recognized. Where there is a multiplicity, the weaker ones are rubbed out as the plant progresses and if any more weak shoots appear, they too must be removed. Eventually flower buds will appear and we embark on the crucial stage of dis-budding.

Fig. 8.2 To be effective disbudding must be completed when the buds are immature.

Hybrid Teas

Because of the very nature of Modern roses, many Hybrid Teas produce a large flower head with many small lateral growths. These side growths must be eliminated at a very early stage in the development of the leading bloom. This exercise is called dis-budding and is done by pinching the buds out when they are very young (Fig. 8.2). Some of the Hybrid Teas of earlier years had a history of producing deformed blooms on a leading shoot and the knowledgeable exhibitor would remove these to allow a strong side bud to develop. This practice does not apply to very modern varieties.

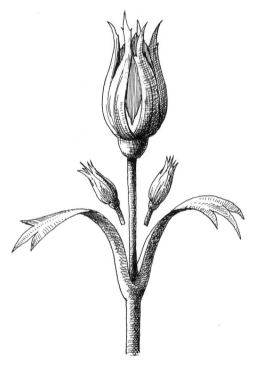

Floribundas

Many Floribundas owe their existence to a parentage that includes strong Hybrid Tea blood. Because of their outward performance in the garden, particularly their floriferousness, they are nevertheless classed as cluster-flowered roses. Many of them produce strong leading blooms which have the intensely annoying habit of flowering much earlier than the rest of the cluster. Floribundas are judged on the quantity of flowers as much as the quality; it is therefore prudent to remove the leading bud of these varieties at an early stage (Fig. 8.3).

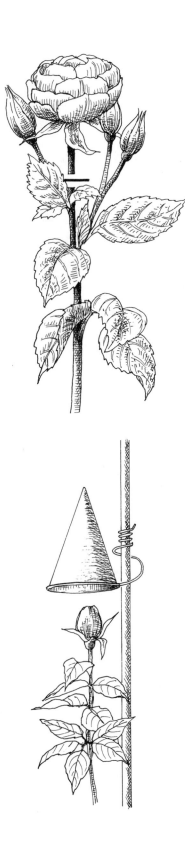

Protecting show blooms

As the exhibitor gains knowledge and skill in staging, he will become aware of the fact that some of his fellow competitors are gaining points with the spotless condition of their blooms. This can be achieved by giving protection to emerging blooms. Small bloom protectors are available, which look like miniature bell tents (Fig. 8.4). Conical in shape with a depth of 15cm (8in) and a radius of 20cm (9in), they are fixed with a spring attached to the stakes, which the exhibitor will use to protect his prize blooms. Rose-growing *aficionados* rightly aver that this form of protection is quite legal, but overall protection is not acceptable. Great skill is required to select blooms early enough in their development to benefit from this practice.

Timing

In theory pruning should be to a timetable enabling a good long flowering flush at the most advantageous times. So much is dependent on local weather conditions that at worst it's a gamble and at best an enormous slice of good luck. The average rose will take approximately 10 weeks to flower from a young shoot to a mature bloom. This growth can be influenced by excessive cold spells and mini heat waves. One of the biggest coups on the show bench happened some years ago when the RNRS Championship Trophy was won by a seasoned exhibitor who meticulously pruned all his plants in a progressive fashion from early to mid-spring. That particular year a neighbouring farmer's sheep broke into his garden and demolished the whole crop of new shoots in late spring. Fortuitously, the climate was very considerate, with long periods of sunshine and warm weather; his fellow competitors' blooms were past their best and he swept the board.

Notwithstanding these frustrations, the finest blooms are normally produced in a climate that is soft, with no extreme variations in temperature. To obtain first quality blooms in the autumn is, curiously enough, never as difficult, but the exhibitor will not have the same choice of varieties or quantities.

Fig. 8.3
Disbudding a floribunda to encourage an even cluster of flower for showing.

Fig. 8.4 Bloom protectors can be adjusted for height.

Fig. 8.5
A class at an important show with six vases, six blooms per vase, six distinct varieties.

Fig. 8.6
A bowl of eighteen specimen Hybrid-tea blooms

The show schedule

A local flower show is not too demanding in the consideration of rose classes and probably there is only provision for:

one vase – 3 Hybrid Tea blooms, two or more varieties.
one vase – 3 stems Floribundas, two or more varieties.
one specimen bloom

and in some early season shows

one vase – 3 stems of Climbers/Ramblers/Old roses.

To the beginner, probably the greatest problem is discerning the difference between Hybrid Teas and Floribundas, as some of the rules may quote large flowered and cluster flowered. These differences are thoroughly discussed in Chapter 2. Nevertheless it is from these first forays into the competitive horticultural world that many lessons can be learnt.

The bigger regional shows and national competitions are as much an exercise in understanding rules and nomenclature as an ability to stage a meritorious exhibit. The competitions are generally divided into *open* classes – that is where anybody, amateur or professional, is eligible to compete – and *restricted* classes for amateurs only. Many societies will divide these further into the potential number of plants the exhibitor is able to cut from: over 1000, 500, 250, and novices.

Apart from the large decorative baskets and bowls, the majority of classes are variations on the basic vase, bowl or box, where the limitations are determined by the number of stems or the eligible varieties.

The main errors quite commonly committed by even experienced exhibitors are few in number but can cause much anguish. The commonest fault is an apparent inability to count. Vase (Fig. 8.5) and bowl (Fig. 8.6) classes are determined by the number of stems – 18, 12, 6 or whatever. This may appear to be a simple rule but is regularly broken. A polite note from the judges NAS (not according to schedule) is small reward for months of work and anticipation. The definition of a cluster-flowered rose (Fig. 8.7) is such a grey area

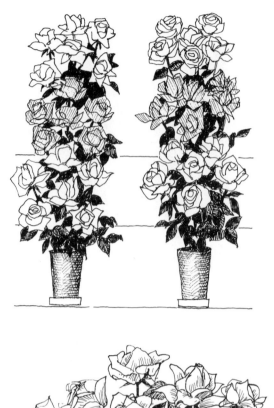

that quite frankly if the rose grown has a vast spray, accept it as such.

If the exhibitor is thinking of attempting to stage a class of Old Garden roses he will be well advised to swot up on his history; some societies/clubs have criteria on the eligibility of a variety by year of introduction.

Competitions for Patio and Miniature roses are becoming increasingly popular. The choice of varieties must command particular attention, bearing in mind that modern thinking defines a Miniature and/or Patio as miniature in both size of flower and foliage.

Fig. 8.7 Vase of six Floribundas; six stems.

Ideally water is best obtained from the rain-water butt or well, but rarely is this possible. Never use warm water and *always* use a conditioner – that is, a chemical that is added to the water *before* cutting commences and encourages the cut stem to take up water. It also acts as a preservative to prevent the cut surface of the stem being contaminated with bacteria and fungus spores. It is not generally realized that a cut flower rarely dies through lack of water, it is the effect of the stem absorbing foreign bodies and air which is usually the ultimate slayer. The chemicals used are well known, containing glucose and various soluble trace elements with fungicides and anti-bacteria agents. The most popular product is Chrysal. There are always instructions with chemicals, which must be adhered to.

Preparing for a show

There can be no doubt that successful showing is the culmination of much hard work and planning. Even the most experienced exhibitor will draw up a list of equipment to be carefully checked every time a show is embarked on. Many of the most experienced trade exhibitors will even produce a rehearsal in their packing shed several times before the bigger events. The beginner is advised to visit a flower show if possible whilst staging is in progress, talk to exhibitors but keep out of the way, observe everything that is happening and go back home resolved to do even better.

The water

Much harm can be done to exhibits if they are not properly maintained from the moment they are cut. This does mean having adequate containers and suitable water. Great care must be taken to scrub buckets thoroughly that are to hold the blooms. The most appropriate are the tall green florists' buckets; they hold about 9 l (2gal), but of greater significance is the depth of water, about 30cm (12in) (Fig. 8.8). Any cut flower must have a good drink once it is cut – this is the foundation for any subsequent success.

Fig. 8.8 A good deep bucket filled to give cut roses an ample drink.

Cutting

This may appear a somewhat fatuous comment but check the date of the show and the time by which staging has to be completed. Arriving at the show venue a day late has been known to happen! Cut flowers in the cool of the evening or early in the morning, dry if possible. High-quality secateurs are acceptable, but a strong, very sharp pruning knife will give a better cut.

Ensure that the bloom is plunged into water immediately – in a matter of seconds rather than minutes. Keep the bloom in the shade and as cool as possible.

There is always the agonizing problem over how long the bloom will last in water and how far ahead of staging the bloom should be cut. A professional will normally cut about 48 hours before staging, but with the use of a cool room this can be extended to a week. There is the temptation to use a freezer, but this can quite seriously damage the petals and a good judge will spot this. (They appear to have the look of blotting paper.) There is no doubt that if kept in a cool room temperature of about 3°C, the petals will appear to elongate. A dark cupboard or cellar is quite adequate, and much can be gained in quality if the bloom is allowed to grow in these conditions for at least two days.

Travelling

Cut flower roses are extremely tolerant and will travel for miles by road, rail or air – but only if they are packed in an orderly fashion. This, in effect, means packing them very tightly. Very rarely will bloom be damaged if packed in this way. This may mean thorning some of the stems which may damage foliage; a torn leaf can mean losing points for presentation. Green buckets, as mentioned earlier, are remarkably stable and if well filled with flower travel successfully. If this is impossible, roll up the stems in newspaper. Never use tissue paper, which if wet sticks to everything and is very difficult to remove. On departure check everything: bloom, spare containers for water if travelling dry, water conditioner if this has to be made up on arrival, stub wires (these may be needed for weak stems), vases and bowls if the exhibition organizers are not providing them. Every experienced exhibitor will always carry a tool box. This will contain bits of wire, hammer, screwdriver, nails and all sorts of oddments which seem invaluable in a crisis.

Although bowls and some vases are wired to give stability to stems when being arranged, there is no doubt that blocks of absorbent polystyrene (oasis) are much easier to handle and can be cut to shape. They are available in a variety of sizes, but the brick shapes are the easiest to handle.

Finally, do not forget that all exhibits must be named and good marking pens and labels are essential, as is a tape measure.

On arrival at the exhibition venue

The primary concern on arrival is the care of the bloom. This is paramount and transcends matters of parking the car or chatting with old friends. If the bloom has travelled dry, containers must be filled with *treated* water and the flower carefully unpacked and plunged into deep well-filled buckets. Travelling wet does not pose quite the same problem, but the bloom will need plenty of air. Assemble your exhibiting gear and bloom at an advantageous position and establish a table to stage on. This is the time to relax, assess the opposition and establish the space allocated to the various classes entered. The most important factor is to allow the bloom to assimilate the atmosphere of the exhibition hall or marquee and warm up after the cool travelling conditions. This is because they will require to be dressed, which is virtually impossible while they are cold and rigid and would easily bruise. If oasis is to be used then make sure that this is being soaked in prepared water. Take some time and do not forcibly submerge the blocks. There is no reason to prepare fresh water for staging, the water used for travelling is quite adequate.

Staging

Establish the containers that will be used in each class, being careful to check that they conform to the criteria demanded. Some societies will provide vases and bowls etc. and in this case it is their responsibility to ensure that they are the required sizes. The sight of show officials measuring containers does nothing for the morale after a long night of staging. As the blooms are arranged in their appropriate classes, an experienced exhibitor will always remove at least 1cm (3/8in) from the bottom of each stem with a sharp knife or secateurs; this is

open, with the petals in perfect concentric circles, with no blemishes and a high point to the formation of the bloom. Some societies will permit a bloom to be wired; a florist's wire (stub wire) is used to give strength to the neck on some varieties of Hybrid Teas by inserting the wire into the calyx and winding round the stem. Fortunately there are few varieties that require this form of artificial support. Points can be lost if wool ties (Fig. 8.11), which have been used to maintain a bloom, or papier-mache plugs, which have been used to persuade petals to assume a better shape, are not removed.

Fig. 8.9 Points can be lost if an exhibit is not staged evenly.

Fig. 8.10 Dressing a bloom to perfection.

to remove any accumulation of air trapped in the stem, or intrusive spores and will become an automatic procedure with experience.

Although technically your exhibit will be judged on the quality of the bloom and the condition of the foliage, there are many methods of enhancing the presentation. First and foremost is the displacement of colour. A vase of six blooms will look lopsided (Fig. 8.9) if there is not an orderly distribution of colour. Two reds do nothing for each other if placed together, and the same can be said for many other hues. A very large bloom of whatever variety can be the pride and joy of the grower but can be out of proportion in a vase with other blooms and may have to be discarded in spite of its quality. A bowl of roses can show an excellence of cultivation but be ruined by overcrowding, a flat arrangement, torn or diseased foliage.

Dressing

The final exercise when staging is to dress the bloom. This can mean teasing a petal out with a soft camel-hair brush (Fig. 8.10) to positively pinching the base of a petal to present a more open effect. Points will be gained with a perfect bloom which *at the time of judging* appears half to three quarters

Fig. 8.11 A good bloom can be preserved by tying to travel. Remember to remove before judging or else it will be disqualified.

Fig. 8.12 A perfect specimen.

On completion of the staging check that your entries are in the correct class and complete by labelling accurately (Figs. 8.12 – 8.15).

Judging roses

The most comprehensive handbook defining the responsibilities of show organizers, rose judges and the rules of judging is *Judging Roses* published by the Royal National Rose Society. There is little merit in repeating word for word much of what is stated in the book, but a few salient points are worthy of mention.

'A rose show is both a competition between those who exhibit and a spectacle for the enjoyment and education of those who come to view it.'

Fig. 8.13 Box of six specimen blooms.

'Judges must always know their roses.'

Methods

'In fairness to exhibitors judging must commence promptly at the scheduled time.'
'In each class the eligibility of the exhibits must first be established.'
'Of the eligible exhibits, all which are manifestly inferior shall be dismissed from consideration before comparing those which remain.'
'Exhibits remaining after dismissal of inferior entries shall then be ranked in order of merit so far as necessary to establish the winners of awards.'

Fig. 8.14 Bowl of twelve decorative blooms.

Standards – form

'A double bloom type in the "perfect stage" – should be half to three quarters open with the petals symmetrically arranged within a circular outline.'
'For any large flowered (H. T.) type (sic) the outer petals should regularly surround an upright and well formed conical and pointed centre. For any other type the outer petals should regularly surround a central formation typical of the variety e.g. rounded, rosette, quartered, pompom etc.'

Cluster

'The inflorescence should be representative of its variety, with the blooms gracefully

Fig. 8.15
Miniatures.
Perfectly
proportioned
palette for the
smallest roses.

Presentation
'The exhibit should be gracefully balanced in relationship to the container for height and width and enhanced by good colour combination. The flowers and foliage should be artistically arranged to avoid either crushing or excessive gaps and without exposing such expanses of stem or foliage that the flowers are not the dominant feature of the exhibit.'

Serious defects
'Individual blooms of irregular outline; having fewer than the average numbers of petals; split, blunt or confused centres; stained or damaged petals; evidence of removal or trimming of petals, immaturity or over-development of blooms; overdressing so as to appear unnatural; blooms left tied or pelleted.'

Miniatures
'Special emphasis is placed upon the requirement that miniature roses are miniatures in all aspects of size of flowers, foliage and stems.'

There is little to add to these excerpts from this valuable publication other than that the purpose of *this* book is both to inform and encourage the proper appreciation, *enjoyment*, showing and cultivation of the rose. Entering competitions with the products of one's own cultivation is a tremendously exhilarating experience which, once enjoyed, is compulsive in its effect and can become addictive. Perhaps the extract at the beginning of this section should read: 'a rose show is both a competition between those who exhibit and a spectacle for the enjoyment and education of those who come to view it but of primary consideration is the enjoyment and satisfaction of the competitors.'

arranged and so spaced as to permit their natural development, neither being crushed together nor exposing wide gaps between them.'

Substance
'This refers to petals. These should be firm, smooth and of good texture, neither coarse nor flimsy and free from blemish.'

Foliage
'This should be adequate in quantity and size; undamaged, fresh and clean in appearance, of good colour and substance for the variety.'

CHAPTER 9

Species, Old Garden Roses and Modern Shrub Roses

The Royal National Rose Society's publication *The Rose Directory* describes shrub roses thus: 'plants usually taller and or possibly wider than bush roses and particularly suitable for use as specimen plants'; and a bush as 'a variety of moderate height particularly suitable for cultivation in groups'. *The Oxford Illustrated Dictionary* describes a shrub as a 'woody plant of less size than a tree and usually divided into separate stems from near the ground', and a bush as 'a woody plant with numerous stems of moderate length'. Many other authorities have completely avoided or refused to define roses in particular and used the pretext of date of introduction to compile rose lists by categories. Mother Nature surely never intended to pigeon-hole each and every plant!

Groups of roses in this chapter have been compiled with only two criteria: they must primarily be an asset to the garden and, probably of equal importance, they can be obtained from a good selection of rose nurseries round the world. There is little merit in growing a variety simply for its historical interest and even less if it is virtually unobtainable.

For the convenience of the reader, the roses are divided into well-recognized groups to enable varieties to be easily traced and using a modicum of common sense allied to accepted garden practices.

Species Roses

Although some botanists have attempted to catalogue this group to the extent of defining some 450 separate species, it is now generally acknowledged that at the present time there are some 150 identifiable species in existence. Some authorities would call

them wild roses, which in many ways they are. Historically all roses have evolved from plants formed in the wild, by a series of mutations, chance hybrids and, latterly, deliberate plant breeding. The plants in this section include some of those which contributed to the status quo and many more that are still grown for their natural beauty as wild forms. Not every wild rose will make a good garden plant. The salient point to remember is that they require the normal cultivation demanded of any garden; some are happier on alkaline rather than acid soils and they are all very hardy. They never require pruning in the accepted sense of the expression but in certain circumstances may need some encouragement to make a good garden plant. This normally means cutting out the occasional dead branch and in exceptional circumstances cutting out complete live stems to encourage new growth from the base.

When purchasing plants of this type, ascertain that they are propagated from an established clone. Some are still sold as 'grown from seed' which unfortunately can make for the cultivation of inferior plants. There is, however, no reason why they cannot be grown on their own roots, but again establish the source of the clone. A unique feature of species roses is their diversity of character and their contribution to the garden. Unlike the ordinary modern cultivar, some of their characteristics have little to do with flower and they are cultivated for their foliage, largesse of hips and in one or two examples, scent of foliage.

They are wild roses; let them grow naturally and never cut them down in a conventional pruning mode or the result will be a horticultural monstrosity.

**Species (wild roses) –
a garden selection**

The dates referred to are the recognized date of introduction.

R. californica **'Plena'** 1894. A mature shrub that will produce a dense thicket of stems about 1.8m (6ft) tall. The rich dark pink, small double flowers are produced in mid-summer. There is some doubt as to its fragrance but selected clones have a memorable scent.

R. ecae 1880. A relatively short dense shrub 1.2m (4ft), which flowers very early with an abundance of very small bright yellow single flowers. It will need some protection in cold areas. Discovered by Dr. Aitchison in Afghanistan, who used the initials of his wife (ECA) to name this interesting plant. Fern-like foliage is a typical characteristic. There are two modern garden forms:

R.e. **'Helen Knight'** F.P.Knight 1966. This is a splendid free-flowering form, rather more robust than its parent, that will produce a plant about 1.5m (5ft) tall and is one of the earliest to flower. Normally it will stand a considerable depth of cold, but has been known to be cut down by the frost. If this should happen, saw it off at 15cm (6in) above ground level and it will produce a rejuvenated plant in due course.

R.e. **'Golden Chersonese'** E.F.Allen 1963. A seedling which counts 'Canary Bird' as a parent. In a good season it will produce swathes of golden yellow blooms and a plant about 1.8m (6ft) tall. It is very hardy.

R. farreri var. *persetosa* 1914. A fern-like graceful shrub about 1.5m (5ft) with dark green foliage which turns crimson purple in the autumn with small bright orange-red hips. The minute salmon-pink flowers appear in early summer and must be the smallest in the rose garden, hence the name 'Threepenny Bit Rose'.

R. foetida 1790. Sometimes called the Austrian briar. This is obtainable in three forms, the single yellow (Austrian Yellow) and the bi-colour (Austrian Copper). They are both interesting roses, pretty shrubs with fern-like foliage, up to 1m (3ft) tall. The third, 'Persian Yellow', is a double form and is the origin of yellow in modern hybrids. Unfortunately it is also the source of black spot. This group must therefore be grown in isolation from other roses.

R. forrestiana 1918. A plant for the autumn. The 1.8m (6ft) stems are smothered in bottle-shaped small red hips in neat clusters. The pinkish-carmine flowers are of little consequence.

R. glauca (R. rubrifolia) Another native of Europe, which can best be described as a purple-foliaged dog rose, but that is an understatement. The clear pink flowers are insignificant but the foliage can contribute to garden design with the deep mauve stems and leaves supporting myriads of bright scarlet round hips in the autumn. An unlikely colour combination which is quite dramatic in its effect. Until recently catalogued as *R. rubrifolia* and may still be traced in lists under this name.

R. highdownensis 1908. This was at one time confused with the *moyesii* family. Now established as a distinct species, the medium single pink blooms are freely produced on a 3m (10ft) shrub with medium-sized foliage and a rich harvest of flask-shaped hips in the autumn.

R. hugonis 1899. A very strong vigorous shrub which is generally described as some 3m (10ft) in height, but will cover a difficult wall to some 6m (20ft). The vigorous bronze stems with fern-like foliage are covered in primrose-yellow single blooms in very early summer and small dark red fruit in the autumn. *R. cantabridgensis* is a coarse form of *hugonis*, with slightly larger and paler flowers. It is probably slightly hardier but this is debatable.

R. macrophylla 1818. A vigorous smooth wooded plant 3m (10ft) tall with flask shaped hips.

R. mirifica stellata 1916. An interesting small shrub about 1m (3ft) tall. The foliage and hips are strongly reminiscent of the gooseberry bush. The simple lilac-pink flowers occur spasmodically throughout the summer. A native of W. Texas and Arizona, it is sometimes known as the Sacramento rose.

R. moyesii 1984. This species is probably the most widely grown of all the wild roses for the superb production of medium-sized flask-shaped hips. A very vigorous plant, in its native habitat it will climb into trees to a height of 12m (40ft); but will normally grow in most equable climates to 3–4m (10–15ft). Easily identified by its bright metallic-red single flowers and dull green foliage. The fecundity of its seeds has given rise to a whole host of hybrids, not all of which are successful. It is as well to establish the source and then clone as many of these as possible.

R.m. 'Geranium' 1938. Probably the most successful form. The mature plant is not so vigorous as the original type, growing to about 1.8m (6ft), with very bright geranium-coloured blooms and a spectacular show of hips in the autumn. There is a pink form, 'Sealing Wax'.

R. multiflora 1800. Although this justifiably has greater prominence as the ancestor of many of our modern Floribundas, Shrubs and Climbers, and as a stock for propagating purposes, it does have the right to be judged on its own merits. It is still useful in environmental planting and has been widely used as a crash barrier on central reservations in road-building programmes; it has been proved to be a soft cushion for erratic motorists! The long thick masses of innumerable canes are covered in myriads of single small creamy-white flowers in the summer and masses of small red hips in the autumn.

R. pomifera (R. villosa) 1761. A medium-sized shrub about 1.2m (4ft) with pretty grey-green downy foliage. The scented flowers of pale pink appear in mid-summer, followed by large orange apple-shaped hips, hence its name Apple rose.

R. primula 1910. (Incense rose.) A novelty among species. The young leaves, when crushed, give off a strong aroma of incense. The 1.5m (5ft) plant, with pale yellow flowers, is happiest in a slightly damp environment where it will emanate a pleasing fragrance on a warm summer evening.

R. roxburghii 1814. (Burr rose, Chestnut rose.) An interesting shrub where buff-coloured stems peel during the winter months to give a fresh dimension to a rose plant. The pretty single white and rose-pink blooms are followed by an extremely prickly hip, more reminiscent of a thistle head. If they are not taken by the birds, they will turn orange-yellow. The leaves are numerous, with as many as 15 leaflets.

R. rubiginosa The Sweet briar or Eglantine is a native of Europe and is quite distinct from its plebeian cousin, the dog rose. It is easily identified by its numerous thorns and the extraordinary sweet fragrance of the leaves. It will repay the trouble of tracking down a good clone. The pretty clear pink single blooms are borne in profusion in early summer. The spectacular oval hips are a great attraction to bird life.

R. sericea pteracantha 1822. There is some confusion with the name, some authorities using *omeiensis*. This is of little consequence, the matter of greater significance is obtaining the true clone of the type that produces a shrub some 3m (10ft) in height with interesting fern-like foliage and small pale white blooms, but most important of all the thorns. These are truly stupendous when young, they are a brilliant ruby colour and semi-translucent (Fig. 9.1). Some 4–5cm (1½–2in) at the base and 2cm (¾in) in length, they are to be seen at their best against the light. Young shoots clothed with these thorns are spectacular. A good strong plant will stand severe cutting back to produce this great contribution to the garden.

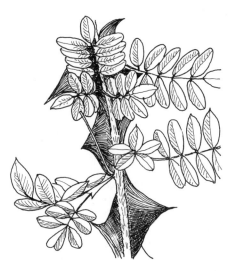

R. soulieana 1896. A wild rose for the big garden. A mature plant can be 3–4m (10–13ft) in height and equally as broad. The grey-green stems and foliage carry medium-sized clusters of ivory-white fragrant flowers borne in abundance. An extraordinarily beautiful spectacle when viewed from a distance. Generally hardy but does have the annoying habit of not producing flower until about five years old. Small orange-red hips in the autumn.

R. spinosissima (R. pimpinellifolia). In garden terms these are generally catalogued as Scotch roses or Burnet roses and at the end of the eighteenth Century were tremendously popular, some nurseries listing as many as 200 names. Largely fallen out of favour, they are still to be found in many old gardens as they are remarkably long living. Because of the tremendous variety, it is difficult to describe with any accuracy specific varieties, but they can still be obtained under their basic colours. They are superb round shrubs, usually 1m × 1m (3ft × 3ft). Some can be half as big again. Their small leaves are a characteristic dark green, with seven to nine leaflets on a multitude of fine stems heavily covered in straight prickles and fine bristles. The basic colours and flower forms are small and globular, with many petals and range from white to pink, dull red and

some mottled varieties. Although yellows do not appear prominently in these lists there is an interesting hybrid *R.* × *harisonii* ('Harison's Double Yellow') which is the legendary 'yellow rose of Texas'.

R. sweginzowii 1909. A truly spectacular vigorous plant some 4m (13ft) tall. The stems are well covered with large flattened thorns and bright pink flowers, but its chief attraction is the large skeins of bright red bottle-shaped hips.

R. virginiana 1760. This is a pretty shrub from North America, with dense green foliage about 1.2m (4ft) tall. The almost perfect pure pink small flowers bloom in mid-summer. A unique feature is the beautiful red and yellow foliage in the autumn.

R. wilmottiae 1904. A beautiful shrub with grey-green fern-like foliage. The arching habit is enhanced by deep lilac-pink flowers with yellow anthers and orange-red hips.

R. xanthina spontanea 'Canary Bird' 1908. Apart from the *moyesii* family, this the most popular species in gardens today. The clear yellow single blooms make a tremendous effect on every arching branch. Growing to about 1.8m (6ft), the main flush appears quite dramatically in late springe and can repeat intermittently in the autumn. On some soils, particularly in wet acid situations, the occasional branch will die back but it is not fatal. A small handful of ground limestone hoed in should cure this frailty.

The ten most popular species are:
R. ecae 'Helen Knight'
R. farreri persetosa
R. glauca (R. rubrifolia)
R. hugonis
R. moyesii 'Geranium'
R. moyesii 'Sealing Wax'
R. rubiginosa
R. sericea pteracantha
R. sweginzowii
R. xanthina spontanea 'Canary Bird'

Fig. 9.1
R. sericea
pteracantha
with spectacular
translucent
thorns.

Old Garden Roses

The rose developed as a garden plant in the Western world and by the eighteenth century some easily identifiable groups could be listed. Although all of them were Shrubs of various types and colours (there were no climbers in the garden at that time), they had one characteristic in common, which was that they were only summer flowering. The introduction of the rose from the Orient, particularly those carrying remontant (recurrent-flowering) genes, gave a fresh impetus to a genus that had lost its popularity. This list of Old Garden roses can therefore be divided quite comfortably into two parts:

Summer flowering:
  Albas
  Damasks
  Gallicas
  Centifolias
  Moss roses
  Sweet briars

Recurrent flowering:
  China roses
  Tea roses
  Noisettes
  Bourbons
  Hybrid perpetuals
  Hybrid musks
  Rugosas

Old Garden roses. Summer flowering

There have been variously catalogued some 1500 hundred varieties which can claim to be eligible to appear in this section and it is difficult to understand why Empress Josephine, who professed to have a considerable collection, could only muster a total of some 200. Apart from the species and their offspring, which must have totalled some 300 or 400, there were at least 200 Moss roses and probably as many more Centifolias. They are all very easy to grow – indeed they must have been – to still be in existence today, and a considerable number can be grown on their own roots.

Because they produce bloom on two-year-old wood, they are very difficult to use

as cut flower for the reason that rose wood of this age will not take up water with the enthusiasm that young maiden wood can. The remedy is either to cut the short stems supporting the bloom or alternatively cut and plunge the long branches into deep treated water for about 24 hours.

Pruning them can be confusing but is made easier by cleaning up a plant in the summer immediately after flowering. This is a simple process of very heavily dead-heading and removing about a third of the old flowering stems every year to allow new growth to develop. If this technique produces the desired results it is a simple matter in the following spring to remove any old or decrepit wood.

Some of them are notorious for mildew but this has very little effect on their flowering potential and any spraying should be limited to preventing the spores from infecting their more modern neighbours. Like all other roses, they will appreciate being fed well, particularly with the early season mulches of organic manure.

The Albas

Characterized by strong upright canes, some of which bow over in a rather splendid fashion with the weight of the bloom. Historically they have been in cultivation since the time of the Greeks and Romans. As their name implies, they are basically white in simple and double forms. Many are flushed with the most delicate pink. They are characterized by their handsome grey-green foliage and consistency of scent. Their greatest claim to fame is that their admirers maintain that a variety of Alba was the White Rose of York, one of the factions in the English 100 Years War or War of the Roses. When peace was declared the Red Rose of Lancaster (*R. gallica*) and the White Rose of York (*R. alba*) were to become the Tudor Rose, the emblem of England today. Naturally, in the course of time there evolved many varieties, probably over 40 in all, which can be identified as possessing unique characteristics. The following six are sufficiently different to warrant listing; some have been in cultivation too long to date.

'Celestial' (*R.* **'Celeste'**). Semi-double blooms, almond pink with a refined fragrance and copious foliage of grey-green. About 1.8m (6ft) high.

'Great Maiden's Blush' 1400. This is the most widely grown of all the Albas and there are many variations, some with the most evocative and descriptive names: 'Cuisse de Nymph Emue', 'Incarnata', 'Mme de Gros de St Germains'. An upright vigorous 1.5m (5ft) shrub with fragrant ivory coral-centred flowers.

'Königen Von Dänemark' 'Queen of Denmark' 1826. Although there is probably some Damask blood in this variety, it is commonly identified as an Alba. The foliage, a silvery blue-green, provides an exquisite backdrop to carnation-scented rose madder blooms. 1.5m (5ft).

'Maxima' 1400. Another Alba that possesses a host of historic names: 'Jacobite Rose', 'White Rose of York', 'Cheshire Rose'. A vigorous creamy-white, very double variety with the Alba scent and grey-green foliage. 1.8m (6ft).

'Mme Plantier' 1835. Convenience has probably caused this rather lovely sprawling shrub to be represented as an Alba. Mme Plantier is extremely vigorous and is quite capable of climbing to 3m (10ft) and will spread to about 1.8m (6ft). The flat double flowers are pale cream.

Small 'Maiden's Blush' 1797. A smaller version of its big sister.

The Damask Roses

There is considerable confusion in the rose world in differentiating between the Damasks and the Gallicas and no definitive description has ever been satisfactorily produced. To the gardener they are both extremely reliable products of the Old World and it is not too difficult to imagine these lovely Old Garden Roses being distributed along the caravan routes from Asia Minor.

'Gloire de Guilan'. A variety rich in fragrance, with an almond-green foliage and a sprawling plant with thickets of stems some 1.2m (4ft) tall and quartered blooms of clear pink.

'Kazanlik' (*R. damascena* **'Triginti-petala'**). Grown as an economic crop in Bulgaria and elsewhere for the production of 'attar of roses'. It is an interesting plant that will provide petals for pot-pourri in more temperate climates. The flowers are a warm pink and double.

'Leda' 1800 (Painted Damask). Probably a hybrid Centifolia but none worse for that. A compact shrub 1m (3ft). Downy grey-green foliage. Shell-pink flowers picoteed with crimson lake.

'La Ville de Bruxelles' 1849. A strong shrub 1.5m (5ft) that will cut well. Pure pink fragrant quartered blooms.

'Mme Hardy' 1832. A splendid Shrub rose with flowers of pure white with a rich green eye as they develop. Very free-flowering with a strong scent. 1.5m (5ft).

'York and Lancaster' 1551. An interesting but disappointing variety which is occasionally mistaken for its superior putative parent *R. mundi*. Grown as a semi-climber, the blooms are mottled or blotched blush pink and white.

The Gallicas

Until the introduction of the new breeding lines from the Far East, this was without doubt the most popular type of rose grown throughout the Western world. The cultivation was easy; many of them are exquisite in flower arrangements and most of them have a superb fragrance. In common with its contemporaries they are sadly only summer flowering but have a long season. The colours range from shell-pink to the deepest purple-ruby. A characteristic of this group is the proliferation of striped varieties, a factor which has recently become very popular again in many modern cultivars. The group includes some fantastic flower formations; the plant style is easy to accommodate and, although they will benefit from the judicious selection of flowering wood (a more appropriate phrase than 'pruning'), they will 'thrive on neglect'. Historically as befits a variety which was the 'garden rose' of the Middle Ages and Renaissance, it assumed in its various forms many titles including 'The Apothecary's Rose', 'Rose of Provins', 'The French Rose' and, not least, the 'Red Rose of Lancaster'.

Many authorities claim that there were as many as 1,000 varieties in existence at one time or another. Apart from its popularity, the group can claim the distinction of contributing greatly to the ancestry of the Modern rose. If one has to point to its weaknesses they are few, but there is a tendency to mildew. Very fortunately, this only appears after the flush of flower and as this has been occurring for some hundreds of years, must prove a point or two. Even today some catalogues will list between 50 and 60 varieties. This list, considerably reduced, gives prominence to those which are both garden worthy and easy to obtain. The first three are considered close to the type and could well appear in the species section.

R. gallica 'Complicata'. This is a rose for the 'wild' garden. A vast sprawling shrub with simple large pink flowers. A mature plant will certainly grow to about 4m × 4m (13ft × 13ft) and will thrive with no attention for many years.

R. gallica var. officinalis (Apothecary's rose). A tidy plant about 1m × 1m (3ft × 3ft) and one which is reputedly valued for its medicinal properties. The light crimson flowers are interesting and have given cause to the notion that this is the Red Rose of Lancaster, a theory that has never been properly authenticated.

R. gallica 'Versicolor' (R. mundi) This is the rose that has sported more legends than any other. The large striped semi-double blooms of very pale pink and light crimson are borne profusely on a rela-

tively short bush about 1m × 1m (3ft x 3ft), usually about the middle of the summer. It is a total contradiction of everything that rose buffs delight in telling the gardener. It suffers the most abominable mildew in late summer and autumn, it will grow very freely on its own roots, which means suckers can be dug up and planted elsewhere. Cut down hard, that is to about 30cm (1ft) immediately after flowering, it will yield a crop of new growth which will produce the most amazing floral display the following season (Fig.9.2). The rose *Rosa mundi* is reputed to be named after Fair Rosamunde, the mistress of Henry II, the Plantagenet king. Legend suggests that when she died the adage 'non rosa munda sed rosa mundi' was placed on her catafalque, which briefly translated implies that 'she was not as pure as the driven snow but was a courtesan'.

'Belle de Crécy' 1840. An almost thornless plant about 1m (3ft) tall. The blooms are variable lotus-pink and orchid turning silvery mauve with a sweet fragrance.

'Camaieux' 1830. Pale pink blooms striped purplish crimson. One of the many striped varieties.

'Cardinal de Richelieu' 1840. The velvety purple fragrant flowers which are produced in modest clusters are smaller than some in this family. The thin dark green stems covered with abundant foliage grow to about 1m (3ft).

'Charles de Mills'. The large purple-ruby blooms form a beautiful pattern as they develop. A plant about 1.5 × 1.5m (5ft × 5ft), which develops as a tremendous asset to any rose collection. The blooms cut well and will grace the most voluptuous flower arrangement (Fig.9.3).

'Du Maître d'Ecole' 1840. From the schoolmaster's garden, a large-flowered pink variety with shades of amethyst and magenta. An upright bush about 1m (3ft).

'Rose des Maures'. Semi-double blooms of mulberry velvet with a lighter reverse. A very old variety with thin stems, almost thornless, about 1m (3ft).

'Tuscany Superb' 1848. One of the best. Semi-double blooms, velvety dark red turning damson plum. The sturdy plant about 1.2m (4ft) will contribute to any border or grown as a specimen plant in the wild garden.

To conclude this section, it is appropriate to quote from an old catalogue:

The renonculiform shape of the fully expanded flowers, the luxuriance of their animated, spotted and variegated shapes and the brilliancy of the stamens added to a fragrance sui generis *constitute the beauty of the French Rose. The blooms retain their variegation of shades according to the soil and exposure; the variegation of shades is most striking in a poor soil, in a dry temperature and on old plants.*

The Centifolias
Cabbage rose (Provence rose). An amalgamation of many strains that the Dutch fostered, collected and propagated in the fifteenth and sixteenth centuries, which appeared with a strong and individual identity in the still life works of the Old Masters. The name cabbage is confusing and is a reminder that they were grown for their cut-flower potential and used by vegetable growers as an added attraction to enhance their produce when they brought the fruits of their labours into the town markets.

R. × centifolia. A lax shrub about 1.5m (5ft) tall with cup shaped flowers of deep pink with a strong scent. There is a white form 'White Provence'.

'Fantin-Latour'. A rather beautiful rose with typical cup-shaped flowers of delicate pink, about 1.5m (5ft) tall.

'Petite de Hollande' 1800 (Pompon des Dames). This could be called a patio of the late seventeenth century. The clusters of small double flowers are clear pink with deeper centres on a tidy bush about 75cm (2ft) tall.

'Robert le Diable'. A small shrub about 1m (3ft) tall which flowers later than most in this group (mid-summer). A crimson red with hints of purple and violet.

'Tour de Malakoff' 1856. A lax plant that can be grown as a semi-climber. The large cabbage-like blooms are magnolia-purple turning magenta grey. Will grow to about 2.4m (8ft).

Fig. 9.3 'Charles de Mills' with the most interesting petal formation in the Old Garden roses.

There are two more varieties which are usually listed in this section and make interesting garden plants.

'Bullata' 1600 (Lettuce-leaved rose). The very large leaves make this a very distinguished and bold plant about 1.5m (5ft) tall. The blooms are similar to the type – very double, cabbage shaped, deep pink with a pleasing fragance.

× *centifolia* **'Cristata'** 1826 (Crested Moss, Chapeau du Napoléon). In some catalogues erroneously listed as a Moss rose. The calyx *only* of the flower carries any pretext of the 'mossy' characteristics of the true Moss rose. A lax grower with pretty deep pink flowers will grow to about 1.5m (5ft). The 'chapeau' alludes to the fantastically shaped calyx which makes it an interesting feature.

The Moss roses
It is difficult to believe that the Moss rose is a relatively recent introduction into our gardens. It first appeared as a mutation of *R. centifolia* about 1600. Although cultivated since that time, they only became a cult in the early nineteenth century and at one time there were as many as 200 catalogued. The terminology 'moss' has been given to the extensive whiskers and glaucous structure of the excrescences on the stems and flower buds which exude a delicate perfume when handled.

As a complement to the garden, they are difficult to place. Only the Common Pink and White make good plants and the foliage deteriorates quite dramatically once the flower is over. There is doubt, however, that they can contribute to the garden. Planted at the back of a border and allowed to grow up over their shorter neighbours, they are magnificent in flower but best forgotten afterwards. They range from white through to pink and red/purple. A yellow does exist but it has a doubtful constitution. It is interesting to observe that the American breeder Ralph Moore has used one of these forms to produce 'miniature' Moss roses. Moss roses, apart from 'William Lobb' are all about 1.2m (4ft) tall.

'Blanch Moreau' 1880. A profuse double white with a tremendous scent. Needs protection against mildew.

'Common Moss' 1700 (Old Pink Moss, Communis. The selection of the correct clone of this variety is extremely important. There are many 'variations' but a well-shaped plant in full flower can vie with the best of other Old Garden roses. Beautifully perfumed with medium-sized pink flowers when in full bloom, it is a sight that is worth growing and looking for. There is a white form, White Moss, of equal distinction and red 'Crimson Globe', which is not so pretty.

'Capitaine John Ingram' 1856. A pretty flower with double blooms of dark crimson purple.

'Mme Louis Lévêque' 1898. One of the larger-flowering Mosses. The soft pink blooms are quite dramatic in their opulence.

'Nuits de Young' 1845 (Old Black). The darkest moss available in the lists today. The black-purple blooms of less-than-average size for the type are borne freely on a plant of slender habit.

'Striped Moss'. There are a few striped Mosses but none of any distinction.

'William Lobb' 1855 (Duchesse d'Istrie, Old Velvet Moss). Probably the most opulent looking of all the Mosses. The large purple flowers are seen to their best advantage when supported on the long stems in the manner of a climbing rose. Erroneously catalogued as a climber, it is nevertheless happier cultivated as a very tall grower, requiring ample support.

The Sweet briars
R. **'Eglantine'** (Sweet briar). The sweet-smelling briar of Shakespeare's sonnets, this is sometimes confused with its common-placed cousin the dog rose (*R. canina*). The type can be distinguished by the higher density of thorns, which are small, and the

young foliage which is highly scented when crushed. The small blush-pink flowers produce a rich harvest of bright red round hips.

There are many forms, some of which do not have the fragrance. Probably the best method, unless a reliable source is known, is to identify a good specimen and collect its hips in late autumn. The seed is slow to germinate but will usually grow true to its parent. The Sweet briars have contributed little or nothing to the development of the modern rose, but in the late nineteenth century the Head Gardener to Lord Penzance produced a host of hybrids using *R. foetida* as the other parent. They were named after various members of the family and characters in Sir Walter Scott's novels. They do not possess the scent of the type and share the other parents' propensity to black spot.

Old Garden Roses. Recurrent Flowering

China Roses

The first plant hunters to visit China were well versed in stories that had filtered back to the West of roses that flowered well into the autumn, a fact inconceivable in the early eighteenth century in Europe. However, by the end of the 1780s the first plants arrived in Europe. But it was to take some time before there was a realization that the genes from this group could provide a basis from which to produce a greater continuity of flowering in our own garden roses. There is little evidence in our gardens today of the proliferation of this astonishing breakthrough, but those that have survived or were a direct result of their introduction, make worthy garden plants.

'**Cécile Brunner**' 1881 (Sweetheart rose). Probably one of the most exquisite roses that has ever been bred. The very small blooms of shell-pink are classically shaped and are reminiscent of Dresden china. The plant is a moderate performer but extremely long lived. There is a pretender to this variety – 'Bloomfield Abundance'. It is a coarse grower with identical

blooms, although younger by 40 years. It is easier to grow than Cécile and is sometimes supplied to the unwary as the original variety. A valuable addition to the garden is the climbing mutation (see under 'Climbing roses').

'**Louis XIV**' 1859. A variety with very dark crimson, semi-double flowers of perfect shape. The bush is a moderate grower but the variety is regarded by many as having high novelty value.

'**Mutabilis**' 1932 (Tipo Ideale). This is an interesting and very pretty single rose. The blooms develop from a pale yellow through to bronze and red. Although it will make a shrub, it is much happier grown as a semi-climber. Obviously of great age, it is curious that it was discovered relatively recently.

'**Old Blush**' 1781 (Parsons' Pink, Monthly rose). This is the rose probably cultivated in China for centuries that has contributed so greatly to the development of the modern rose. The silvery-pink flowers with a good scent are produced in a bush of moderate height. Young hybridists could do worse than use this pollen with some of our modern cultivars. A question of 'back to the drawing board' and lots of patience.

'**Perle d'Or**' 1884. This rose is remarkably similar to the variety 'Cécile Brunner' but for the colour which is Indian yellow.

'**Sophie's Perpetual**' 1960. A tremendously free flowering bush about 1m (3ft) high with cup shaped blooms of lilac pink with deeper shades. The perpetuity is quite astonishing.

'**Viridiflora**' 1833 (Green rose). A strange rose, almost a botanical freak. The sepals or bracts are a confusion of rosettes grape-green in colour, which turn brown as they age. A modest plant, about 1m (3ft) high, which has been found to be useful to the flower arranger.

Tea roses

These rather sophisticated varieties were the immediate ancestor of the modern Hybrid Teas. By derivation they can well be described as the ultimate in garden forms of the China roses, from which they were obviously developed in their country of origin.

A peculiarity of this group is the name, which is typical of a whole genus where so much folklore finds itself surfacing as fact. Before the invention of the Wardian Case, which was used so effectively to bring plants back from the Far East, a long and arduous journey 200 years ago, the most suitable method of plant transport was the old tea chests. It does not require much imagination to realize that very quickly they became to the gardener whose responsibility it was to resuscitate them in Europe 'the rose plants that arrived in tea chests'. They certainly do not have any affinity to tea-scent as in the beverage.

The tea roses were tremendously popular towards the end of the nineteenth century, presumably as a foil to the coarseness of the gross Hybrid perpetuals. Their biggest drawback was an inability to withstand the winters of northern Europe and many manuals of that time give elaborate details of their protection from the frost. One or two varieties have survived, presumably on the merits of their hardiness.

'**Gloire de Dijon**' 1853. More, fully described in the climbing section, it is worthy of recognition here to remind ourselves that at the time of introduction the buff-apricot blooms were the closest colour that had been achieved in the quest for a yellow rose in the public imagination. The dream of many brides at that time, according to contemporary literature, was a bouquet of 'Gloire de Dijon'.

'**Lady Hillingdon**' 1910. Rather a beautiful deep apricot with bronze foliage and a lovely perfume. The plants require some protection in hard climates. There is a climbing form that grows well on warm walls.

'**Niphetos**' 1843. The creamy buds mature to a pure white. A florist's rose 100 years ago and benefits from some protection. There is a climbing form.

The Noisettes

With the proliferation of breeding lines there were inevitably quite a number of developments, not all of which have stood the test of time. Originating in the USA in the middle of the last century, they found favour in many gardens and have bequeathed a number of varieties which are still grown in numbers today.

'**Alison Stella Gray**' 1894. Pale yellow.

'**Manetti**' 1837. Used as a stock for forcing varieties.

'**Maréchal Niel**' 1864. Fragrant golden yellow.

'**Mme Alfred Carrière**' 1879. White.

'**William Allen Richardson**' 1878. Apricot.

These are all climbers and are found in the appropriate section. Worthy of mention is 'Mme Alfred Carrière', probably still one of the finest climbers and 'Maréchel Niel', which was grown extensively in India during the Raj.

The Bourbons

The history of the development of the rose is a curious mixture of fact and legend, which is still happening today. The introduction of the family of Bourbon roses is a classic example of this phenomenon. On a small island in the southern Indian Ocean, the 'Old Blush' China was planted up with a Damask. The resulting seed harvested and sown produced a variety of rose that was commonly used as hedging material. The director of the local botanical garden sent some of the seed from this crop back to France in 1817, where it was successfully raised and became the foundation of a new strain of roses called Bourbons, named after the little island in the Southern Indian Ocean, the Ile de Bourbon, now Reunion. The potential of this cross was quickly recognized and in a short time a recurrent flowering shrub with abundant well-formed blooms, with quite of lot of fragrance, was being produced.

The group has developed in two directions. One with a predominance of China blood is relatively thornless; the old favourite 'Zéphrine Drouhin' is a Bourbon. The other line is rather more upright in growth with the thorns of its Damask ancestors. Many of these interesting varieties are still in commerce today. They are all very hardy but will require heavy dead heading to maintain a continuity of flower. Some of them do require support and can be called semi-climbers. The majority are subject to some mildew and other frailties of the rose but none suffer enough to deter their culture. In many respects they are pure Victoriana, their large incurved blooms providing models for embroidered cushion covers and similar needlework.

'Boule de Neige' 1867. Pure white globular balls of bloom. Moderate in size with a strong fragrance. The foliage is a healthy dark green on a medium-sized bush. Best treated as a short shrub.

'Honorine de Brabant'. A big shrub about 1.8m (6ft) which gracefully falls with globular blooms of wisteria pink with stripes of fuchsia. Will cut and decorate rather beautifully.

'La Reine Victoria' 1872. A slender bush with large pale green leaves and generously sized deep lilac-pink blooms. Rather lax in habit, which will require some support. The plant responds to being planted in a very fertile pocket of soil with plenty of garden compost. It will require some protection from black spot but this does not appear to have deterred its many admirers. There is a pale pink sport, 'Mme Pierre Oger' (1878), which is identical in habit and which will occasionally revert to its parent. Both admirable subjects for large flower arrangements, e.g. in church.

'Louise Odier' 1851. A graceful shrub about 1.5m (5ft) tall with slightly flatter blooms than its contemporaries. The rose-pink camellia-shaped blooms are very fragrant. Probably healthier than the two preceding varieties.

'Mme Isaac Pereire' 1851. Without a doubt one of the most fragrant roses that have have ever been introduced. The shrub or large bush has many attributes of its Damask parent, with large deep green leaves and thorny stems. The blooms are more reminiscent of a big blowsy modern Hybrid Tea and are a deep pink, shaded red. The early blooms have an annoying habit of growing a green eye, but this is quickly forgotten with the abundance of large heavily scented flowers. Light annual pruning in early spring will produce a magnificent and shapely bush.

'Souvenir de la Malmaison' 1843. A beautiful rose which will produce the most stunning blooms of peachy cream in a good summer. Normally a large shrub about 1.8m (6ft) tall, there is a climbing form which does not have the 'flower power'. The wise purchaser will establish that the nursery stocks the true bush form.

'Variegata di Bologna' 1909. A large undisciplined shrub producing a rich harvest of white striped, deep crimson blooms, smaller than some of this type.

'Zephrine Drouhin' 1868 and **'Kathleen Harrop'** 1919. Although these are well described in the climbing section, they are worthy of comment in their 'family' section, to emphasize the point that they will make rather beautiful lax shrubs.

Hybrid Perpetuals

With the benefit of hindsight it is not too difficult to trace the way that Hybrid Perpetuals evolved. Many authorities speak with enthusiasm over the plant form of the Bourbons, with their delicacy of presentation of the bloom, but there was a hint that the bigger and brasher blooms derived from the Damask parent would attract attention. Inevitably the plant breeders saw the potential of the larger blooms and in modern day parlance threw the pollen at potential breeding material from a variety of sources to produce in a relatively short space of time, the most extraordinary population explosion of new varieties. One of the most knowledgeable commentators of that time, Paul, makes the biting comment in the second edition (1860) of his famous book on roses that the previous year some 100 new varieties had been introduced with a plea, 'where was it all going to end?'

Basically there evolved a plant coarse in habit. Although called bush roses they had little in common with the orderly plant style we expect in our plants today. The emphasis on the size and novelty of the bloom is a legacy which we still suffer today with some of our keener exhibitors. Little regard was made of plant style. The result was gross plants with even grosser blooms, a commentary on the philosophy of the Victorian *nouveau riche*.

The name Perpetual has been queried recently because of the absence of autumn bloom. This is a curious observation and is as much a comment on lack of rose culture today as the shortcomings of some of those Victorian monstrosities.

The Hybrid Perpetual is very easy to grow, is hardy and has a gross appetite. There is a great art in producing a high flower production. Basically they should be allowed to grow naturally, tall stems included, and not cut down very hard. Advantage is then taken of the old method of pegging down. This is in essence bending the big stems over to produce a plant with a multitude of horizontal growth. The flower production from them is quite astonishing and on a good plant with this practice continual new growth can achieve a remarkable show from early summer to mid-autumn. Space is the criteria but that is something gardeners 150 years ago did not lack. Such was the rivalry to produce the biggest and the best that most successful exhibitors were reluctant to divulge the secrets of their triumphs. Most varieties were budded on R. canina but a considerable number were propagated on *multiflora*

and *manettii* cuttings. We have inherited a few of the more remarkable seedlings produced at that time before the pure flower form and finesse of the modern Hybrid Teas usurped their popularity. They include some blooms of extraordinary size and a smattering of victorian oddities, of which there was a propensity. The number of Hybrid Perpetuals that at one time or another were marketed must run into some thousands.

'Baron Giraud de l'Ain' 1897. Although technically a sport, this is an interesting novelty which has stood the test of time. The slightly cupped deep crimson blooms are scalloped with silver. The whole appearance may look slightly ragged but there is an interesting beauty and novelty in the formation.

'Empereur du Maroc' 1858. A plant of shorter stature than many of its contemporaries, possibly predicting the introduction of the Hybrid Teas. Dark velvety maroon, the blooms are of moderate size with a rather splendid scent. The colour is variously described as the first red to have purple shadings.

'Ferdinand Pichard' 1921. Rather a latecomer to the Hybrid Perpetuals, but is always listed in this section because of its vigorous growth and flower form. The medium-sized cup-shaped blooms are pink, heavily streaked and laced with crimson. Quite a startling combination and considered by many connoisseurs to be the finest striped rose yet produced.

'Frau Karl Druschki' 1901 (Snow Queen, Reine des Neiges, White American Beauty). Probably the whitest rose that still exists from that period. The variety of names give a story of strong anti-Teutonic feeling in 1914 then there was a trend to give more acceptable names to a patriotic public. An extraordinarily vigorous plant with pale green leaves and very large blooms. Lack of scent is a disappointment and very soft petal texture does mean that it is not happy in wet weather.

'Gloire de Ducher' 1865. Huge blooms which were once described as 'great purple plums ready to burst with vineous juices'. A vigorous bush that will pay good dividends if well fed and pegged down.

'Hugh Dickson' 1905. A true rose for the exhibition box. Considerable skill is required to attain perfection with this variety. The very vigorous shoots must be pegged down to achieve the quality which it has the potential to produce. The large scarlet crimson blooms, well disbudded, are still a tribute to the Dickson family who were breeding roses commercially many years before their UK competitors. There is another darker variety 'George Dickson' (1912) which has been equally successful on the show bench but does not have quite the same scent.

'Paul Neyron' 1869. The enormous blooms of deep rose pink with a delightfully sweet scent are produced on a vigorous plant. The stems and foliage are strangely reminiscent of 'Peace' and suggest that its affinity to that variety is not great in distances of breeding.

'Reine de Violettes' 1860 (Queen of Violets). One of the prettiest roses that have been bred. The medium sized blooms (small compared to some other Hybrid Perpetuals) are an exquisite amethyst and purple which opens flat with quartered petals. Heavily perfumed blooms are produced consistently throughout the season.

'Roger Lambelin' 1890. Another sport similar to 'Baron Giraud de l'Ain', with which it is very often compared. The crimson blooms are edged and streaked with white. Quite different to the Baron, whose colouring is scalloped. Does not possess the vigour or robustness of health of its peers.

'Souvenir de Docteur Jamain' 1865. Rather a pretty rose whose dark velvety wine coloured blooms can easily be burnt in the hot sun. On a good day worth a lot of trouble and very good as a cut flower.

'Vick's Caprice' 1897. Large fragrant blooms, soft pink which are flecked and striped with strawberry. The plant is almost thornless and compact. Healthy but does not like wet weather.

Top ten old garden roses
'Cécile Brunner'
'Charles de Mills'
'Common Moss'
'Mme Isaac Pereire'
'Mme Pierre Oger'
'Mme Plantier'
'Paul Neyron'
'Reine des Violettes'
'Rosa Mundi'
'William Lobb'

Hybrid Musks
At the beginning of this century a Reverend gentleman, Joseph Pemberton, developed the hobby of rose breeding in an Essex garden. He obviously had his own ideas and used as his stud a shrub he had collected in Germany sometime previously: 'Trier'. He used the pollen of several contemporary Hybrid Teas and bred an interesting group of shrub roses. Originally called Pemberton Hybrids they are listed today as Hybrid Musks, a misleading description as their pedigree has little to do with *R. moschata*. In some respects they were 'born before their time'. The early 1900s are more associated with the proliferation of Hybrid Teas and shrub roses took a back seat. When Pemberton died he left his breeding stock to John Benthall, his head gardener, and Mrs Ann Benthall. Now sadly overtaken by building estates, they persevered with the parson's progeny for another 20 years.

Basically the Hybrid Musks are vigorous shrubs about 1.5m (4ft) tall with a spreading habit. They produced clusters of scented bloom and with maturity a plant should be well proportioned as wide as it is tall, and a mass of flower in mid-summer and early autumn. They are used in great numbers today for landscaping purposes but need some attention to produce an autumn flush. Apart from the normal mulching and feeding they do respond to an additional 'push' (fertilizer) in mid-summer and require to be heavily dead headed immediately the summer show is over. Do not prune but rather cut back any long shoots to produce a well shaped plant.

'**Buff Beauty**' 1939. This was probably bred by Pemberton but not marketed for a number of years. Quite distinct with beautiful buff yellow sprays of scented blooms it can be disappointing when first planted as the shoots appear to go off at a tangent; it is however well worth persevering with to produce a beautiful shrub.

'**Cornelia**' 1925. The bronzy foliage is a good background to the large clusters of medium-sized blooms of coral and shell pink with old rose; it has a lovely fragrance.

'**Felicia**' 1928. This is probably the most underrated of all the Pemberton hybrids, the large clusters of shell pink flowers are produced in prodigious quantities. An ideal subject for hedging, about 1.2m (4ft) tall and as wide, or as a specimen plant (Fig.9.4).

Fig. 9.4 'Felicia', a Hybrid Musk which will produce lovely lax growth.

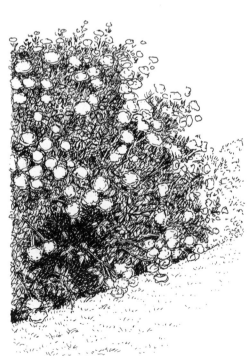

'**Moonlight**' 1913. One of Pemberton's early successes. Clusters of creamy white small flowers. Vigorous and scented.

Pax (1918). Very large semi-double flowers, creamy white. Repays judicious dead heading.

'**Penelope**' 1924. Marvellous clusters of pale salmon pink blooms which turn to a beautiful pink as they develop. A mature plant with an abundance of flower which is replicated in the autumn, a memorable sight.

'**Prosperity**' 1919. A rather more upright plant than many in this group. Looks at times rather like an overgrown Floribunda. The clusters of ivory white flowers have a pleasing fragrance and weather well.

'**Robin Hood**' 1927. The only red that Pemberton bred. The bright scarlet single flowers are produced in small clusters. An important rose as it has been a successful parent to some good modern varieties.

'**Trier**' 1904. The purists would not have this variety here but as it is a parent of the preceding varieties it deserves to be mentioned. The single flowers are produced in clusters. They have a pleasant scent and the plant is upright in stature, very free and hardy.

The Rugosa family

This family of plants is probably the most interesting in the rose family. The type are identified by dark green leathery foliage and the deeply etched veins which appear wrinkled, hence the name *rugosa* (*ruga* is the latin for 'wrinkled'). The other familiar characteristic is very bristly prickles that cover the stems. A form was collected in Japan (hence the name in some lists 'the Japanese Rose'), at the end of the eighteenth century. It grew in the northern part of the country as a plant of coastal regions. It quickly escaped in Europe and is sufficiently widespread to assume the title of an indigenous plant, particularly in the Scandinavian countries. A recent publication has listed some 120 varieties or forms which has been quite a revelation in commerce, although not surprising when one considers the fecundity of the seed. The important factor that has greater significance than any other is the remarkable resistance to disease that many rugosas possess. The aim of hybridists must be to use this welcome characteristic in future breeding programmes. There is unfortunately evidence that this has not been successful so far. The other factor which is dominant in using the genes of the rugosas is the extraordinary dominance of the spines. Nevertheless there are ample grounds for thinking that roses of the future, particularly the bigger shrubs, will have a lot of rugosa blood in their make up.

The majority of the rugosas are ideal subjects to make hedges requiring no maintenance, they produce thickets of impenetrable shrubs; many have a good scent, and some have the most amazing large tomato shaped hips. Those closest to the type are very hardy and in fact relish a very cold winter. One or two can become 'straggly' and tend to take over small gardens. A simple solution to this problem is to cut them down about every five or six years to within 30cm (1ft) from ground level in midwinter; a drastic step but one which will produce a rejuvenated plant which will flower the next season in profusion with at least 60cm (2ft) of new growth.

Do not prune. Rugosas must never be pruned in the conventional sense. If this is done they will proliferate short ugly growth and destroy the concept of a well balanced shrub.

Before describing the most popular cultivars it is worth noting that there is a selected form that is used as a standard stem. The production of these stems in quite prodigious numbers is a significant industry within the rose-growing world. Their merits are discussed in the chapter on propagation. This type of rugosa is quite alien to its cousins and has no merit as a garden plant.

'Agnes' 1922. This plant has a singular claim to fame as the first yellow rugosa.

An upright shrub 1½m (5ft) with dense foliage and double scented amber yellow blooms.

'Blanc Double de Coubert' 1892. An extremely popular member of this family. The large semi-double pure white flowers are richly scented on a plant that can become an embarassment in some gardens due to its vigour. A mature tree can be 1.8m (6ft) tall but is ungainly at that height and needs cutting down hard every three or four seasons to make a better shaped plant.

'Conrad Ferdinand Meyer' 1899. Fragrant silvery-pink flowers on a robust plant with large leaves and thorns. Unfortunately, is prone to disease quite early in the season.

'Fru Dagmar Hastrup' 1914 (Frau Dagmar Hartopp). One of the most useful and beautiful rugosas in the garden today. A compact plant which matures at a height of about 1m (3ft) producing typical rugosa foliage with lovely soft light pink flowers throughout the season, with a bonus of bright crimson round hips in the autumn. The young maiden plants from the nursery are disconcertingly small but planted 1m (3ft) apart, they mature to make a beautiful hedge.

'Hansa' 1905. A very vigorous and tough variety with crimson-purple scented flowers and large red hips. Used extensively for environmental planting in northern Europe.

'Hunter' 1961. Very bright crimson flowers on a medium-sized plant 1.2m (4ft); well shaped with luxurious foliage and an abundance of thorns.

'Mrs A. Waterer' 1898. A broad thorny bush with semi-double crimson flowers and deep green foliage.

'Pink Grootendorst' 1923. This, one of three rugosa seedlings with clusters of small double flowers whose forms are remarkably similar to garden pinks (dianthus). The plants make pleasant specimen bushes about 1m (3ft) tall and the pale green rugosa foliage is supported by very spiny stems. There is a red form 'F.J.Grootendorst' (1918), from which the pink is a mutation and the two revert from one colour to the other quite frequently. There is also a white form 'White Grootendorst' (1962).

'**Robusta**' 1982 (Kordes Robusta, Korgosa). One of a new generation of rugosa seedlings. The plants are vigorous with beautiful dark green foliage. The single bright scarlet flowers are produced freely throughout the season. In northern Germany, where it was bred it is grown to about 3m (10ft) in the most astonishing hedges of scarlet and green, but generally elsewhere it is kept down to a 1.2m (4ft) plant. There is a seedling (not a sport) 'Pink Robusta' (1987), 'The Seckford Rose', 'Korpinrob', with large double glowing pink flowers on a very upright plant.

'**Roseraie de l'Hay**' 1901. One of the most popular rugosa hybrids. A magnificent shrub that is adaptable as a specimen shrub or for hedging purposes planted about 1–1.2m (3–4ft) apart. A prodigious grower, 1.5m (5ft) that fills out well. The semi-double large royal purple flowers are heavily scented, but unfortunately are sterile. This is more than compensated for with a good continuity of bloom and a dark green foliage that turns a beautiful yellow in the autumn.

R. rugosa '**Alba**' and *R. rugosa* '**Rubra**'. These two varieties are linked together as they are identical in every respect apart from the colour of their flowers. Although many of the rugosas are good hedging plants these two excel in this respect. The robust rounded plants will grow to about 2m (6ft) with single flowers of either pure white or crimson purple with a delightful scent. They are both recurrent and produce very large tomato-shaped and coloured hips, with luxuriant dark green foliage.

'**Sarah Van Fleet**' 1926. An upright free-flowering pink rugosa with large double blooms. It has now probably been superseded by 'Pink Robusta', as it unfortunately succumbed to the ravages of rust which appear after the first flush of flower.

'**Scabrosa**' 1950. A dense upright shrub with deep mauve pink single flowers. The dense growth contributes to a good plant for medium-sized hedges 1.5m (5ft) tall and gives an abundant crop of orange-scarlet hips in the autumn.

'**Schneezwerg**' 1912 (Snow Dwarf). One of the smaller flowering members of this family. The clusters of pure white flowers are produced on a plant that matures to about 1.25m (4ft); the abundant perfume and high yield of small red hips makes this a useful plant in the smaller garden.

'**Vanguard**' 1932. An upright, very gross plant with salmon/bronze blooms. Different to many in this group, it is probably happier as a climber.

'**Yellow Dagmar Hastrup**' 1987 (Gelbe Dagmar Hastrup, Topaz Jewel, Moryelrug). One of the newest arrivals, and most welcome to this famous group: unfortunately named as it has no resemblance or association with the pink form and the introducers claim that it is the first yellow rugosa! Nonetheless, the clear yellow very double medium-sized fragrant flowers are very pretty. Shorter than most, but will grow to about 1m (3ft).

Modern Shrub Roses

Collectively this group is very difficult to define; some of them obviously have a close affinity to the groups that have already been discussed but nevertheless are too distant in appearance to be identified with their peers. Others are so modern in flower form and shape that this is the only practical section for them to appear in. They all have one thing in common, they do not take kindly to harsh pruning and are much happier grown naturally with heavy dead heading to encourage a good plant shape.

Summer-flowering Modern Shrub roses

The title of this group is slightly incongruous as one usually associates the term 'modern' when describing roses as an obligatory characteristic of flowering in recurrent mode. Nevertheless there are a few that have appeared recently that are too good to be refused garden room. They all make huge plants if allowed to grow naturally and may require staking if grown in windy positions. In common with all roses they respond to the normal seasonal feeding and spraying programmes.

'Alchemist' 1958. A vigorous very double fragrant yellow with shades of orange. The plant will require support to encourage a good plant and is grown as a climber in Europe.

'Cerise Bouquet' 1958. A truly astonishing shrub that requires no maintenance and will develop into an enormous plant, well over 4m (13ft) tall and equally as broad. The slightly arching habit and grey-green foliage are a frame work for clusters of cerise crimson double blooms of medium size. The plant is apparently sterile and dead heading is a fruitless exercise.

'Constance Spry' 1960. The bright pink large loose flowers have an old fashioned appearance as befits a variety which claims a Gallica as one of its parents. This can be a big sprawling plant which requires some support and is occasionally grown as a climber when plants 6m (18ft) wide are common.

'Fritz Nobis' 1940. A medium sized but substantial plant 1.5m (4.5ft) that produces clusters of soft blush pink perfectly formed blooms. The grey-green foliage is slightly arching and the autumn show of small orange hips is impressive.

'Fruhlingsgold' 1937. Some 60 years ago the famous German rose breeder Wilhelm Kordes raised a range of shrub roses crossing modern varieties and a form of one of the Scotch briars. They are all very free flowering shrubs which if allowed to grow naturally can be 4m (13ft) tall. Smothered in early summer with large single blooms with a good scent they are an extremely valuable plant in the garden, they all have the prefix 'Fruhlings' (spring). Probably the most successful and most popular variety is 'Fruhlingsgold' with canary yellow flowers turning primrose as they age. They require no pruning whatever and are robust enough to grow unsupported. Others in this range are: 'Fruhlingsanfang' (1950), white; 'Fruhlingsduft' (1949), lemon-yellow flushed pink; Fruhlingsmorgen (1942), cherry pink/white centres; 'Fruhlingszauber' (1942), silvery pink.

'Scharlachglut' 1952 (Scarlet Fire). A big arching shrub with astonishingly big single flowers of brilliant scarlet crimson. A plant in full colour is a memorable sight, with a bonus in the autumn of large urn-shaped bright orange hips that last well into the winter. Although generally grown as a shrub, it is equally spectacular as a pillar rose, which can give extra colour and height to a big border of herbaceous plants.

Modern Recurrent-flowering Shrub roses

This group of plants has a curious history of nomenclature caused by the 'human factor'. In the 1950s and 1960s shrub roses, apart from the really Old Garden roses, suffered a reversal of fortune simply because to call any Modern rose a shrub was tantamount to damaging its sales potential. The consequence was that many of the more vigorous Floribundas, whose rightful place in any list was here, found its way to the bush section of catalogues. There is still a legacy of this with certain countries using the term 'grandiflora'. Even worse now that the descriptive word shrub has been accepted, there is a reluctance to use the title 'ground cover'. The prospective customer must be aware of some of these frailties.

Because of this greater rationalization and a more realistic approach this group has now gathered together many of those very vigorous varieties that were a source of embarrassment when a compiler of catalogues attempted to place short growing varieties like 'Trumpeter' or 'Regensberg' in the same section as 'Fred Loads' or 'Mountbatten'. In truth, to attempt an overall description is a practical impossibility: however a good guide is to determine the majority as 'Floribundas that are not pruned'. Ranging in height from 1.5m (5ft) to 3m (10ft), they are invaluable to give colour to rose and shrub borders where colour is at a premium and it is this group that will be described first.

'Bonn' 1950. One of the first of the new very vigorous roses. The tall upright canes 1.8m (6ft) have large handsome leaves. The clusters of medium-sized flowers are a bright orange red which was considered a very modern colour when it first appeared.

'Chinatown' 1963 (Ville de Chin). The vigorous canes 1.5m (5ft) have light green glossy foliage. Truly recurrent deep yellow blooms turning pale with hints of scarlet as they age in medium-sized clusters.

'Dorothy Wheatcroft' 1960. Brilliant vermilion red clusters of medium-sized blooms that require careful placing in the garden with this difficult colour.

'Fountain' 1970 (Fontaine, Red Prince). A rose that made history in the UK, when it became the first shrub rose to be awarded the highest honours. The blood red flowers of Hybrid Tea quality are produced on well clothed stems with large dark green leaves and makes an upright shrub about 1.5m (5ft) tall.

'Fred Loads' 1967. Another bright red vermilion-orange with the most extraordinary vigour, which is quite capable of growing to about 3m (10ft). Planted in a small group at the back of a border, it will make a tremendous splash of colour.

'Joseph's Coat' 1964. This rose was

originally introduced by its raiser as a climber but was not happy in that position, looking very thin. However, as a shrub with the yellow flowers that turn pink and red with age it has become very succesful. The plant will require severely dead heading to encourage autumn bloom, about 1.25m (4ft) high.

'Lavender Lassie' 1960. A pretty rose delicately coloured lavender pink with a lovely scent.

'Miss Pam Ayres' 1982 (Bonanza, Kormarie). A free-flowering shrub with clusters of yellow flowers turning red as they mature, revealing an affinity to an ancestor – 'Masquerade', which was the first popular variety to possess this colour character. The 1.2 (4ft) shrub is a spectacle of colour which must be dead headed.

'Mountbatten' 1982 (Harmantelle). Originally catalogued as a Floribunda, this variety is obviously much happier pruned lightly and grown as a shrub. The large double yellow blooms are produced in big clusters and provide good splashes of colour.

Fig. 9.5 'Westerland', a modern Shrub which illustrates its Floribunda origins.

'Remember Me' with its perfectly shaped blooms has a good pedigree, coming from 'Troika' and 'Silver Jubilee'.

'Royal William'
has been
described as the
healthiest crimson
red with a
fragrance,
a description
it fully merits.

This standard
'Nozomi' has the
most elegant plant
form which
demonstrates the
adaptability of
some of the
Modern Ground
cover roses to
different uses.

Weeping standard 'Excelsa' has been a favourite for many and gives credence to the description of this type of plant as the umbrella rose.

Standard 'Iceberg' is probably the most successful Floribunda to be grown in this mode and will give a long period of flower.

'Golden Showers' is the most widely grown re-current Climber with large open blooms and a very long flowering period.

'Rambling Rector'
with clematis
'Hagley Hybrid'
and *Solanum crispum*
'Glesneven' make
a good splash of
colour.

'Mermaid' is the most exquisite yellow climber to ever grace the garden but can be difficult to grow in very cold situations.

'Compassion'
is the heaviest
scented modern
recurrent Climber
with large blooms
and a robust plant
structure.

'**Sally Holmes**' A pretty shrub, pale pink single flowers about 1.2m (4ft) tall.

'**Uncle Walter**' 1963. A bright crimson red that was first introduced as a Hybrid Tea but its vigour was an embarrassment and it is now generally accepted as a shrub rose. The dark green foliage contributes to a handsome plant about 1.5m (5ft) tall.

'**Westerland**' 1969 (Korwest). A vigorous and hardy shrub with semi-double blooms variously described as an apricot or a bright golden orange. The clusters of flower contribute to a splendid shrub about 1.2m (5ft) tall (Fig.9.5).

Shrubs

This group can be justifiably be called true shrubs. They are not overgrown Floribundas as in the previous section. They all have an identity of their own with a good round shape rather than vertical in appearance.

'**Angelina**' 1976. A pretty flower, single bright rose pink, usually produced in large clusters on a healthy plant about 1.25m (4ft) tall.

'**Ballerina**' 1937. This can well be described as a bye-blow from the hybrid musk stable of the Rev. Pemberton. Some authorities even list it with them. However this is a totally different plant. Although coming into flower rather late in the season the plant about 1m (3ft) high and as broad is a mass of small single flowers, pink with a white eye, that have a peculiar visual affinity to phlox. Their continuity is extraordinary. Dead heading will keep the plant nice and fresh but severe pruning is not recommended as the shape of the plant should be allowed to develop quite naturally. There is a red seedling 'Marjorie Fair', not a sport which is usually described as a 'Red Ballerina'.

'**Cardinal Hume**' 1984 (Harregale). A violet-purple more reminiscent of the Gallicas in colour but fortunately recurrent. The semi-double blooms in clusters are scented and the plant which is slightly spreading is about 1m (3ft) high.

'**Elmshorn**' 1951. When this was introduced many admirers described it as a perpetual-flowering 'Dorothy Perkins'. A description which is slightly over the top but accurate when describing the flower form. The vivid pink sprays contribute to a slightly spreading 1.2m (4ft) plant with medium green foliage.

'**Golden Wings**' 1956. A superb plant that meets every criteria a shrub should have. A mature specimen is about 1.5m (5ft) high and wide and in mid-summer is a mass of open clear golden yellow single flowers reminiscent of the famous climber 'Mermaid'. Very little pruning is required but an attention to dead heading will encourage a continuity in its flower production.

'**Kathleen Ferrier**' 1955. Great clusters of deep salmon pink double flowers. The arching growth gives a pleasant relaxed effect which can give colour for a long period in the summer.

'**Lichtkönigen Lucia**' 1966 Probably the most underrated yellow shrub that has ever been raised. The intense lemon yellow blooms of Hybrid Tea quality are produced on well proportioned shrub about 1.8m (6ft).

'**Mary Hayley Bell**' 1987 (Korparau). A delicately scented bright pink shrub with a great continuity of flower. The well shaped trusses make up to a plant about 1m (3ft) high.

'**Nevada**' 1927. A fantastic shrub which requires a large garden. A mature plant is quite cabable of growing 4m (13ft) high and as wide. The open creamy white semi-double flowers can smother a plant in early summer to produce an unforgettable sight which is replicated to a modest degree in the autumn. Allowed to grow naturally, it should never be pruned, does not require to be dead headed (it is sterile), and is a valuable contribution to the garden. Under certain climatic conditions the petals can assume a pink tinge which is slightly disconcerting. 'Marguerite Hilling' (1959) is a pink mutation which is identical in every respect apart from colour.

'**Pearl Drift**' 1979 (Leggab). The blush single blooms give an interesting colour to the rose border with plants about 1m (3ft) in height. Could be mistaken for a Floribunda which it is not, and does not take kindly to pruning.

'**St Dunstans**' 1991 (Kirshru). Pretty lemon yellow clusters of medium-sized flowers give good colour to a medium-sized plant with very healthy foliage.

New English Roses

Some years ago David Austin had the brilliant idea of crossing some of the Old Garden roses with modern varieties. The success of this venture has been phenomenal. The plants are a curious mixture of plant and flower forms but as a generalization it can be said that they are tall Floribundas or short Shrubs. They must receive only the lightest pruning to give a good shape. A selection of them is described here but there are many more. One or two are susceptible to the usual frailties of the rose family and the potential purchaser is advised to see them growing before making any decisions.

'**English Garden**' 1986 (Ausbuf). Soft apricot yellow with a pleasing fragrance.

'**Gertrude Jekyll**' 1986 (Ausbord). Rosette-shaped blooms of glowing pink with a deep fragrance.

'**Graham Thomas**' 1983 (Ausmas). Probably the best variety on this list and certainly one of the finest fragrant yellow shrubs of recent years. Named after the doyen of writers on old garden roses, a distinction richly deserved. The 1.2m (4ft) shrubs must be allowed to grow naturally and will provide a valuable splash of colour,

it is also very useful as a cut flower for decorative purposes.

'**Heritage**' 1984 (Ausblush). Heavily reminiscent of the older roses with cup-shaped blooms of clear shell pink with a lovely fragrance.

'**Mary Rose**' 1983 (Ausmary). Really a bush rose with a lovely Damask fragrance and large pink blooms.

Climbers as Shrubs

Some of the new generation of recurrent-flowering climbers make stunning shrubs. Planted in groups or singly and cut down every spring to about 1.2m (4ft), the effect is truly amazing. They will require little or no support.

Name	*Colour*
'Aloha'	Coral pink
'Altissimo'	Velvety Red
'Compassion'	Salmon shaded gold
'Danse de Feu'	Orange red
'Dublin Bay'	Deep red
'Golden Showers'	Bright yellow
'Handel'	Creamy white edged pink
'Laura Ford'	Yellow and amber
'Mme Alfred Carrière'	White
'Pink Perpétué'	Rose pink
'Summer Wine'	Coral pink
'Swan Lake'	Silvery white
'Sympathie'	Scarlet
'The New Dawn'	Flesh pink
'Warm Welcome'	Orange vermilion
'White Cockade'	Ivory

Shrub Roses as Standards

Rather like many other garden plants, the rose has enjoyed the ups and downs of fashion and popularity even with the meteoric rise to universal acceptance in the last 100 years. Within the rose-growing fraternity there is even now a wide range of opinion on the merits of certain plant shapes and forms. This is well illustrated by the choice of appropriate varieties that can be grown as standards. Much of this is related to plant form and compatability. It is now a well-established fact that many successful roses just do not grow when propagated on a standard stem. The reason still has to be explained. There are also some varieties whose shape do not make good standard heads. Two examples of this will explain the problem. The Queen Elizabeth rose, which is regularly listed as a standard, is totally unsuited to make a good head with its upright growth. Similarily in another respect 'Paul's Scarlet' is propagated as a weeping standard which is a total disaster. The stems are not lax enough and the effect, unless persuaded with heavy and ugly 'umbrellas', is most unnatural.

We are fortunate with the rising popularity of shrubs to have a large selection of varieties to choose from and some can make a valuable contribution to the garden. They are normally budded at about 1.2m.

'Ballerina'. This shrub will make a beautiful round head of flower.

'Bonica'. The slightly lax growth can give very pleasing results.

'The Fairy'. A well-grown plant of this variety is a truly astonishing sight. The slightly lax growth will give the impression of a recurrent flowering weeping standard!

'Graham Thomas'. A well-established standard with a good track record of flower production and pleasing growth.

R. mundi. This is quite a novelty on a standard and produces a nice round head of striped bloom.

***R. xanthina* 'Canary Bird'**. This very early flowering species can make the loveliest specimen in the garden. The big heads of bright yellow flower are complemented by delicate fern-like foliage.

CHAPTER 10

Bush Roses and Standards

Hybrid Teas and Floribundas, the subjects of this chapter, are only babies when compared to the rose itself. Acknowledged as the first of this race of Modern roses was the 1867 introduction 'La France', which brought together the best of the Hybrid Perpetuals and the Tea roses – hence the name of Hybrid Tea. It also brought with it a new type of growth – less boisterous than the Hybrid Perpetuals and stronger than the Teas. The flowers, too, brought together the best of shapes, giving us what we call 'classic' form in a rose.

And yet how much luck played in all this has seldom been discussed. M. Guillot, the raiser of 'La France' indiscriminately planted a whole collection of rose seeds and one day, among the weak and spindly ones, he saw a two-toned pink seedling that was standing out way above all the others. He knew it had promise and entered it for a competition organized by the Society of Horticulture of Lyons for a rose that would carry the country's name. M. Guillot's rose was chosen, which was lucky for him because in subsequent trials and competitions it came nowhere! However, it went on to become the rose that saw in the twentieth century. It was planted everywhere; its soft pink flowers, its pleasant fragrance, and its relatively good growth won it international admiration.

That was the start of the Golden Age of Roses – hybridizers of the late nineteenth and twentieth centuries evolved a race of roses that would have bewitched the rosarians of old. They blended together the blood of Musk, Bourbon, Damask, Gallica, Tea, China – roses from every part of the world and from every description. These were the cornerstones of a new race.

The roses produced from all this intermingling of the ancient and the old gave us bushes that were not just beautiful to look at but also had the ability to go on flowering all season long. In other words where most roses had been spring and early summer-flowering, now we had many varieties that would bloom twice, even three times between spring and autumn.

The colours also mingled and took their cue from the rainbow, as combinations that could only have been dreamed about emerged. Individual colours, too, that had never been seen, came to the forefront – colour breakthroughs such as the first true yellow 'Soleil d'Or', which was achieved in 1900.

And the shapes of the flowers changed. They became larger, high pointed with a symmetry no other flower could approach. Perfection was just about on the doorstep when one of the great rose writers, the Rev. Dean S. Reynolds Hole, wrote in his magical *The Book of the Rose* a definition of perfection in a rose bloom. It should, he said, have:

Beauty of form – petals abundant and of good substance, regularly and gracefully disposed within a circular symmetrical outline.
Beauty of colour – brilliancy, purity, endurance.

'Peace'

The Modern rose has provided all that, and more. It seemed to edge its way through the early part of this century until in 1946 when 'Peace', the rose that was to change the whole outlook for the gardener, was introduced. Here was a new variety that had everything that Dean Hole might have wanted, as well as enormously vigorous growth on a bush that kept itself well within the accepted proportions and did not shoot away to the skies.

Indeed 'Peace' heralded for gardeners the final twist to make it truly the golden age. Since its appearance roses have gone on and on improving beyond all bounds of the imagination until today there is a whole bevy of wonderful beauties there for selection. A bush rose now means that – it is a true bush; not carrying straggley, long growth to make it look halfway towards a Climber. It is a plant that is acceptable anywhere in the garden – and can be found high enough to reach your knee or tall enough to top the tallest human.

Floribundas

In its own way the Hybrid Tea has tempted hybridizers into more and more imaginative combinations, one of which produced the Floribunda rose. Here was a rose that was different again: it produced clusters of blooms in neat trusses, almost in the tradition of Polyantha roses. But it was different again – it had vigour and far more flowers. The year was 1911 and 'Ellen Poulsen' and 'Rodhatte' came on the market. But there was little fuss about them, even though the flowers had a long life on the bush which was winter hardy, and they were called Poulsen roses. The First World War interfered with rose breeding and it wasn't until the mid 20s that the Poulsen roses went to win more and more admirers.

No one knew where or how they should be classified – they were like Polyanthas but they were growing to 1.2m (4ft) high. Eventually they were called Hybrid Polyanthas, near enough I suppose to their true origins but not really good enough for commerce. Then one day Charlie Perkins, one of the partners of the now famous Jackson and Perkins company was telling a journalist, Ed Seymour, that he needed a good name for the new roses. Immediately Seymour responded with: "Why not call them Floribundas?"

Charlie Perkins loved it, but the horticultural world doesn't like anything that smacks so much of commerce and the name was denigrated. Perkins knew what he, and they could do – he had a number of very fine roses now available and he would not allow any other nurseryman to use his colour plates unless they called the roses Floribundas. He stuck it out longer than those who digressed. The name is still with us, despite humourless suggestions to call

them cluster-flowered roses, a committee nominated name that wants to ignore history for personal glory. But then the same committees want to change the term Hybrid Tea to large-flowered roses – a group title that today is proving totally unsuitable and unacceptable.

Grandiflora

The Floribunda has made its mark in the rose world with devastating effectiveness so that today no garden could be without some. Its story has been written into history by every rose breeder in the world. And today the intermingling of blood from the Hybrid Teas is producing another type of rose – one with larger blooms than the Floribunda and smaller than the Hybrid Tea, produced in clusters unlike either. This has been called – in places – Grandiflora, and there seems little doubt that the way roses are going it is a name that will be used more and more frequently for yet another race of roses, similar but different.

Bush roses

It is just another phase in the evolution of the rose, a development that means today bush roses can have a place in any and every garden. Whether they be grown in formal beds or mixed informal borders they give a wave of colour that no other flower can give over the same length of time. As specimen plants or as hedges they can be allowed to grow into sturdy bushes that will continually present not just great flowers but very effective foliage too. In herbaceous borders they can add their own very different plant form and colour that never makes them look out of place. There are no rules about where you grow them – place them where you can get the most enjoyment from them, where their fragrance and their colours add enjoyment to the garden and our lives. It is for this that the rose was created (Fig.10.1).

Floribundas (Cluster-flowered)

'Amber Queen' (Haroony); Harkness 1983; British Rose of the Year 1984; Genoa GN 1986; Orleans GM 1987; AARS 1988.

Probably one of the most successful roses raised by Jack Harkness, winning approbation all over the world. In all it has won 21 top awards in 10 countries. What made it so successful? Was it the colour? Was it the lower growing type of bush? Was it the sweet and spicy fragrance? Probably you have to put all three together to have a really good variety. The colour is fashionable, a soft double-whiskey amber in flowers that have 25–30 petals, good substance and decorative shape. They are carried in clusters of 5–8 blooms (and in cooler climates even more). The bush is low growing, rounded and slightly spreading. The foliage is shiny and productive – making it a good all-round variety, especially for the front of borders or for low beds, and it produces its flowers happily in rain or sun.

'Angel Face', Swim and Weeks 1968; AARS 1969. A truly lovely rose – but then I have to admit again to my bias toward mauve/lavender roses. It has been one of the widely grown Floribundas in the United States for over 20 years, but strangely enough it did not infiltrate Europe. The only place outside the States where you will find it widely grown is Australia. To give an idea of how popular it was in America, its first reviews called it 'very fragrant, very prolific, very disease resistant' and gave it a rating of 8.2 (out of 10). Afterwards, however, some spotted problems with mildew, but it has not slowed down the appreciation of the mauve buds with tips of ruby on the petals. The bush is low and rounded, varying in vigour from area to area but generally doing quite well. It is a colour that has not been repeated successfully in the Floribundas.

'Anisley Dickson' (DICkimono, Dicky, Muncher Kindl); Dickson 1983; RNRS PIT 1984. Despite winning the top prize from the Royal National Rose Society, this rose was slow to take off, but now is regarded as one of the finest possible Floribundas for garden show, for cutting or exhibiting. Maybe it was the name: some said that they found it hard to pronounce, but it was named after Pat Dickson's wife and when a grower names a rose for his wife it generally is very good. However, someone somewhere decided to call it Dicky, a name that it still labours under in the United States and Europe. Now everyone believes it should have retained its family name and the main producers in the United States, Edmunds Roses, refuse to deviate from that. It's a salmon-pink blend or a warm coral, whichever you choose, with perfectly shaped flowers grown in marvellous trusses and with stems strong enough to hold them upright. Also very disease resistant.

'Anne Cocker' Cocker 1970. Named for Mrs Anne Cocker, widow of Alex Cocker, who produced some of the best British roses for years, including 'Silver Jubilee' and 'Alec's Red'. This is one of the top flowers of recent years for flower arrangers in search of medium, shapely blooms of 36 petals in a vivid luminous vermilion. The flowers have the wonderful ability of long life after cutting which also makes this a highly prized decorative variety. The bush is upright and vigorous, the foliage mid-green and glossy.

'Anna Livia' (Kormetter, Sandton Smile, Trier 2000); Kordes 1985. A rose that has been so widely accepted that it is named for 'Trier' in Germany, 'Sandton' in Johannesburg and the 'River Liffey' in Dublin, which James Joyce once called 'Anna Livia'. It carries orange-pink, finely defined blooms in very attractive clusters and has the ability of almost always being in flower, which makes it a very useful bedding variety. Foliage is semi-glossy and the bush grows very evenly with disease-resistant foliage. It also makes a very fine cutting rose and for flower arrangers the small buds are excellent.

'Ann Aberconway' Mattock 1976. If you want a tall rose that delivers well-shaped trusses of blooms that have good shape and last well, then this is a rose for you. The flowers begin with apricot yellow and that is the time to cut them for arrangements. The blooms are bigger than those generally found on Floribundas and the

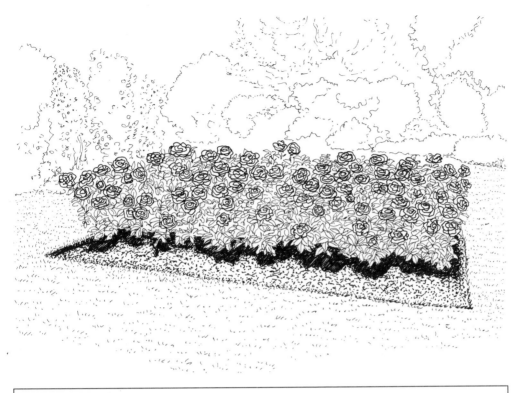

Fig. 10.1
A well-proportioned rose bed is pleasing to the eye.

Key to entries

Commercial name, followed by Code name and alternative names which are often given in other countries. Breeder and year of introduction. Then International prizes won; these include AARS = All American Rose Selection, an annual award for roses to be introduced in the United States; GM = Gold Medal. RNRS PIT = Royal National Rose Society's President's International Trophy. To the top Gold Medal rose after three years' trials at St. Albans. In some cases awards from the same society are marked (R)NRS to denote it was made before the Society became the Royal National. ADR = Anerkannte Deutsche Rose, the top designated German variety.

Height It is almost impossible to assess the height that roses attain in different climates where soil and cultural conditions will affect their growth and performance considerably. Therefore I have given guidance where a rose is generally going to grow lower than most by calling it 'compact'. 'Medium' means that it will stay at a reasonable height in most environments and certainly will not run away with very long stems. 'Tall' means that growers will have to give the bush room to expand.

Grandiflora This is a recognized classification but is generally only in use in the USA and some parts of Europe. It is given to varieties that fall between Hybrid Teas and Floribundas; they carry Hybrid Tea type blooms in clusters, with a branching growth. I do feel that it will not be very long before the classification is generally accepted – even though the American growers are tending to turn away from it. British hybridizers have to find a spot for many good roses that at present do not fall into the established categories.

In the context of these lists the roses that fall into the American classification have been noted.

dark foliage makes a fine foil for them. The advice to cut early should not be ignored because as the flower ages, so it fades fairly rapidly. But caught at its best, it is spectacular.

'Arcadian' (MACnewye, MACneweye, New Year); McGredy 1983; AARS 1987. This beautiful, bright apricot yellow excited American rose growers when it won the AARS award in 1987 as a Grandiflora, a term seldom used in Europe. It took a long time getting to Europe but here it took on a new name of 'Arcadian' – after all, very few rose growers ever have blooms around new year. It makes such a good shrub that the flowers could be regarded as a bonus – it gives lots of good clusters all spring and summer long. The blooms are small to medium with a lovely shape and are carried in medium-sized trusses. It needs watching for mildew, but again the advice of prevention being better than cure is important to remember. Spray at the beginning of the season when foliage is just appearing, and again in mid-season and this one should well live up to its award.

'Arthur Bell' McGredy 1965. Although it is growing old by today's standards of change in the rose world, 'Arthur Bell' is still a great favourite. And it is likely to continue in that position if only for the marvellous fragrance it carries – probably stronger than any other Floribunda. The almost continuous flowering also puts it at the top of the class. Its 20-petalled, large, golden yellow blooms have a very good bud stage, eventually opening flat. Unfortunately the colour fades to creamy-white as the flowers age, but in everything else the variety is capable of holding its own. Resistance to disease is good; the glossy, medium green foliage, is leathery and off-putting for pests. The bush itself is upright, medium to tall in height.

'Bridal Pink' (JACbri); Boerner 1967. Still one of the top-selling Floribundas in the world, probably as much for its great ability to produce bridal bouquets of long elegant, tight, pointed buds in the soft creamy pink, that are perfect in size for the purpose. Bred by 'Papa Floribunda', Eugene Boerner, in the USA, you can find it still among the lists of the world's top growers. The plant is bushy, vigorous, healthy and prolific. While the blooms tend to be short stemmed, the flowers have a great lasting quality. This variety needs, however, to be grown in a sunny spot to give of its best.

'Brown Velvet' (MACultra, Colorbreak); McGredy 1983; New Zealand GM 1978. This rose was being applauded long before it made its way into general commerce. Obviously the New Zealand judges were overcome by the russet/brown velvet colours of the flowers. It is a colour in which the McGredy family have always shown an interest (see 'Spiced Coffee' in Hybrid Tea section) and this one lives up to its name in cooler climates.

Unfortunately, like many browns it changes colour under strong sunshine when the brown tones become orange. This becomes obvious in the USA, where growers see it as orange that develops a purplish hue (but even that is a unique colour.) John Martin in New Zealand calls it 'a modern rose in an old world guise', with many petalled blooms that have an old-fashioned quartered look. The bush everywhere gets points for good vigour and a fine plant with healthy bronze foliage.

'Bucks Fizz' (POULgav, Gavno); Olesen 1988. A very attractive clear orange rose that carries its well-shaped blooms in nice clusters of buttonhole-sized flowers. The bushes grow upright and tall with dark, glossy foliage. As a bedding plant it is eye catching especially if grown on its own where its height can be controlled by regular pruning. It has good disease resistance.

'Cherish' (JACsal); Warriner 1980; AARS 1980. A unique winner of the AARS award in that it was one of a trio of roses by Bill Warriner, hybridizer for Jackson & Perkins, to be named for the award – the first time one breeder won all the prizes in the same year. This turned out to be the best rose of the three. The flower is of a lovely pastel soft pink on a creamy white base. It is big for a Floribunda, having about 30 petals, but then many American-bred Floribundas carry bigger flowers and fewer clusters than their European counterparts where the inclination is towards flowers of a more informal nature. Very large dark green foliage that begins a bronze-red, on a bushy spreading plant, makes for a good garden variety and also an impressive cutting variety.

'Class Act' (JACare, First Class, White Magic); Warriner 1988; AARS 1988, Portland GM 1989. Bill Warriner was a man who was heavily into the softer shades of roses (see 'Cherish' above and 'French Lace' later). Here he produced a real charmer. It begins with creamy coloured buds and opens to snow-white blooms that delightfully show off their lovely yellow stamens and their frilled blossoms. Blooms are borne in neat sprays and are informal, semi-double and flat which, if you like that sort of flower, will mean you will give it a top rating; on the other hand if you want the 'classically' shaped high-centred bloom, then it won't appeal. The bush grows large for a Floribunda and is vigorous and disease resistant with glossy, dark green foliage.

'Champagne Cocktail' (HORflash); Horner 1983; Glasgow GM 1990. Raised by one of England's leading amateur breeders, Colin Horner, this one attracted judges to such an extent that it was awarded the Torridge Award for the best rose raised by an amateur in 1985. It certainly deserved the award because it was quite a break into the 'hand-painted' roses (see 'Picasso') but with a real bubbly effect (hence the name). The colour is a base of creamy yellow that becomes flecked and splashed with carmine and deep pinks. Add to the beauty of the flower the fact that it has a strong fragrance and you can see how it attracted such attention. The plant is bushy and vigorous with dark green foliage and it is very free flowering.

'Charisma' (JELroganor, Surprise Party); Jelly 1977; Portland GM 1976; AARS 1978. Bred by Bob Jelly, who is best known in America for his production of cut flowers for the commercial grower. But this one became a dual delight with its brilliant orange-red and golden yellow blooms being produced in a huge numbers of flowers per bush. The colour was called noisy by one reporter at its introduction but since then it has shown its value as a good garden plant where the full double multicoloured blooms are always effective. The bush is tough, medium and compact with very glossy, dark green foliage.

'Columbus' (WEKuz); Carruth 1990. One of the first varieties to go on the market from a new young hybridizer, Tom Carruth, who works for the very famous Weeks Wholesale Nursery in California. The rose commemorates the 500th anniversary of the Columbus landing and has received wide approval. The old-rose pink blooms are perfectly formed and would almost rate in Europe too big for a Floribunda, but they are also grown in clusters that make them very attractive. The bush is rounded, vigorous and the foliage is light green.

'Colwyn Bay' (FRANblue); Cowlishaw 1992. In every breeder's greenhouse there is a small corner devoted to a batch of seedlings that it is hoped will one day produce the first true blue rose – before the scientists baffle everyone with their gene manipulation. This is one from a leading British amateur breeder, Frank Cowlishaw, and is said to be well into the blue race. The flowers certainly have an overlay of blue on the mauve background and are perfect in shape, making them ideal blooms for the flower arranger. The introducers of this rose, C&K Jones, say that in the three years they tested the variety, it never once showed a sign of disease. The bush is lowish to medium and vigorous too.

'Edith Holden' (CHEWlegacy, The Edwardian Lady); Warner 1988. Russet and orange blend have been the two inadequate colours offered for this rose. In fact it is far more impressive, being a sort of polished mahogany, deep brown, and bright golden eye with foliage that looks as though it has been highly polished too. It is a marvellous bloom for flower arrangers, having an urn-shaped bud that allows its 15 petals to open flat. It can also be appreciated for mixed borders where the robust growth and continuity of flowering makes it happy in any conditions. It is true Floribunda, with clusters of 10–15 blooms and has very few prickles. The bush is upright, tall and has robust growth.

'Elizabeth of Glamis' (MACel, Irish Beauty); McGredy 1964; (Royal) National Rose Society PIT 1963. One of the world's most beautiful and most fragrant Floribundas. The colour is a soft mixture of salmon with a golden base to each petal and the flower starts with a very acceptable bud shape and then opens to a delicate flat flower that makes its truss one of the prettiest sights of the summer. There has, however, to be a fault even with the most perfect of nature's gifts and this rose can be tender in hard winters and show dieback. It needs TLC to keep its beauty going, and this means giving it a place in the garden where it will be protected from cold cutting winds yet gets warming sunshine. It also performs well with a little extra cultivation and fertilizer in the spring. It was named for Her Majesty the Queen Mother.

'Escapade' (HARpade); Harkness 1967; Baden-Baden GM 1969, Belfast GM 1969, ADR 1973. Jack Harkness, who bred this rose, has never been backward in saying how much he enjoys it. With good reason, too, it is a real summer rose of lightness, delicacy and beauty. The flowers are a sort of rosy violet that softens with age and when fully open shows a distinct white eye. The 12 petals have a pleasing fragrance; the medium-growing vigorous bush, and its hardiness make it a lovely flower for bed or border. In his book *Modern Roses*, Peter Harkness writes about the pleasure this rose gives him and says that breeders have long ago come to learn that an 'intrinsically good rose is not necessarily

a popular one'. For those who have doubts, the message should be to try it while it is still with us.

'Europeana' de Ruiter 1963; The Hague GM 1962, AARS 1968, Portland GM 1970. Here is a rose that takes up over an inch of space, listing the nurseries who grow it, in The Combined Rose List, that annual and so invaluable list of roses in commerce – as well as providing a link for those who want varieties that seem to have slipped out of popularity. There is not much hope of 'Europeana' slipping out of commerce all that quickly even though it has been called 'just another red Floribunda'. But I will dispute that – it is not just another red Floribunda, it is still one of the finest of them all. It probably gives the heaviest crop of all Floribundas, huge trusses of dark red flowers covering the bush from top to bottom. But that is part of its misfortune – it is too generous with its flowers and often the trusses flop to ground level where they can be damaged when mud splashes up after rain. But for a rose so prolific in flowering that should bother no one. The flowers frequently win at shows, too, where one truss can easily fill a large bowl. Its other bonus is the foliage, which is so rich as to make it worth growing even if it never had a flower. Fault? Yes, mildew can be a visitor but remember that spraying need not be constant – prevention is always better than cure.

'Fellowship' (HARwelcome); Harkness 1992; RNRS GM 1990. A very new rose that has yet to prove itself in our gardens but one that promises very well. It has already received the blessing of the RNRS with a gold medal and there may well be more to follow for a rose that is robust, bright, compact, hardy and has a fragrance. The colour is an orange-red with flowers that cluster well with brightness and ruffled petals. Harkness said in their introduction of this rose that 'it was impossible to overlook in the seven years of testing'. It will certainly get public prominence as it is a good international name, as well as being named by Rotary International.

'French Lace' (JAClace); Warriner 1980; AARS 1982, Portland GM 1984. Ah, talk to me of elegant roses and I will immediately name this beauty. It is labelled a white rose, but the creaminess of beauty tends to surround it, even suggesting in some places the ghost of apricot over the blooms. The flowers of 35 petals have the classic high-pointed centres that make them in a cluster almost impossible to pass by; they are crisp on long stems and very prolific in flower bearing. The bush is pleasing too, medium to tall and slightly upright. The foliage is quite distinctive, being serrated something like holly. If there is a problem with the rose, it is that it takes a little time to get established and does not prove totally hardy in very cold climates. It's still a great pity that it never really moved far beyond the USA.

'Geraldine' (PEAhaze); Pearce 1982. A slow-moving variety that is now beginning to be appreciated much more widely. Bred by Colin Pearce in Devon, its great attraction is the clear orange colour of well-shaped blooms that are carried in neat trusses on strong stems. They have a slightly fresh fragrance. The plant, neat and compact, grows upright and vigorous with glossy foliage. Quite recently this variety has worthily crept into the top ten with a number of nurseries as gardeners find out that it not only makes a good bedding variety but is also long-lasting when cut.

'Glad Tidings' (TANtide, Lubeckerr Rotspon, Peter Wessel); Tantau 1988; British Rose of the Year 1989. Here's a really strong contender for the best in the red Floribunda stake. The strong crimson blooms form themselves into almost perfect rosettes, large enough to be noticed and strong enough to withstand any rain, wind or sun. They are also produced in clusters that are big and bright. The flowers are quick to repeat and it is the sort of bush that is hardly ever without colour from spring to winter. The foliage is dark and glossy and the bush height is medium and well rounded. When it won the privilege of being named Rose of the Year in Britain, it

was at the time a winner by the largest margin of points since the trials began.

'Gold Medal' (AROqueli); Christensen 1982; New Zealand GM 1983. The first dilemma is that this is rated a Grandiflora in the States but as that term does not apply in Europe, I have to put it with the Floribundas. If I didn't give it a place in this collection, one of the best American-produced roses of the 80s would be missing. It is tall, upright, deep green foliaged plant that is highly disease resistant. The buds begin golden yellow and the flowers stay that way right through their bloom cycle.

This one is a workhorse and a thoroughbred too. It will give you lots of blooms whether you want then in trusses or singly; it will make a great garden show and it will win awards galore on the showbench. The big surprise is that it never won an AARS award, but its appreciation by gardeners has made up for that. When it comes to pruning, it is one variety that does not like to be hard cut – after all it spent a whole year building itself into a great bush so why deprive it of that ability?

'Hannah Gordon' (KORweiso, 'Raspberry Ice'); Kordes 1983. Will the real Hannah Gordon please stand up? This very fine Floribunda has suffered all sorts of

Fig. 10.2 'Hannah Gordon' illustrates the novel colour disposition of the 'handpainted' rose types.

impostors during recent years. Three or four different Floribundas came on the market and were somehow muddled up, not all of them doing 'Hannah Gordon' any favours. Now, however, the problem seems to be resolved and as long as you don't take the official colouring of pink blend too much to heart, you will probably get the right plant. My description of this rose (prompted no doubt by an admiration for the actress for whom it is named) is of a delicately beautiful, full, well-formed blooms of silvery white, edged with light raspberry or cherry pink. The lovely clusters of flowers show up well against a glossy, green foliage. One of my top six of British Floribundas which is also grown well in the USA but does not have a commercial outlet there (Fig.10.2).

'Hiroshima's Children' (HARmark); Harkness 1985. This is a rose that has been dubbed the perfect one-to-a-stem Floribunda in the States, where its perfection of bloom has won hearts and frequent top prizes at shows as far apart as Ohio and California. It is exactly this fact that is, however, against it in Britain, where it was bred by Jack Harkness and where a Floribunda, to merit the name, must carry clusters of bloom. American shows have classes for perfection in one-bloom Floribundas and this is where this yellow, slightly touched pink lovely excels. The blooms are absolutely 'classic' in shape on a neat bush and it is a variety that gets raves from those who demand perfection.

Unfortunately it was almost lost to commerce, but now more nurseries are picking it up. The rose commemorates the work of Dr. Tomin Harada who returned to his Hiroshima home in 1945 and dedicated his life to rebuilding the lives of survivors of the first atomic bomb.

'Iceberg' (KORbin, Fee des Neiges, Schneewittchen); Kordes 1958; (R)NRS GM 1958, World's Favourite Rose. Probably the rose with the widest sale in the world, and a rose that never lets a gardener down, provided it is treated with knowledge. This knowledge insists that the bush should

never be pruned hard until it is well established, when it can be cut back to about half its height. If this advice is followed it will always flower in perfection. Sam McGredy, once asked to name his favourite rose, asked that the question be switched to the best rose in the world. His answer to that was 'Iceberg'. It is planted everywhere in the world. The most fantastic planting I have seen was in the Valley of Fransshcok in Cape Province where there must be 10,000 bushes of it surrounding the memorial to the Huguenots. In roses it holds the same position as 'Peace' – almost historically untouchable. The flower is immaculate white, carried in clusters on long stems. It has a fresh fragrance rather than a perfume. Foliage is glossy and green and the bush will grow vigorously to be taller than medium.

'Intrigue' (JACum); Warriner 1982; AARS 1984. Not too many Floribundas win the All-American Rose Selection award but when they do you can be sure they will excel. This rose had to overcome the problem of being mauve to plum . . . not the most widely acceptable colour for commercial use. But it has many other things in its favour, especially in the petallage which is ruffled, often leaving the blooms looking like a cup and saucer. But this alone is not enough, it has a delicious fragrance and grows on a bush that is upright with shiny foliage. It should not be mixed up with another rose of the same name – a Kordes dark red Floribunda that can be more generally found under the name of 'Lavaglut'.

'Judy Garland' (HARking); Harkness 1977. A rose that was just saved from extinction by the American Judy Garland fan club, who originally negotiated with Harkness for the rose to be named in the star's memory. However, by the time the necessary and various forms and importation regulations were complied with, the rose had been taken off the catalogue by Harkness. However, Rearsby Roses still had a few bushes and they were quickly sent to the United States where today it is firmly established. Indeed the rose seems to do much better in the American climate where the bright yellow and red-tipped flowers are so much brighter and even bigger than they were in England. It also seems to have overcome a disease problem and is producing good bushes which brought the comment from Tom Carruth of Weeks roses: 'It's an outstanding performer!'. And that is backed up by comments about a good fragrance. A medium to tall rounded bush and "glossy 'Oz' green leaves".

'**Korresia**' (Sunsprite, Friesia); Kordes 1977; Baden-Baden GM 1972. When it comes to nominating a personal batch of Floribundas I always put this rose very high on my list. My reasons are simple enough: the bright yellow is unfading, the flowers are fragrant, the bushes are disease resistant, the growth is medium to low and vigorous with it, and continuity of flowering is very good. It is also long lasting either in the garden or in a vase where the trusses keep on flowering for a long period. For my money, you cannot expect anything more from a good rose and this is backed up by polls which still make it first class, especially in Britain where it is widely grown.

'**Liverpool Echo**' (Liverpool); McGredy 1971; Portland GM 1979. Roses named for newspapers don't have a reputation of being the most successful, probably because carrying one paper's name restricts the amount of general publicity a variety can get. However, here is a rose that survived all that and has proven itself both a good garden and an exhibition variety. It has even survived lack of mentions in books on Modern roses, something that will surprise those who grow it. I have seen it really at its best in New Zealand where the big bushes were laden with the orange-pink flowers that seem to vary from area to area. Still, a useful medium to tall variety, to grow where its vigour can be appreciated.

'**Many Happy Returns**' (Harwanted, Prima); Harkness 1988; Geneva Gold Medal 1987. This is being regarded in many places today as a Modern shrub – with all the good points of a Floribunda. It

is being put into the shrub category in some countries because of its slightly sprawling bush size where it can give you a height of 1m (3ft) and a spread of about the same. The flowers, which clothe the plant right to ground level, are handsome, well shaped, opening from small bud to a wide flower of 18 petals. It carries continuous trusses of creamy-rosy pink blooms making it a very suitable subject for a hedge or a border plant. It can be allowed to grow into a fair-sized specimen in either the garden or a large container.

'**Margaret Merril**' (HARkuly); Harkness 1977; Geneva GM 1978, Monza GM 1978, Rome GM 1978, Edland Fragrance Medal 1978, James Mason GM 1990. Only one year old and this rose swept Europe. Today it is still among the top Floribunda roses where its fragrance makes it much sought after. But it isn't merely the perfume it exudes, the form of the flower is classical, high pointed and always good looking as a silken sheen of pink overlays the white bloom. The blooms are small to medium sized with 28 petals; foliage is dark green and glossy. If you want to have it perfect, cut flowers before rain can spot them or find something to cover them.

'**Matangi**' (MACman); McGredy 1974; RNRS PIT 1974, Rome GM 1974, Belfast GM 1976; Portland GM 1982. It's a red blend; it's an orange blend; it's 'hand-painted'. No matter where you go you get a different version of the colour of this very handsome plant. It came from the hand-painted line of Sam McGredy but displays far less of the variety of colouration than varieties like 'Picasso' and others. The weather-proof flowers are well shaped in the bud, opening wide and flat and attractive to show a small white eye in the centre of the orange-red bloom. Flowers are produced in huge numbers in the first flush; slightly less as it continues to flower all season long. A great bush for the garden with upright, vigorous growth that can grow tall if not kept under control by pruning. It does not have good lasting qualities when used as a cut-flower.

'Melody Maker' (DICqueen); Dickson 1990; British Rose of the Year 1991. In recent years the Dickson output of roses has tended to be in the pink-orange and yellow categories, and have always been widely appreciated. They are renowned for their flower power, producing lots of blooms right through the year, something that certainly applies to this one. The flowers are above-average size and have a soft fragrance. They certainly make a garden look bright and if they follow the standard set by earlier Dickson roses such as 'Memento' and 'Anisley Dickson', they will keep the famous Irish name well to the forefront. The plant is bushy and rounded, which makes it an ideal bedding variety that grows to medium height.

'Memento' (DICbar); Dickson 1978; Belfast GM 1980. This coral-salmon Floribunda has won acclaim everywhere for massive and continuous flowering all season long. The flowers are smallish with very little fragrance but what they lack in size they make up for in quantity with clusters that are as big as any variety could be expected to carry. Stems take up water well, making it good for cutting. With all these attributes it is a great bedding variety where an upright medium-to-tall rose is needed. Preventative spraying is needed where mildew and black spot are prevalent.

'News' Le Grice 1968; RNRS GM 1970. This rich purple-red-mauve rose (you take your own pick of the colour chart in roses of this description) is still unique although falling quite quickly down the popularity charts. It was bred by Edward Le Grice who was one hybridizer always chasing after the unusual colours, and who gave the world varieties in greys, browns, lilac and silver. 'News' tends to be a spreading bush with no great height but very suitable for the front of a border where its colours will draw all sorts of admiring comments. 'Don't be afraid to mix it with other colours', Edward Le Grice himself said. 'This colour blends or contrasts pleasantly with all rose colours and offers a new dimension for the rose garden.' However, it

is liable to be caught by rust, although today new chemicals are being developed all the time to tackle this nasty problem and one spray in early summer usually saves it from disaster – and it deserves it.

'Orangeade' McGredy 1959; (R)NRS GM 1959, Portland GM 1965. When 'Orangeade' arrived on the market there were few flowers in such a sparkling, even dazzling colour. It is a tone on the red side of orange-peel but a great producer of blooms. I have often read that it is prone to disease but that is relative: a couple of preventative sprays a year is advocated not just for this rose but all others too and, if it gets that, there is little or no need for special concessions. It carries lots of 10-petalled flowers with a slight fragrance in well spaced trusses. The foliage is a very good bronze when young, ageing later on to a dark green.

'Oranges'n'Lemons' (MACoranlem); McGredy 1992. A rose that positively named itself. It is a mixture of orange and lemon stripes, the likes of which has never been seen before – and one that will cause a sensation in any garden. It has to be the best novelty rose for a number of years. The flowers are bright and double, in clusters of several blooms. The bush is upright, of medium height and has a moderate scent. But it will always be the colour that excites. No doubt there will be many more in this type of rose but this is the first and is as attractive as you could hope to get.

'Peppermint Ice' (BOSgreen); Bossom 1991. Yes, it is green, with an attractive flower that will certainly be a winner with flower arrangers as well as being an eye catcher in the garden. The green is as green as any of the modern Floribundas, with a suggestion of creamy overlay. The word peppermint does cause American eyebrows to raise because there peppermint sticks are historically red and white, but in Britain peppermint is green. This rose was named as a result of a competition in *Garden News* in conjunction with its raiser, amateur Bill Bossom.

'**Piccolo**' (TANolokip, Piccola); Tantau 1985. Looked upon often as a Patio-type rose, this must surely fit in as a distinct and a very good Floribunda. It is low growing, but what a sight it makes with its deep bronze foliage that would make it a worth-while shrub on its own. The flowers are 20-petalled, medium-sized, almost small Hybrid Teas in a bright red, produced singly and in clusters of 2–3 flowers. It deserves wider attention and certainly should have been among the award winners of recent years, but no doubt it was denied a top prize by the uncertainty about its growing habits – the bush is low enough for Patio but the flowers and the foliage are too big for that classification.

'**Playboy**' Cocker 1976; Portland GM 1989. Here is a story of a wonder rose in the USA, yet almost a forgotten variety in Britain where it was bred in Scotland and is called 'Cheerio'. It wasn't until it got to the land where people love single roses that it found success. In the States no one thinks of a 5-petalled rose as 'looking like a wild rose'. They accept its rare beauty for what it is, a lovely gift of nature. But even in America the rose was slow to become appreci-ated – it was 13 years before it won a top prize! But before that Ralph Moore was promoting it, which was quite a plaudit as Moore is king of the Miniatures and sells very, very few other roses. Since then it has been praised, admired, even adored as it has figured in every garden where the sun shines. The colour is truly eye catching, with orange and scarlet adorning a deep yellow eye. It is easy to grow, clusters well, the foliage is glossy, it has a sweet fragrance – and you have to see it to believe it.

'**Playgirl**' (MORplag); Moore 1986. If you have a 'Playboy' you surely need a 'Playgirl'. That is exactly what Miniature rose expert Ralph Moore felt. Having made 'Playboy' such a success among growers, he set about watching for a rose that could accompany it. Appropriately he found a hot little rosy-pink darling that has certainly delighted a lot of people. Flowers are pro-duced in large clusters on a rounded bush that goes on and on producing great blooms. Even Ralph Moore calls this one an 'exhibitionist' and there can be no doubt that it will be only a short time before she is showing her counterpart a thing or two.

'**Pink Parfait**' Swim 1960; Baden-Baden GM 1959, Portland GM 1959, AARS 1961, (R)NRS GM 1962. One of the great and most beautiful rose stayers still being appreciated world-wide, at a time when age should be bowing it out. But 'Pink Parfait' is grown everywhere – either as a Flori-bunda or a Grandiflora, as it is classified in America. Hybridizer Herb Swim under-stood the classification in Britain. After see-ing a bed of it in London's Regents Park he said it was easy to understand its pop-ularity there. 'A soft pink, it made the most effective bed in the park and it was defi-nitely a Floribunda there.' The rose is a clear pink, softening with age. Flowers are well shaped, cup-like, and produced in good numbers. Growth is bushy, foliage is bright green – and its flair and colour have still not been truly matched.

'**Pleasure**' (JACpif); Warriner 1988; AARS 1990. Here is another rose to prove my theory that when the AARS deigns to give its top award to a Floribunda, they usually pick a good one. This was the only winner in 1990 and is so far doing every-thing it should to be a success. Again, in the style of American-bred Floribundas, the bloom size is bigger than European flowers and double with it, making it a very accept-able flower either in clusters or when car-ried singly on the bush. Colour is an attractive warm pink with ruffled edges. Foliage, too, is attractive being dark green and quite disease resistant. Bush is com-pact and rounded – an ideal plant for the large number of flowers carried. From what I have seen it has the makings of a very good garden variety.

'**Princess Alice**' (HARtanna, Brite Lites, Zonta Rose); Harkness 1985; Dublin GM 1984. Don't ever mention the name 'Brite Lites' if you happen to speak to breeder Jack Harkness. He hated it from the moment the American introducers gave it the name. But it is a bright light in anyone's garden. The breeders call the colour Empire Yellow, which just means that the colour is true and even. The flowers are produced in big trusses, each one big enough to fill a bowl on its own. And each flower of 25 petals is individually well shaped. The bush is tallish; the general effect is very good but it is low on fragrance. However, a good variety for bedding.

'Picasso' (MACpic); McGredy 1971; Belfast GM 1973, New Zealand GM 1973. This was the starter of a fabulous series of roses presented to the world by Sam McGredy. He called them hand-painted roses, because of the unusual spots and blotches on the petals. They arrived through a quite staggering train of breeding but he feels that the hand painting comes from 'Frulingsmorgen', a Kordes shrub from 1942. 'Picasso' was immediately different, with petals red and white, always changing from season to season and flower to flower. This is a characteristic carried through most of the roses; indeed it has often astonished gardeners to find that what they thought was going to be a startling mass of purple, red, whites and yellow began its life as an innocuous pink. Its growth was bushy and good, its flower production excellent and its flower startling enough to catch anyone's attention.

It still remains one of the favourite bushes in my garden. It was also the precursor of a whole batch of other roses in every shade and shape from Sam McGredy. Among the ones that caught public attention were 'Priscilla Burton', 'Old Master', 'Regensburg', 'Sue Lawley', 'Little Artist', 'Maestro' and the very recent introduction 'Tango' (also known as 'Rock'n'Roll' and 'Stretch Johnson'), a rose that swings between a well-clothed Floribunda, a Grandiflora and a Shrub.

The gift of 'Picasso' to the rose world was not as well appreciated as it should have been; certainly there can be no doubt that it will be carried through many parentages and will produce further worthwhile novelties for the rose world.

'Sexy Rexy' (MACrexy, Heckenzauber); McGredy 1984; New Zealand GM 1984, Auckland GM 1990. One of the star roses of the 1980s, despite the rather risqué name. But while a name can add prestige to a mediocre rose, a name will never kill a good one, a point which is emphasized here. 'Sexy Rexy' has risen above everything with its large trusses of rosette shaped, pure pink blooms. It has become a standard in catalogues now, where it is constantly recommended as a bedding variety of exceptional qualities. It also makes a lovely rose for showing, as the stems cut well and the blooms have good holding power. The flowers are carried in clusters of 9–10 which make a marvellous sight as the very full blooms open fully to over 5cm (2in) wide. It is a sturdy little grower, making a compact bush to around about medium height.

'Sheila's Perfume' (HARsherry); Sheridan 1982; Edland Fragrance Medal 1981. An amateur-bred rose from John Sheridan in Catford, London. Just to emphasize that you don't need a large garden to breed a winning rose. This one was germinated in a seed tray on a kitchen window sill and is now a worldwide favourite. The colour in Britain is exceptional; bright red and yellow blooms that could easily be entered among the Hybrid Teas because of their size and their very good shape. However, in places like California, South Africa and New Zealand, the strong sunshine can lighten the colour. But one thing this rose will never lose is its perfume; a true lovely fragrance. It is a vigorous bush, too, generally growing to a strong medium height.

'Showbiz' (TANweieke, Bernard Daneka Rose, Ingrid Weibull); Tantau 1983; AARS 1985. So what is it that makes this red Floribunda better than all the others that have gone before it? First of all, I suppose, is that it won the AARS award and that, as one grower once said, is like being handed an open cheque. Certainly the winning rose gets magnificent publicity, but then it has to live up to it. This one has. The colour is a bright red – someone dubbed it fire engine red. Trusses are heavy, the bush is low, compact and rounded. The blooms of about 25 petals make an eye-catching sight in a bed or along the front of a border; they also have a reputation for long life. The foliage complements all by being dark green and glossy.

'Shocking Blue' (Korblue); Kordes 1974. This rose was attracting lots of attention from the time it was named, but the public had to wait almost ten years before it became available. The reason was that it was being used merely as a cut flower, until someone with the courage took it into the garden. There it flourished and has now a place in catalogues of Britain, the USA, Canada, Australia and South Africa. I must declare an interest, as any rose in this colour attracts me. This one, however, is something less than its name: it is nowhere near blue but is a mauve lavender that softens to a creamy lavender – if you know what I mean! Certainly it is always attractive. It carries medium-sized blooms of about 32 petals in a neat truss and a good scent.

'Simplicity' (JACink); Warriner 1978; New Zealand Gold Medal 1978. A rose that was being grown by the million for American growers and being offered as the 'perfect' hedging variety. This is true (I have seen one area in America where there is a 5-mile hedge of 'Simplicity' right around a property). The name does tell it all: it is a simple pink flower carried in clusters on a good, disease-resistant bush. But the enthusiasm of some growers has carried distinction too far by nominating it as the Pink 'Iceberg'. It is nowhere in the hunt where 'Iceberg' is concerned. It would never marry with the height of the white rose; neither is the display in the same style or abundance. But having said that, I must revert to the comment that it is a pretty and vigorous rose for a hedge.

'Summer Serenade' (SMITfirst); Smith 1986. Bagatelle GM 1986; Geneva GM 1986. A rose of distinction that has never been given the chance to shine by growers. For a variety that took two of Europe's top awards in 1986, it has limited distribution although it can be found in Switzerland, France, Britain and India. The colour of the flowers is quite unusual and does not seem to bring people close to agreement – some find it deep apricot, others call it a yellow blend. These flowers are outstanding, being carried in large clusters on a bushy plant. It makes a tremendous bedding plant and is a credit to former train driver Ted Smith of Nottingham who has had other winners since he became attracted to hybridizing when looking at wild roses growing along the railway lines.

'Sun Flare' (JACjem, Sunflare); Warriner 1981; Japan GM 1981, AARS 1983, Portland GM 1985. For yellow rose lovers this is one that must have a place in your garden. For landscapers it makes a bright dash of colour, and the plants are willing and strong but never over medium height. It also makes a very fine bedding variety with an abundance of ruffled, spicy-perfumed flowers of 25–30 petals; flowers do not mark or spot in the rain. The plants are rounded, filling themselves with heavy clusters of bright blooms that, despite their size, are generally carried very well by the bush.

'The Queen Elizabeth' Lammerts 1954; Portland GM 1954, AARS 1955, (R)NRS PIT 1955, ARS GM 1957, Golden Rose of The Hague 1968 – etc, etc! If it hadn't been for 'Queen Elizabeth', there would never have been a classification called Grandiflora. It had to have the classification created for it. Bred by Walter Lammerts in the USA, it was so successful and so different that it could not be properly classified as either Hybrid Tea or Floribunda. It was a totally new sort of rose, with flowers not quite big enough for one class and not clustered enough for the other; it was also considered too tall for the Floribunda class but not tall enough for a Climber!

'Queen Elizabeth' is a once-off and, although other roses have been entered as Grandiflora, none has ever reached its wonderful proportions of position. The flower is pink with good form, fine foliage and quite free of disease. It will grow anywhere: inland, on a high and windy hill, facing the sea, on ground where other roses would be unhappy. It can also be cut to ground level and still bring inspiring growth in a couple of years. It was, of course, named for Queen Elizabeth II at the beginning of her reign and was so good that, although it was not entered for them, it was awarded the Gold Medals of the then National Rose Society in Britain to add to its American Rose Society Gold and the Gertrude M. Hubbard Gold Medal of the American Rose Society.

It always was one of the world's favourite roses and is planted worldwide, frequently being found in catalogues as a Floribunda – but you can expect a very tall Floribunda if you treat it that way.

'The Times Rose' (KORphean, Mariandel, Carl Philip, Kristian IV); Kordes 1985; RNRS PIT 1982, Golden Rose of The Hague 1990. Here is a real red rose that is quite different to all those that have already been named on these pages. First of all it makes an ideal bush with large clusters of crimson red blooms on a bushy, slightly spreading plant that is perfect bedding material. The flowers are carried elegantly in large trusses, strong enough to stand upright. The blooms are a good Floribunda size, packed with petals that shine in the sun. Anyone who doubts its ability should look at the beds of it that are growing at The Gardens of the Rose at St Albans in Hertfordshire – they are superb and should have the effect of making more people plant this lovely rose.

'Trumpeter' (MACtrum); McGredy 1977; New Zealand Gold Medal 1977, British Rose of the Year 1977, Portland GM 1981, James Mason GM 1991. You want my number one Floribunda? This is it. Whenever I get a request from someone who has never grown roses before and wants a splash of colour I have no hesitation in naming this orange-red that just bursts with enthusiasm and health. It was bred by the inimitable Sam McGredy who intro-duced this rose in his book *Look to the Rose* with these words: 'Modesty doesn't become the Irish so I'll go straight on and say that 'Trumpeter' is just about one of the best scarlet Floribundas grown today'. Very few people would disagree with this. It was bred, appropriately enough, from another good red of his, 'Satchmo'. The details of the plant are: medium-low, rounded, very vigorous, foliage is disease-resistant, glossy; the flowers are ruffled and medium sized. For the greatest effect you are likely to achieve with any Floribunda, plant this in masses.

'Wishing' (DICkerfuffle, Georgie Girl); Dickson 1985. One of the many fine roses produced by the Dicksons in the 80s. This one falls somewhere between two stools, being good enough for a small Hybrid Tea but often not producing enough flowers for a Floribunda. However if you want a bush that grows well and goes on producing good flowers all summer long, this is the one for you. The peachy-orange-pink blooms with a touch of yellow at the base of the petals will delight you – and they don't fade. The flowers too have good shape in the tradition of a rose that is bred from the marvellous Hybrid Tea, 'Silver Jubilee'.

Hybrid Teas (Large-flowered)

'Alec's Red' (CORed); Cocker 1970; RNRS 1970, ADR 1973, Edland Fragrance Medal 1969. Bright crimson flowers, very large and very double. Highly perfumed. Flowers up to three-quarters open bloom stage have good form, after which they tend to flatten out, but retain their colour and scent right to the very end. Flowers are produced singly and up to three per stem. The bush is vigorous and sturdy, with medium to lightish green foliage. It is more hungry than many roses, so needs a little extra feeding. It does have a tendency to fall victim to black spot in areas where the disease is particularly bad, but this problem is generally easily controlled by a fungicide spraying immediately after pruning and another soon after first foliage emerges. After that, another spray mid-summer is generally all that is required. A very worthwhile rose to have in the garden.

'Alexander' (HARlex, 'Alexandra'); Harkness 1972; Hamburg GM 1973, ADR 1974, Belfast GM 1974, James Mason GM 1987. The brightest of all vermilion roses – even brighter than its parent, the once widely planted 'Super Star' ('Tropicana'). It is also extravagantly stronger and taller, frequently growing in normal conditions into a 2.1m (7ft) high, upright bush. Although the blooms have only 20 moderately scented petals, they have great lasting power on the bush and as cut flowers. It is most attractive as a bud to the halfway open stage; after that you realize that just another row of petals would have made it an even greater rose. Quite disease resistant, with light green glossy foliage. The bush often responds best with early spring pruning which gives its blooms a chance to keep up with the vigorous growth.

'Aotearoa' (New Zealand); (MACgenev); McGredy 1989. The first part of the strange name is the Maori name for the Land of the Long White Cloud. The delightful soft pink rose carries a great perfume. The large flowers are carried singly and in small clusters with petals that are soft and can be liable to damage from rain. The ideal cutting time for the blooms is when they are still in tightish bud but have good colour; they open well as cut flowers. The bush is of medium height and vigorous. Foliage is lightish green and quite disease resistant.

'Blessings' Gregory 1967. An English bred variety that has never been taken as seriously as it should. Blooms carried in clusters 3–5 are soft coral-pink in colour with a slight scent. While the blooms are large, they can be improved in quality greatly by disbudding early in growth. Its real value can be seen in massed plantings: the strong upright bushes with medium-green foliage make a continuous splash of colour up to a height of about 1.2m (4ft).

'Bride's Dream' (KORoyness, Fairy Tale Queen, Marchenkonigin); Kordes 1985. The lightest of pink that often pales to white on a bush of the most impeccable blooms you can find. Each flower is perfection, with the high-pointed spiral bloom of 25 petals that is the hallmark of many of the Kordes-bred Hybrid Teas. In sunshine it thrives, but can spot somewhat in wet weather. For all that, the petals are quite tough for a rose so beautiful and pale. Growth is good, foliage must be protected with a fungicide for best results. Introduced by Ludwig Taschner of Pretoria, South Africa, who made this comment: 'This is the bride's as well as the cutflower enthusiast's dream. Plant a row or two in front of a wall, at the back of the rose garden; as a specimen in a mixed shrub bed or in an adequately sized pot or, if space allows, grace a whole area with the charm of her presence.' Since that introduction, it has also made its way right into the heart of American rose growing where it is a frequent show winner.

Fig. 10.3 Some of the more vigorous Hybrid Teas and Floribundas will develop into splendid shrubs if lightly pruned.

'**Brigadoon**' (JACpal); Warriner 1991; AARS 1992. This winner of the All America Rose selection award is categorized as a pink blend, a description that tells nothing about its real colour which is a creamy blush spreading from the centre into deep pink coral. It makes a marvellous bed of blooms in ever changing colours. Very shapely, mildly scented blooms produced one to a stem, are best up to the halfway stage where the bud is perfection itself. As the flower opens it holds its shape but does tend to drop the immediate central petals – something that will only bother an exhibitor. As a flower for decoration, it is a real eye-catcher. The bush is medium-tall, slightly spreading with large deep green foliage.

'**Cary Grant**' (Maimanger, Bushveld Dawn); Meillands 1987. A luscious orange-blend Hybrid Tea that has been winning accolades as both a garden bedding rose and as a show variety. Its large blooms are high pointed and spiral in what is often called the classical Hybrid Tea bloom – the sort that wins best bloom in many shows. It is thorny on a vigorous plant which can produce gross growth if it is over-fed. It needs watching too for mildew.

'**Congratulations**' (KORlift, Kordes Rose Sylvia, Sylvia); Kordes 1979. A rose that has experienced mixed fortunes the world over – but is renowned everywhere for its growth and flower power. Its deep pink, very large, high centred blooms are high on the exhibitors' lists in New Zealand and Australia, while in the USA and South Africa it is frequently seen on the show benches. However, as a show rose it has not made any great impact in Britain, although it is a flower arranger's dream variety. That's only one part of its make-up; it is a rose that produces continuous and abundant flowering on very vigorous growth. The foliage is glossy and quite disease resistant all of which makes it a very desirable variety.

'**Die Welt**' (DieKOR, The World); Kordes 1976. Orange blend is a description which doesn't do the vivid, sunburst orange and yellow blooms justice. Its 25 petals frequently produce the best bloom in show as it holds a magnificent high-centred bloom. For a rose with such large flowers, it produces an abundant and continuous crop on vigorous upright and bushy plant. The glossy foliage is fairly disease resistant but care should be taken to spray early on and thus prevent black spot making an appearance.

'**Doctor Dick**' (COCbaden, Dr. Dick); Cocker 1986. Orange-pink and very distinctive the large, almost globular blooms can also produce high centred and eye-catching blooms. It is fragrant and grows on a medium sized bush to medium/tall proportions. While at its seedling stages, it became a great favourite of a leading Scottish exhibitor, Dr. Archie Dick, for whom it has been named. Now an accepted variety for showing in both Britain and the United States.

'**Double Delight**' (ANdeli); Swim/Ellis 1977; Baden-Baden GM 1976; Rome GM 1976; AARS 1977. Voted into the gallery of the World's Favourite Roses by the World Federation of Rose Societies. Without doubt the most beautiful of all dual-coloured roses. Its raspberry and cream blooms make a marvellous eye-catching bed. Its perfume too is renowned – a super spicy fragrance that cannot be misplaced. The blooms can be perfection itself with high centres that open to a full lovely flower that can easily become queen of a show. If you get the bush in the right place in the garden where it has sunshine (lots of it), air, water and feeding, it can be perfection but under less good conditions it does – despite what many people say – mildew. However that is a mere 'cold-in-the-head' type aggravation and a little care will clear it up.

'**Elizabeth Taylor**' Weddle 1985. A rose named for one of the world's top female movie stars, this deep pink has been a slow starter but now has a place of honour in most American exhibitor's gardens. The bloom is of classical shape with 35-petalled high-pointed, spiral and fragrant flowers that are usually borne one-to-a-stem. Growth is upright, medium vigour with large, dark, semi-glossy foliage.

'Esther Geldenhuys' (Korskipei); Kordes 1987. A rose of almost total perfection of bloom with every flower producing light pink, high pointed, spiral flowers that are perfect for flower arranging. If it has a fault it is that there can be quite a variation in the size of bloom – from small to medium-large. Originating in Germany, it was taken by South Africa's leading grower, Ludwig Taschner, and named for the first lady of that country's roses. Its fame, however, soon spread and it has become a leading variety in many American gardens, especially those in the sun belt. It also makes a very good cutflower variety and is widely used by commercial growers, as well as being a very useful addition to any garden.

'First Prize' Boerner 1970; AARS 1970. For years and years the classical show rose of American gardens, this very large, high centred rose-pink and tinted ivory flower was seen everywhere. It carries its almost perfect high centred blooms singly and on long, strong stems. Very little fragrance but abundant upright growth. In the USA it has proven itself in the top grade but in climates like Britain and Ireland, every fault is revealed as it dislikes rain and falls quickly to disease – hence it has not made the same impact everywhere. But when it can be grown in warmth and sunshine, with good watering around its roots, it is a superb variety.

'Fragrant Cloud' (TANellis, Duftwolke, Nuage Perfume); Tantau 1967; (R)NRS PIT 1964, Portland GM 1966; chosen as one of the World's Favourite roses. One of the roses by which the strength of fragrance is measured. The perfume is distinctive: once sniffed never forgotten. The flowers back up the perfume, being a sort of smoky-red, a colour that every rose writer tries to clarify, but all seem to fail. The flowers are large (often up to 13cm (5in) across), usually very well formed, especially in the second flush. Growth is medium to about 90cm (3ft); foliage is large and plentiful, being very tough and dark green. This rose is another of those that flourish in good weather; in cold it goes blue, in rain it can ball – but for all that anyone who enjoys a perfumed rose of quality can still not be without it.

'Fulton Mackay' (COCdana, Maribel); Cocker 1988. Official colour descriptions of roses seldom do justice to them, and this is a case in point. It is said to be a yellow blend which could be anything; in fact it is a whole confection of peachy, apricot, creamy and golden tints which makes it a very attractive rose from Scotland. The flower quality is stupendous as a garden variety. With only about 20 petals, it could be said to be too thin but this means that in wet weather the rose stays as lovely as ever, opening up from bud to full flower in absolute beauty. And you can add a strong fragrance to that, a fragrance reminiscent of still-to-ripen peaches. Foliage is big and glossy; a rose that will enhance any garden.

'Grandpa Dickson' (Irish Gold); Dickson 1966; (R)NRS PIT 1965, Golden Rose of The Hague 1966, Belfast GM 1968, Portland GM 1970. This lemony yellow Hybrid tea was a standard rose for exhibitors within two years of its launch in London. It sometimes made a place for itself in the US but it was Britain and Ireland where it really succeeded. Not the most vigorous rose bush you will meet, the blooms it produces are first class in size and generally a good shape; to get perfection of bloom they should be cut at the halfway stage of flowering which generally eliminates split blooms. The upright bush, however, needs to be fed, fed and fed again. One grower once said you could shovel the fertilizer on to it and it would still ask for more. Light coloured foliage and a height to about 90cm (3ft).

'Ingrid Bergman' (POULman); Poulsen 1984; Belfast GM 1985, Madrid 1986; The Golden Rose of The Hague 1987. A dark red rose that quickly won acceptance for its huge specimen blooms of classic form, and its ability to go on and on producing almost continuous blooms. It is best when cut at about the halfway stage as the blooms often begin to open loosely after that. As a red bedding variety it is almost unbeatable in its colour and with a vigorous, bushy but medium-height plant it is very popular in most gardens. It suffers, however, from the missing factor in many modern red roses, which is a lack of heavy perfume. It was one of the tricks of nature that took the scent from the red roses and placed it elsewhere. Now hybridizers will have to go back through pinks and whites to rescue the perfume.

'Joanne' Poole 1985. A rose bred by an amateur, but an amateur who knows what a real Hybrid Tea should look like. Lionel Poole was for many years champion exhibitor of Great Britain until he changed over to hybridizing his own roses. This was one of his first and it is proving itself all over the world where the orange-pink colour places it as quite a distinctive arrival. It got the accolade from top American exhibitor, Peter Schneider, of being his best new rose for 1991, while in Britain it frequently appears in the top spots in shows. The blooms are, of course, big and classically shaped, while the bush exhibits its parentage of 'Chicago Peace' with bushy growth and large dark green foliage.

'Julia's Rose' Wisbech Roses 1976; Baden-Baden GM 1983. Easily one of the most distinctive roses on the market, its russet-coffee cream blooms looking like left-over silk roses from a lady's hat from the last century. It has an almost porcelain-like shading, delicate and beautiful. As it unfolds it takes on a softer, lighter colour but at all stages it is a marvellous rose for flower arrangers who want something different, which was the reason it was named for Julia Clements, the doyen of British arrangers. The bush tends to be spreading with not over-vigorous growth. But for all that it remains a rose that will bring novelty into the garden.

'Just Joey' Cants 1972; James Mason Medal 1986. Everything good that has been said about roses has been said about this buff-orange beauty. Everywhere in the world it has been acclaimed and deserves to be among the list of the world's favourite roses. In very warm climates the colouring is slightly less intense but it retains its unique frilled petals. Even its growth and the deep colouring of the foliage complements the beautiful flower. The bush is vigorous and free flowering. The flower can achieve great size and wlll last for days in a vase. It was named for the wife of the managing director of Cants of Colchester, Joey Pawsey – a perfect match (Fig.10.4).

'Keepsake' (KORmalda, Esmerelda, Kordes, Rose Esmerelda); Kordes 1981; Portland GM 1987. When this rose was first introduced to growers in the UK at the Royal National Rose Society's Summer Show in 1981, it attracted immediate attention. Its rich blending of pinks in a large

Fig. 10.4 'Just Joey' introduced a new dimension into the flower form of Hybrid Teas.

well-shaped flower was what drew attention. The flowers are carried 1–3 on a stem and the buds are ovoid opening with well reflexed petals. It also has a medium fragrance. Very soon it was making its place in international gardens, from New Zealand to California and right over Europe. It does, however, have one fault: in one garden it will grow into a vigorous bush while in another it will just barely linger. If yours happens to be unhappy, move it to a place where it gets sun and the soil is fresh and well fed. It is quite disease resistant, with medium green, glossy foliage.

'Las Vegas' (KORgane); Kordes 1981; Geneva GM 1985, Portland GM 1988. While 'Keepsake' was making a name for itself in 1981 the Kordes hybridizers introduced this vibrant orange and yellow rose much more quietly. It makes a marvellous bedding rose with colours that glow in the sunshine, the perfect foil for any large area of lawn. It is good where the sun shines but has been found to be remarkably hardy in colder parts of the world. Its 26-petalled, high pointed bloom is also weather proof and opens quickly. However, the blooms do have a tendency to hang down due to a weak neck. The vitality of the bush makes up for any slight deficiency in the bloom, being vigorous and bushy with slightly glossy medium green foliage.

'Limelight' (KORikon, Golden Medallion); Kordes 1984. A rose that also slipped quietly into commerce. Obviously bred as part of the Kordes cut-flower operation, it has been found to be quite happy in the great outdoors. The blooms are light yellow, large double with 35 petals, and a very strong fragrance. It has not, surprisingly, gone on sale in the UK, but is regarded as a very important rose in Australia, South Africa and France, with this comment coming from Ohio writer and grower, Peter Schneider: 'Limelight is more than a rose, it is a genuine phenomenon. It wins Challenge Classes, it wins Queens. It wins Queen of the District Show even when it has no foliage. Catching the eye of the judges because its colour is anything but

light, 'Limelight' coasts to victory with form that is perfectly symmetrical but seldom classically high centred'. You can't very well improve on a review like that.

'Liverpool Remembers' (FRYstar, Beauty Star); Fryer 1990. An emerging star that was named to commemorate the tragedy of 95 football fans who lost their lives at a British soccer game in April 1989. Its large perfectly formed buds of tangerine orange make a spectacular display when growing or when cut for display. It brought Wini Edmunds of *Roses by Fred Edmunds* fame, to exult 'Gorgeous, gorgeous, gorgeous'. It is a rose that stands up to wind, weather and other enemies of the rose, holding its blooms high and colourful until the very end. It also has the great ability of constantly producing first class blooms.

'Lover's Meeting' Gandy 1980. One of those wandering souls in the rose world, as no one can be sure whether it is a Hybrid Tea or a Floribunda. Its flowers are generally carried in clusters of bright, medium-sized orange tangerine blooms and the majority of gardeners treat it as a Hybrid Tea. The colour of the bloom is the really attractive feature, bright and glowing, calling from one grower the description of it being 'a sensational new rose in a gorgeous new colour.' The foliage is an added attraction, being bronzey-green and the stems are strong and long on an upright bush. The variety also has another great recommendation – it is extremely disease resistant.

'Loving Memory' (Korgund, Korgund 81, Burgund 81, Red Cedar); Kordes 1981; Dublin GM 1981. When it comes to my personal recommendation for a red rose that is easy to grow, I always put this one first. The reasons are many: the bush is strong, upright, bushy and as tough as you can find. It is quite disease resistant although I have heard some growers say that it mildews (but not with me). It is full of good medium green, semi-glossy foliage but most of all it always seems to be in bloom, carrying one flower per stem and that flower is big and bright red. The petals are large and full and it has a soft perfume. If you have anyone who ever says they cannot grow a rose, give them a gift of this one: in one year it will be shoulder high, stretching higher later. Surprisingly, it still does not figure in nearly enough catalogues.

'Madame Violet' Teranishi 1981. A rose with a very small distribution yet one that is closer to the blue-mauve than any other. It moved from its Japanese hybridizer to the USA where it has been taken up, albeit slowly, by those who love its colour. Being a strong upright plant, it has brought the comment that it looks stiff and unnatural but there is nothing unnatural about the perfection of the bloom. It swirls magnificently to a high pointed centre that is perfection itself. To get the best from these blooms they should be disbudded; otherwise you get too many, too small flowers. The foliage looks very good, being greyish-green, and it is very disease resistant. It is also very weather hardy, which is quite unusual with this colour of rose.

'Margaret Thatcher' (KORflug, Flamingo, Veronica, Veronika); Kordes 1979. Two roses were named for former British Prime Minister, Mrs Margaret Thatcher, but the first one from a Japanese grower was not registered. It may not have generally pleased the lady that she eventually got a second-hand rose to carry her name but the re-naming of roses has taken a huge shift in recent years, with multiple names being given to the same variety. The identifying factor, as it goes from country to country, is the Breeders' denomination, in this case KOR for Kordes. This rose proved itself both in the garden and as a cut flower, but it needs warm weather to be at its best. The colour is very light pink with a silver reverse; the shape is extremely good and the cut flower will last for days in water. Plants are vigorous and flowers are carried on long stems.

'Marijke Koopman' Fryer 1979; The Hague GM 1978. Long before this rose came into commerce I was stunned by the sight of it in the fields of the Fryer family in Cheshire. The bloom was big, elegant with long pointed buds. It seemed to shout that here was a winner, and yet for all that it has never achieved the top placing it should in the UK. In other parts of the world, it is much prized both for garden display and for exhibition. The 20-petalled flower, which is bright satiny pink, also has a fragrance, blooms over a long period and it is carried in abundance on long strong stems. The bushy growth has tough, leathery foliage, all of which demonstrates why this British-bred rose has won so many fans in the USA, Australia and South Africa.

'Mister Lincoln' Swim & Weeks 1964; AARS 1965. One of the legendary roses, not just of the USA, but the whole world, especially where dark red roses with a huge perfume are appreciated. This rose has been one of those 'impossible beauties' that now and again are sent by nature. There is one amazing story about it and its parentage. It was bred by Herb Swim & Ollie Weeks as a result of a cross between 'Chrysler Imperial' and 'Charles Mallerin'. They got two seedlings from the cross, one 'Mister Lincoln', and the other the even darker and also scented 'Oklahoma'. On the other side of the world the same crossing was repeated about the same time by the House of Meilland and from their crossing came another wonderful, almost black, highly scented rose, 'Papa Meilland'. The roses were all so good that even today they are quoted whenever superior-scented roses are talked about. In selecting between the three, I opted for 'Mister Lincoln' because the bush is a better grower; upright with urn shape and lots of flowers. In the bud stage it is very dark but as it opens the petals become lighter and, when fully open, it is a joy to behold as it shows off its bright golden stamens. When the roses are as great as this family, then no one should complain. Certainly Herb Swim never did. 'This', he once told me, 'was my bread and butter rose.' In other words, the royalties from it paid for many years of good living.

'Mullard Jubilee' (Electron); McGredy

1970; RNRS GM 1969, The Hague Gold Medal 1970, Belfast Gold Medal 1972, AARS 1973, Portland GM 1973. There was hardly another major award left for it to win when 'Mullard Jubilee' (alias 'Electron' in the USA), swept the boards even before its introduction. It still goes on being a top seller worldwide. All of which justified Sam McGredy's contention to the Mullard Electronic Company that he would give them a rose that was a world-beater. They paid for it, something like $25,000 – a lot of money at the time – even before it won anything! Some people find a problem with its extreme thorniness but others, myself included, believe that a rose is not rose if it doesn't have thorns – which is not to say that I like them as prolific as they are on this variety, especially when it comes to pruning time!

'Mullard Jubilee' answers all the questions that a really good rose should: it is a stocky grower with strong stems, good disease resistance, leathery foliage, and it's hardy. The bloom is something else, 3–5 flowers are on each stem but when disbudded is quality personified. The quality, one-to-a-stem bloom is a perfectly formed, vibrant rose pink which can be slightly harsh in moderate climates but glows in the sunshine. Add to that the blessing of a great fragrance and you will see why it was such a great winner for New Zealand-based Sam McGredy.

'National Trust' (Bad Nauheim); McGredy 1970. The saddest thing to say about a rose as good as this one is that it doesn't have a real fragrance. Every rose has a fragrance of some sort, but often so slight as to be undetectable to the normal nose, and that is the misfortune of 'National Trust'. Otherwise it is an exceptional rose, both for bedding and, in some countries, for exhibition. The bloom is a clear, bright red of medium size – that is, too big for a buttonhole and too small for a show specimen bloom. But it still wins top show awards in countries like the USA (especially California) and South Africa. In the garden it is an impeccable performer, making a lovely bedding rose because of its

habit of growing upright, neat, well balanced and healthy. To give you an enthusiast's comment it is worthwhile quoting Ray Reddell from his book *Growing Good Roses*: 'It ('National Trust') has a way of quilling its petals as though the world's best rose groomer had taken a camel-hair brush to coax it to the limit. And for all its individuality 'National Trust' looks good with other roses; its highly distinct form doesn't clash with anything.'

'Nightingale' (HERgale); Herholdt 1970. A South African bred rose that is an absolute show winner no matter where it appears. However, it has something of a dual personality. There was a mix-up during the transportation of budwood to England from the Johannesburg breeder that resulted in 'Nightingale' becoming 'Gary Player' for British gardeners, while the other rose was never grown to any extent. The result is that it is still wrongly named in Britain but exists quite happily in the rest of the world under its real name. And under that name it is quite a big winner, both in the garden and on the show bench. Its soft rose-pink colouring is shown off to perfection of a large, high-centred, slightly fragrant bloom. The bush is free blooming but needs care and attention to make it grow vigorously.

'Olympiad' (MACauck, Olympiade); McGredy 1983; AARS 1984, Portland GM 1985. What a magnificent rose this would have been with a deep fragrance. Alas, it isn't possible to have everything in a rose and even without that much appreciable perfume, 'Olympiad' has become one of the top selling red roses for garden use in the world. Mind you it had everything going for when it was named the official rose for the Los Angeles Olympic Games. It is red, the top-selling colour in roses; the bush is well behaved – it could grow tallish but not too danglingly tall – and the stems are long and firm, mainly carrying one flower. And that flower is still one of the best to grow in a warm climate, which accounts for its success in the USA and its general lack of appearance in the UK.

'Paradise' (Wezeip, WEzip, Burning Sky); Weeks 1978; AARS 1979, Portland GM 1979. Here is a rose which, in my opinion, is very properly named. But then I love the mauve/lilac/bluey tones – though ambivalence exists even in the wonderful world of roses and you can find as many people who hate it! The colour is really a sort of deep silvery lilac, moving to deeper lilac and then splashing red on the rims of the petals. It has to be one of the most unusual colours in the rose world – and it adds a deep fragrance to it all. The bloom form is wonderful, with 26 to 30 petals arranged perfectly around a nib-sharp centre. But for all that, it isn't perfect. It tends to fall prey to mildew (which to me is nothing more than a floral cold-in-the-head) and with preventative spraying can be kept happy – but do not over-do it as the spray can easily damage the foliage. It also has a slight tendency to die back, but it still goes on to produce enough strong growth for those of us who love it.

'Pascali' (LENip, Blanche Pasca); Lens 1963; The Hague GM 1963, Portland GM 1963, AARS 1969, World's Favourite Rose 1991. The Queen of the white roses – comment that is easily borne out by its continued winning ways. Few roses have existed since the 60s with such an untramelled reputation. No one says anything bad about 'Pascali'. Some may say that its bloom is not quite big enough for them but after that it is all applause. What can you really say bad about its crystal clear whiteness, its purity and its perfect form, very rarely showing split centres? When a bloom is cut it will go on and on growing for days when its size and freshness will rival most of the other contenders. The bush is disease resistant, may seem spindly in growth but stems hold themselves high, especially when disbudded down to an individual flower. In its favour also is the fact that the blooms despise all sorts of weather and even in anyone's summer showers they very seldom show any signs of spotting. In white roses it is a marvel, among all roses it is beautiful.

'Paul Shirville' (HARqueterwife, Heart Throb); Harkness 1981; Edland Fragrance Award RNRS 1982. A rose that has attained the title of the 'Most photographable and most photographed rose in the world'. Certainly its pastel orange-pink blooms look perfection themselves and they add a great quality to any border, while in a bed they are superb. The only distressing thing – or maybe its great attraction – is that it draws all sorts of discussions about what it is. Is it a Shrub? Is it a Floribunda? No, it's a Hybrid Tea, although it could qualify as any of the others. The bush produces flowers that in the USA terms might be likened to a Grandiflora but in growth is only medium height. It has shiny, strong foliage and seems as healthy as they come. It has form, not great size but a fragrance to captivate.

'Peter Frankenfeld' Kordes 1966. It is one of the surprises of the rose world that this rose was so slow to attract attention. Maybe it was its colour – it is that deep pink that may seem harsh in some climates but I forgive it that. Maybe it was the name which didn't immediately attract. But now, despite its age, 'Peter Frankenfeld' appears in catalogues all over the world. And the main reason that it does is that, by word of mouth, gardeners have found that it produces long stemmed, perfectly formed blooms, generally one-to-a-stem which means that it does not need disbudding. It goes on producing these blooms all season long on a hardy, disease-resistant medium to tall bush. In other words if it was another colour with maybe another name it would have topped the polls long ago. I'm just glad it has made it at last.

'Pink Favorite' vonAbrams 1956; Portland GM 1957. A great rose that was overlooked for most of the world's awards but has lived and been successful much longer than many of the more vaunted varieties. Its great attraction is the spreading, strong growth with foliage that can be immaculate and untouched by disease. Some years ago a farmer, totally disinterested in roses, visited my garden and was thrilled by the sight of this rose – in the middle of winter. He said that with growth like that it deserved its place among the great shrubs of the world. Unfortunately, in places recently it has begun to show signs of black spot and rust but this can adequately be kept at bay by preventative spraying early spring and mid-summer. The flower is fragrant, medium pink and produced like a Floribunda, which means that to get the real quality of bloom it must be disbudded heavily and early.

'Polar Star' (TANlarpost, Polarstern); Tantau 1982. Rose of the Year in Britain 1985. A contender for 'Pascali's place as the top white but never reaching the same heights of approval. For all that it is a super-resistant variety that seems to laugh at normal rose troubles. The bloom has that greyish-green frosty look until it opens up, when it becomes large and high centred and white, with just a hint of yellow at the base. Unfortunately for those who want constant high quality blooms, it happens that now and again the flowers are ill-formed, which can often be rectified by a change in the fertilizer. Blooms are produced one-to-a-stem and are spicily fragrant. Foliage is a lush dark green and dense.

'Peace' (Gioia, Gloria Dei, Mme. A. Meilland); Meilland 1945; Portland GM 1944; AARS 1946; Golden Rose of The Hague 1965. World's Favourite Rose. The most famous rose in the world; a rose named and dedicated to peace at the end of World War II; a rose with more stories told about it than any other. Even a book has been written about it: *For Love of a Rose* by Antonia Ridge. The essential part of the story is that some budwood was smuggled out of France in the last diplomatic bag before the fall of the country to the Nazis. It certainly re-echoes the words of the Duke of Windsor of the time who said that it was the most beautiful rose in the whole world. What more can be said about it now? Well, it is on sale in every country of the world; the flower is large, well shaped, light yellow with a touch of pink on the edges of the

petals. Indeed the flower was so unbeatable on the show bench in the 1950s that it was banned in many places from general rose classes. It is a spreading bush with good foliage. Historic and still peerless.

Fig. 10.5 The perfect form and stamina of 'Peace' contributed to the extraordinary popularity of the rose in the 1950s.

'Peaudouce' Dickson 1983; (DICjana; Elina – now the more acceptable name for this rose); ADR 1987; New Zealand GM 1987. In my opinion one of the finest Hybrid Teas of the 80s and proving this by being a best seller everywhere it goes on sale. It has everything going for it: size; quality blooms produced constantly; a bush that is strong and effective without getting lanky; foliage that is dark and glossy and resists disease well. One writer put it well when he said: 'It is a dream of a rose – hardy, healthy and prolific'. However the blooms are not always up to exhibition standard as they tend to open loosely, but that said, they stay fresh until the stamens are fully revealed when it looks as nature intended it to look – a great rose. Oh, yes, the colour is very light yellow and often looks white at a distance but there is a golden heart there. If there is one fault it is that it spots slightly in rain.

'Perfect Moment' (KORwilma; Jack Dayson); Kordes 1989; AARS 1991. A perfectly stunning rose that has proved an eye-catcher at exhibitions of roses everywhere. In 1992 there was a display of it at the famous Elgin Rose Festival in South Africa that was so effective it was a battle to get close up to see the blooms. The colour is a great blending of orange red and golden yellow in blooms that are so big they look unreal. The blooms tend to be perfect up to about the three-quarters open stage but then tend to show petals that fold into the centre ... however, this seems only to happen in cooler, damper climates. The bush is big and bright causing Wini Edmunds to write: 'As a garden rose it is awesome, with colours so bright that you will need sun glasses to prevent retina damage.' For all that it has yet to prove itself in the colder parts of the world.

'Pink Pearl' (Kormasyl, Fee); Martens 1987. A very light pink sport of 'Congratulations' that brought with it the long pointed elegant buds of its parent. The blooms are smallish which makes them very good for flower arranging, where their shape holds very well after cutting. Bushes are upright and tall (one grower calls them columnar). Needs a place where it can get plenty of air circulating around the bush – also likes the sun. Needs to be watched for the arrival of mildew.

'Pristine' (JACpico); Warriner 1978; Portland GM 1979, Edland Fragrance Medal 1979. Not every American bred rose travels well (the same can be said of other roses from other countries), but this one has proven itself everywhere. Its soft light pink-white bloom looks like tender porcelain in a bloom that is elegant, graceful, with about 28 petals. It gives the impression of being a bloom that opens very quickly – not so. From full coloured bud until three-quarters open the bloom does quickly but then it holds itself. After that it gently opens to provide the perfect open flower. But it isn't just as an open bloom it shows perfection; it is also a top prizewinning show rose. The bush is strong

and will tend to grow tall unless controlled, but height is no problem when there is a marvellous bloom at the end of it. The foliage is dark and tough. Whether it deserved the Edland Medal for Fragrance is often debated but there is no doubt that on a scale of 1 to 10 every nose will put it over the halfway mark, and that's not bad for such a handsome flower.

'Red Devil' (DICam, Coeur d'Amour); Dickson 1970; Portland GM 1970. If only this rose had arrived any other year than when there happened to be a whole galaxy of great roses, then it would have won far more awards. However, when it came to winning it certainly provided the British rose exhibitors with a tally that probably has never been topped.

Practically every year since its arrival in commerce, it has been topping the poll of exhibition roses, but that isn't surprising because its bloom is, in 90% of cases, perfection itself. However, it has not been a great traveller and to see it shown at its best you will have to visit a British Rose Show. It is big, bright scarlet bloom with slightly lighter reverse, and very full. As a garden Hybrid Tea, it deserves commendation too – the bush is strong without going too tall, the foliage is a beautiful glossy green, the flowers are carried on long stems and there is a fragrance.

'Remember Me' (COCdestin); Cocker 1984; Belfast GM 1986. If there were awards for unusual colours in roses, then this would be heaped with them. It exhibits the most beautiful coppery-coloured flowers. But that description does not do justice to the tones of orange, pink, tan and gold that blend into each in a suffusion of pleasure. If that suggests I like the flower, then I am happy because it is to me a most original creation. The reason it has not really made the top spots in any country is simplicity itself: the flowers vary in size so that you can get some very good-sized ones, while others will only make buttonhole size (but good ones for all that). The flowers are almost perfection itself with high pointed centres. The bush grows to about medium size in most areas, with very neat and acceptable bushy growth and abundant foliage. A new generation rose that can delight.

'Rose Gaujard' (GAUmo); Gaujard 1957; NRS GM 1958. One of the hardiest, most disease-resistant roses of our time. Produced in France by Jean Gaujard, the successor to the great and famous Pernet Ducher, this rose is still stocked worldwide by nurseries who know that it has not been surpassed by the thousands of other roses that have followed it. The flower begins temptingly tall and narrow in the bud but grows almightily large with 80 petals. Blooms are high centred but because of the number of petals frequently produce split centres – but this will only worry the exhibitors. For the general gardener it is still hard to find a rose so robust, so floriferous, or so vigorous. The flower too is still unique in colouring being cherry-red with a silvery-pink reverse. A rose that just wants to grow.

'Royal Highness' (Konigliche Hoheit); Swim & Weeks 1962; Portland GM 1961, Madrid GM 1962, AARS 1963. Even today there are few roses to match the stately elegance of the urn-shaped flowers of this lightest of all pink roses. From delicate bud to immaculate bloom it can provide stunning qualities, unless you happen to live in a rainy part of the world when it will ball, go brown and nullify everything that has been said good about it. In the UK the pinkish tinge is not in evidence and sometimes the flowers are exhibited snowy white. The bush always looks elegant too with strong stems and one good flower at the top, unless it is allowed to fall foul of mildew. However, I find mildew no great problem with this rose and one or two preventative sprays provide all the care it needs. But it can also be a rust catcher, so take care and do the necessary spraying.

'Royal William' (Korzuan, Duftzauber 84, Fragrant Charm 84); Kordes 1984; British Rose of the Year 1987. A deep red rose with the shape and substance of this one is hard to find these days but Royal William fills the bill. The flowers, carried singly on strong stems, are medium sized with a very good shape, and a soft fragrance. They make ideal blooms for cutting and flower arranging. In the USA where blooms for exhibition tend to be smaller than in Britain it is very much a show rose. The bush is a sturdy, upright grower with dark green foliage that is very disease resistant (Fig.10.6).

Fig. 10.6 Cut flower varieties are bred to produce a perfect form and a long vase life.

'Savoy Hotel' (HARvintage); Harkness 1989; Dublin GM 1988. One of the prettiest pink Hybrid Teas for a number of years, it is also a large, well-proportioned shapely bloom. It makes a very fine bedding rose, being very even in its production of new growth on a bush that is medium height and has good foliage. This helps to put it in line for a good edging or hedging rose where a compact effect is needed. Blooms are carried on medium length stems and, when cut, grow on well in water as well as having good lasting value. Named for London's Savoy Hotel in celebration of its centenary in 1989.

'Selfridges' (KORpriwa, Berolina); Kordes 1984; ADR 1984. A non-fading yellow Hybrid tea that has never achieved the prominence due to it, despite the fact that it is named after a leading British store. It is widely sold in the United States and New Zealand under both the names of 'Berolina' and 'Selfridges'. The fact that Kordes, who bred it, have kept it in their catalogue gives proof to its ability to grow. The blooms are large, with classical exhibition shape that has won many best blooms in show awards. The plant has dark green foliage and is upright and so vigorous that in parts of the USA it can grow almost like a Climber. It is very hardy and also disease resistant.

'Sheer Bliss' (JACtro); Warriner 1985; Japan GM 1984, AARS 1987. When you talk of a rose being acceptable all through the USA, you expect that it will be sun happy and winter hardy, but that doesn't always happen. Many of them fall to the rigours of winter even when they are wrapped up snug and warm. But here is a newish rose that seems to have all the ability to come through fairly tough winters. It carries very large, lovely pastel-type blooms in the creamy-pink tones that are widely acceptable. The flowers are carried one-to-a-stem on an upright bush with medium green foliage. It grows medium to tall and needs to be controlled by judicious pruning.

'Sheer Elegance' (TWObe); Twomey 1989; AARS 1991. Elegance is what personifies this rose, which was bred by amateur Californian-based breeder, Jerry Twomey, who got back-to-back AARS winner with 'All that Jazz' in 1992. The colours are in shades of the early nineties – soft pink and coral lightly blended with cream; both warm and subtle. The flower too is perfection, immediately being regarded in the States as a possible contender with 'Touch of Class' for the top Hybrid Tea spot. Blooms of 35 petals are large and full and carried on long straight stems on a bush that is upright in habit with large and dark green foliage. It has still a long way to go but if initial enthusiasm is any criterion, this lightly fragrant rose will be around for a long time.

'Silver Jubilee' Cocker 1978; RNRS PIT 1977, Belfast GM 1980, Portland GM 1981. One of the very best Hybrid Teas for both consistency of flowering, growth and perfection of bloom. This comment may come as a surprise to many American growers who dislike it for its short stems, but the ordinary gardener who is not worried about showing will treasure its other attributes. And for those in the UK it still makes a magnificent show bloom in classes where length of stem is of no importance. It is a soft, satiny pink with a warmer pink reverse, and the bloom is classical. When it first arrived in my garden on trial, I showed a magnificent bloom to a nurseryman friend and he took a lot of convincing that it was real! The difference in the breeding programme of American and British breeders is that 'Silver Jubilee' has been used extensively on the eastern side of the Atlantic but the hang-up about its short stems has generally kept it out of American hybridizing. Many hybridizers believe it is the best offering to breeders since 'Peace'.

'Simba' (KORbelma, Helmut Schmidt, Goldsmith); Kordes 1979; Belgium GM 1979, Geneva GM 1979. One of the very best yellow roses whether you want it for a near perfect bloom or to fill out a bed. You could go on and on just adding to the great comments about this rose except that just about everything has been said. As the pointed buds unfold, they usually present a bloom of unrivalled class, except on occasions when the centre petals fold into the rose giving it a rounded appearance. There are more fine blooms on it than there are poor ones and they make very good cut flowers, giving blooms large enough for the show table. It produces masses of blooms (they do need disbudding for quality) on a vigorous bush that is compact and upright and clothed with large grey-green foliage.

'Spiced Coffee' (MACjuliat, Old Spice); McGredy 1990. You can call this a russet rose, or you can look around you and wonder at the pale amber, flushed lavender pink buds that open to shapely beige-coloured, largish blooms that still retain that strange look of lavender-edged coffee. Whatever you call it, it will certainly catch anyone's attention, not just the flower arrangers who find it so useful but also the gardener who wants novelty in his roses. In a way it goes back into generations of the McGredy family who once had a rose they called 'Grey Pearl' but was better known as 'The Mouse'. It was loved by some, hated by others – and reminded one writer, Roy Hay, of a Grand Guignol scene 'where the lights are masked with a green shade to emphasize the macabre'. Macabre this is not – it attracts attention everywhere. It loves the sun and is also happy in the rain, a perfect combination for any rose grower. Roses in this type of colouring tend to be grown on weakly bushes, but this one is strong and vigorous with plenty of flowers and a spicy fragrance.

'Sutter's Gold' Swim 1950; Portland GM 1946, Bagatelle GM 1948, Geneva GM 1949, AARS 1950. 'This seedling bloomed for me in 1942 and immediately I knew I had something special' Herb Swim, one of America's greatest hybridizers, once wrote to me. It was winning awards before it was named, a name that is historically associated with California. San McGredy wrote in his *Look to the Rose* that this rose seemed almost too good to be true. Here was a yellow rose (well, yellow brushed with golden orange), with a fragrance 'almost overpowering'. He feels that today this rose is not a front runner but it is still high on the rose lover's appreciation list. It can still produce those elegant long buds that swirl into fantastically perfumed 25-petalled blooms, and the bush itself is dark-foliaged and reasonably strong growing. If you live in a very hot country, it will benefit from a little shade in the afternoon.

'Tequila Sunrise' (DICobey, Beaulieu); Dickson 1988; RNRS GM 1988. Offered as the new wave of Hybrid Teas, this rose is the perfect offering for anyone who does not expect an extravagant bloom with lots of petals. It holds a very good shape until half open; the fully open bloom is flat. It loves the sunshine where the corn coloured flowers take on a lot of red. It makes a very good bedding rose, continuing with flushes of blooms in large clusters right through the season. Blooms last well on the bush and when cut.

'The Lady' (FRYjingo); Fryer 1987; Baden-Baden GM 1987. It is simply called a yellow blend rose by colour classification but that does little to tell the real truth about its delicious and delicate colouring. It is a lovely confection of pastel shading, soft honey with edging of salmon that in the sun seems to pick up some deeper touches of yellow. It is highly scented and each bloom has a perfect shape with petals that reflex totally of their own accord. The bush needs a little extra fertilizing to make it grow big and strong, but when established it asks for nothing other than worship. Bred near Manchester, England – an area noted for rain – it is perhaps appropriate that wet weather does not bother this rose which was named for a British magazine.

'Touch of Class' (Kricarlo, Marechal le Clerc); Kriloff 1984; AARS 1986, Portland GM 1988. Here is a rose that might never have been but for two keen-eyed young rosemen searching France for new varieties. Jack Christensen and Tom Carruth saw the rose in a field and were dazzled by it but were told that it was already under trial in America. Their wonder at the magnificent bloom was such that they pleaded with the grower that should the company in America turn it down, they would get the option to grow it. They never gave up the chase and when the rose was eventually turned down it came back to them. Their insight was rewarded, as it went on to become one of the great show roses of the USA where its high-centred, reflexing, warm coral bloom won everything. Soon it was number one in all top tens and it established itself as a good garden rose too – if you can remember to give it a preventative spray for mildew. It is one of those roses that just loves the sun and when it came to

England it disgusted one gardener so much that he sent the plants back the next year as impostors! He reckoned they were hardly up to second-class plants. Fame is a fickle thing!

'Tournament of Roses' (JACient, Berkeley, Poesie); Warriner 1988; ARS 1989. Yes, so this is a Grandiflora but that is a grouping that is not internationally recognized so I was in a dilemma. However, having seen the rose grow I decided that there was no way it could be a Floribunda – the blooms are too classy for that – and the bush was not tall and straggly so into the Hybrid Tea section it goes. It carries shapely warm pink blooms in clusters of 3–5 which make a fragrant bouquet. The upright bush is vigorous and blooms freely making it an easy-to-grow variety. It is named for the famous New Year's Day tournament of roses at Pasadena, California which celebrated its centenary in 1988.

'Whisky Mac' (TANky, Whisky); Tantau 1967. Sam McGredy aptly summed up this rose when he said that it is 'beguiling, beautiful, fragrant and annoying'. He was commenting on the fact that despite a whole series of faults, it continues to be one of the top sellers the world over. And the faults? It falls under the spell of mildew (but that is curable) and then allows some of the inside wood to die-back. Fairly frequently the whole bush dies. But by then it has made its mark; the gardener is entranced and decides that it wasn't the rose that was to blame – after all it is too beautiful and fragrant a flower to be fallible. So it is planted again and the romance goes on. A romance with the colour, the marvellous blooms when they are cut – and a blind eye for the faults. As Ludwig Taschner in South Africa once wrote: 'It is not a rose for the novices'. But then novices have been known to flirt . . .

'Woods of Windsor' (KORprill, KORhanbu, Belami); Kordes 1985; Dublin GM 1983. Here is another rose that has not really taken off in the UK, despite its association with the famous firm of perfumers. It has achieved a greater impact in the USA where as 'Belami' it has been said to be the closest rose to perfection of bloom. Certainly the blooms are large and classically shaped, which make them ideal for exhibiting, flower arranging or just for decorative cutting. They are the softest possible pink, with a deeper pink rim around the petals. The bush itself is vigorous and free blooming, with glossy reddish-green foliage. It grows on the tall side of medium.

Vintage Varieties

In drawing up the list of Hybrid Teas and Floribundas, I was constantly conscious of missing many favourites: roses that have just gone out of fashion but still make wonderful plants for any garden. The question may be asked why they have gone out of fashion? Well, that is hard to tell. Some have shown a tendency to fall victim to disease after a few years; others are just dropped as growers feel new varieties are better (not always true). So here is a short, personal list of roses that I would like to think of as vintage varieties and that will produce blooms still capable of thrilling even the most cynical gardener.

Hybrid Teas

'Bewitched' Lammerts 1967. Still a staple American variety; a classic among perfumed pink roses.

'Casanova' McGredy 1964. Still a great South African favourite; vigorous, healthy and prolific, deserves a wider recognition.

'Charles Mallerin' Meilland 1951. One of the great dark red roses, whose name is found in the parentage of most of the modern perfumed red varieties. A poor, untidy grower, but what a stunning bloom! Put it at the back of a border.

'Crimson Glory' Kordes 1935. Put it in the warmth of the sun and you get a marvellous dark red rose with strong Damask perfume.

'Albertine' is a popular Rambler that will cover fences, decorate arbours and give pleasure everywhere in the garden.

'Queen Mother' has an appeal as a Patio rose which with its slightly lax growth is also suitable for tubs and pots.

'Angela Rippon' is typical of Modern Patio type roses which will conveniently give colour to small beds and borders.

'Sweet Magic' has the perfect miniaturized flower formation of the true Patio with the bonus of a pleasing fragrance.

Miniature and Patio roses give pleasure to the pretty secluded terrace garden at the Rose Society's garden at St. Albans.

The miniature rose garden at Hyde Hall uses the smaller type of rose bush to advantage with a valuable contribution of good garden architecture.

'Surrey' is a free
flowering Ground
cover that will
grow in many
difficult situations
and has a long
period of flower.

The 'mountain' of Ground cover roses at St. Albans is a graphic demonstration of the adaptability of this type of rose.

'Pheasant' has the potential to sprawl over quite a distance and produces high quality scented bloom.

'The Fairy' may
be an old rose
historically but is
not out of place
as a Ground cover
in the modern
garden.

'Diamond Jubilee' Boerner 1947. Large exhibition flowers in light buff yellow, often touched by shades of pink. A rose that stretches back to great parentage – 'Marechal Neil' × 'Frau Pernet-Ducher'.

'First Love' Swim 1951. The softest pink buds in a beautiful urn-shaped bloom. Once seen, never forgotten.

'Josephine Bruce' Bees 1949. One of the great lovelies – dark, velvet-red blooms with magnificent fragrance.

'La France' Guillot Fils 1867. The starter of the modern rose; now looks distinctly old-fashioned but for history alone deserves a place for its pink, pink flowers on a thin bush.

'La Jolla' Swim 1954. Vigorous, prolific, healthy with blooms that mingle pink, cream and yellow in a marvellous confection.

'Madame Butterfly' Hill 1918. One of the great buttonhole roses; soft pink with gold at the base and a delicious perfume.

'Madame Louis Laperriere' Laperriere 1951. One of the underestimated roses of the wonderful 50s. Dark crimson blooms with a great fragrance.

'McGredy's Yellow' McGredy 1933. Still one of the finest yellow Hybrid Teas. Beautiful flowers in profusion backed by marvellous fragrance.

'Mojave' Swim 1954. Fragrant, vigorous with long elegant buds that open to sunset tones of orange and pink.

'Mrs Sam McGredy' McGredy 1929. A rose in colours that have not been repeated – coppery, orange and salmon. Bush lost out when a climbing sport was found, but is still worth a place where beautiful roses are appreciated.

'Peer Gynt' Kordes 1968. A fine yellow, red tipped Hybrid Tea of solid growth. Still widely grown.

'Piccadilly' McGredy 1960. A superb early-flowering variety, orange-red and gold flowers that are first class.

'Prima Ballerina' Tantau 1957. Rose pink with a deep, lingering fragrance but overtaken by more disease-resistant varieties. Still widely sold.

'Shot Silk' Dickson 1924. Elegance in bloom, perfumed, good grower by the standards of the 20s. Colour unsurpassed – a bright cerise, shot through with golden yellow. Very aptly named.

'Silver Lining' Dickson 1958. Still grown in parks and gardens where a vigorous, fragrant rose is needed. Pink with a silver reverse.

'Super Star' Tropicana; Tantau 1960. A runaway winner with superb vermilion blooms, until mildew and other diseases stalked it. It is still widely sold but needs a lot of protection against disease.

'Troika' (POUmidor, Royal Dane); Poulsen 1971. A beautiful mingling of orange, bronze and red flowers on a strong-growing bush which can still produce first-class bedding plants.

Floribundas

'Bonfire Night' McGredy 1971. As bright a Floribunda as you can find with red and yellow beautifully shaped blooms. Needs a little care to protect it from diseases.

'City of Leeds' McGredy 1966; RNRS GM 1965. Rich salmon-pink bloom on a bush that is easy to grow, and vigorous. A great rose in the sunshine.

'Frensham' Norman 1946; (R)NRS GM 1943, ARS GM 1955. Despite its age, this is one of the great crimson Floribundas. Early on became prone to mildew but in recent years with more emphasis on prevention, it is growing as vigorously as ever.

'Lili Marlene' (KORlima, Lilli Marleen); Kordes 1959; ADR 1960. The almost black buds open to deep red blooms which are carried in trusses. A bushy, lowish growing, weather-proof variety.

'Masquerade' Boerner 1949; (R)NRS GM 1952. The first of the multi-coloured roses in which the yellow buds age to red, giving a really colourful bush. Prone to mildew.

'Molly McGredy' McGredy 1969. A standard setter for elegant red with silver reverse blooms on a Floribunda bush that is among the most disease-resistant available.

'Sea Pearl' (Flower Girl); Dickson 1964. Truly the colours of a sea pearl – massing pink, peach and cream – but not as happy as the pearl in water. Spots in the rain but if grown under cover, produces well-shaped blooms.

'Southampton' (Susan Ann); Harkness 1971. Apricot-orange flushed red made this one of the great flower arranger roses of the 1970s and 1980s. A tall grower it is vigorous with good disease resistance.

'White Pet' (Little White Pet); Henderson 1879. Although classified a Polyantha this little rose deserves a place especially where small cluster-flowered roses grow. A great producer in the Miniature style.

'Redgold' Dickson 1971. Not an old rose but one that should be cherished. The name totally reflects the colours that are produced in lovely Floribunda trusses.

'Yvonne Rabier' Turbat 1910. Another that is classified a Polyantha but its white double blooms would be equally at home in a patio situation or fronting a bed, wherever a compact plant is required. It is very fragrant.

CHAPTER 11

Climbers and Ramblers

On the evidence of a sampling of growers' catalogues and the popularity polls of national and district rose societies world wide, the choice of varieties readily available to the home gardener is somewhat limited. While the range of Hybrid Tea and Floribunda bush roses, together with the shrubby types is numbered in hundreds, the Climbers and Ramblers can only be measured in tens. But what they lack in numbers is more than compensated for by their beauty and versatility. They have the great merit of providing a considerable quantity of aerial colour and form in return for the occupation of relatively small areas of ground space. One cannot escape the feeling that their value as essential 'third dimension' garden furnishings has yet to be fully exploited by park and garden owners and designers.

The most widely available varieties appear to organize themselves into two main groups. The first group comprises those modern hybrids that can be said to represent the 'New Dawn' (almost literally) era of climbing roses and which followed the introduction of the rose of that name in 1930. The second group, mostly introduced much earlier, encompasses a diverse assortment of what might be termed vintage roses that have arisen from a number of different parental backgrounds.

The 'New Dawn' of the Modern Climber

The 'New Dawn' era traces its origins back to two wild roses, *R. wichuraiana* and *R. rugosa* from the regions of Japan, China and Korea, the re- distribution of which into the Western world was the opening chapter in what may be described as the saga of the modern garden Climber.

The saga began in 1860 when Dr Max Wichura, a Prussian botanist, was included in a diplomatic mission to Japan, a country which was in a state of political uncertainty at the time and whose people were not always kindly disposed towards foreigners. Despite these difficulties, Dr Wichura collected and sent home what has come to be accepted as the type specimen of the wild rose that commemorates him, *Rosa wichuraiana*. Eventually, the species reached America and it was here, many years later, that Dr W Van Fleet bred from it a very lovely but only once-blooming double-flowered and sweetly scented pale pink Climber, to which he gave his name. He introduced this rose in 1910 and, such are its qualities, it is still widely grown today.

The saga might have ended there had not Mother Nature taken a hand in the proceedings. A genetic mutation or 'sport' produced a remontant form which the American grower, H. A. Deer, was quick to spot and to recognize as the great breakthrough the rose world was waiting for. With complete justification, he named this wonderful sport 'New Dawn'. This rose soon became, and still is today, one of the world's favourite Climbers, having the great merit of succeeding in almost every climate. It also has the vital quality of being an exceptional parent, as can be seen from the numerous very popular Climbers that have emanated directly from it.

At this point the story switches to Europe and to the efforts of that great German rose breeder, Wilhelm Kordes. Working towards breeding roses of exceptional health and hardiness, he became very interested in one of *wichuraiana*'s offspring, a variety that arose from a mating with *R. rugosa*. Raised by G. Bowditch in America and named 'Max Graf' this seedling has an arching and sprawling habit that enables it to be used as either a Ground cover or Climbing rose. Its pink, pleasingly scented flowers appear for only a few weeks in mid-summer, but its thick glossy foliage and its health and hardiness are noteworthy. Herr Kordes dearly wished to breed from this rose but, as it possessed an odd number of chromosomes, it was of course, sterile and all efforts failed. Then, for the second time, a timely miracle of nature occurred; a doubling of chromosomes enabled 'Max Graf' to pollinate itself and produce viable seed. Thus it was that, in 1940, *R. kordesii wulf* entered the picture and, proved to be, as Herr Kordes himself was pleased to record, 'a very fertile parent'. New varieties raised directly from *R. kordesii* are usually described as being Kordesii hybrids. Some are world-renowned Climbers, such as 'Dortmund', while many others are recognized as desirable Shrub roses.

As the second half of the twentieth century unfolded, the famous Irish breeder Sam McGredy took up both 'New Dawn' and Herr Kordes' hybrids and used them to exceptional effect. In various combinations, the genes of these roses were transmitted into a string of highly successful remontant Climbers, several of which have become world-wide favourites. Notable among these are 'Dublin Bay', 'Casino' and 'Handel'. During this period many other breeders made good use of the *wichuraiana* genes; Boerner's 'Aloha', 'Coral Dawn' and 'Parade', Gregory's 'Pink Perpétué'; Cocker's 'White Cockade'; Harkness' 'Compassion' and Kordes' 'Summer Wine' are merely a few examples of the excellent work of the modern school of international hybridists.

Miniature Climbers

The last chapter of the saga that can be written today – for it will most certainly extend far into the future – concerns the arrival on the scene of the range of Miniature Climbers being bred by C. H. Warner in England. Some are already in circulation ('Laura Ford' and 'Warm Welcome') and several others will be seen in the near future. I could be taken to task for assuming that these are descendants of *Rosa wichuraiana* but, seeing that they all trace back to the variety 'Heidelberg', which Wilhelm Kordes himself denominated a Kordesii Climber, I feel confident.

Sideshoots

As with most family sagas, there are numerous lateral developments, each one serving to emphasize the great debt owed to Dr Max Wichura. On one branch are those great once-blooming favourites of yesteryear, like 'Albéric Barbier', 'American Pillar' 'Crimson Shower', 'Dorothy Perkins' 'Excelsa' and many more. Several of these, being of lax growth, are employed not only to clothe pergolas and the like but as specimen weeping standards. On another branch are the most recent Ground cover roses, the origins of which are described in Chapter 12. These, too, can often be trained as Climbers but, more commonly, as weeping standards. The more compact prostrate growers are often budded on shorter than usual standard stocks and present the garden designer with new opportunities for imaginatively furnishing almost any style of garden.

Climbing sports of bush roses

While we are in the twentieth century, it is worth examining a range of Climbing roses that nursery catalogues usually identify by prefixing the word 'climbing' to the variety name. These have arisen as genetic mutations or 'sports' from varieties that started life as bush roses. Unlike the rare mutations previously described that doubled the number of chromosomes, or caused a once-flowering rose to become remontant, those which result in changes in flower colour or habit of growth are relatively common. The latter change is the one which creates climbing versions of Hybrid Tea and Floribunda type roses.

While they appear on the face of it to be attractive propositions to the garden designer, there are two problems that can arise. First, there is the well-known tendency among Climbing sports to revert to their original bush form if subjected to any degree of severe pruning. The second problem is the unpredictable flowering of a number of varieties; in some gardens a variety may bloom freely and reliably; in others it may flower spasmodically, only in summer or, in some instances, stubbornly refuse to flower at all. The famous rose,

'Peace', has long been recognized as being inexplicably liable to do any of these things. Whether this is a matter of climatic differences, or the existence of different strains of the Climbing form, is not known. The few varieties listed in the A–Z are those generally considered to be the most reliable in the UK with Climbing 'Iceberg' being an almost universal favourite. Garden designers who consider using any of the other Climbing sports are advised to discover local experience before committing themselves.

The 'Vintage' Roses

The varieties that I have chosen to designate 'vintage' roses are of diverse origins and, in contrast to the modern roses of the 'New Dawn era' are mostly of some degree of antiquity. Each has succeeded in retaining a place in nursery catalogues by virtue of possessing one or more specially attractive qualities and in spite, in many instances, of presenting the gardener with management problems of one sort or another. Geographically, they can trace their ancestry to almost every global zone from which roses have been found growing in the wild. Some of them attracted the attention of breeders during the eighteenth and early years of the nineteenth centuries but, in recent times, most have not figured in commercially successful hybridizing programmes.

The Banksian climbers

These Climbers, named after Lady Dorothea Banks, wife of the famous Sir Joseph Banks, came to the Western world from China early in the nineteenth century. There are single and double once-flowering varieties and it is the deep yellow double-flowered *R. banksiae lutea*, usually referred to as Banksian Yellow that, to many connoisseurs, is the most desirable.

Although generally considered not to be hardy, the Banksians have been known to succeed in gardens where, in theory, they should not survive. That said, it would not be wise to expect them to tolerate the severities of locations where wind frosts occur regularly. They possess the attractive qual-ity of reliably producing their one massed display of flowers very early in the spring. This comes on relatively thornless wood made in the previous summer, hence the concerns about winter hardiness.

Bourbon roses

Bourbon derivatives, the origins of which are described in Chapter 9, include among their numbers three very beautiful climbers; 'Blairii Number Two', 'Kathleen Harrop' and 'Zéphirine Drouhin'. They are characterized by being strongly scented, remontant and conveniently short of flesh-tearing thorns. They tend, also, to be prone to frost damage in colder areas and susceptible to attacks by disease. In gardens where these faults can be minimized, they have so much to offer that their inclusion in the overall design should be given careful consideration. 'Kathleen Harrop' (Dickson 1919) is the most recently introduced of the three; the other two are products of the middle period of the nineteenth century.

Noisette roses

A French breeder, Philipe Noisette, living in the US, is credited with developing the group of Climbing roses usually accorded the appellative 'noisette'. Further developing the valuable work of a nearby American breeder, John Champneys, he introduced in 1817 the variety, 'Blush Noisette', the first of this group. A number of other Noisettes were bred and introduced during the nineteenth century, the most widely grown today being 'Gloire de Dijon'. The value of these varieties as garden plants lies in their twin merits of spicy scent and remontancy but they do need to be provided with the comfort of sheltered sites.

Rosa sempervirens

Rosa sempervirens, an evergreen native of areas around the Mediterranean Sea, was used by a French breeder, A. A. Jacques, to produce, among others, the rather tender but very lovely 'Félicité et Perpétue' (which should, correctly, be written as 'Félicité Perpétue', we are told). This was introduced more than 160 years ago, since when *sempervirens* has not figured in the immediate parentage of our garden climbers. There are, however, hopes that it may again serve parental duty in this cause. It is recorded as being a parent of some very recent ground cover roses, from which climbing forms should be but a small step away.

Some other notable vintage roses

These have arisen from a variety of sources, mostly from areas of China and the Himalayan mountains. Worthy of consideration for planting in gardens, where a suitable environment can be provided, and described in detail in the A–Z lists which follow, are seven varieties of more than average merit. These are 'Mutabilis' (*R. chinensis* 'Mutabilis'), with its fascinating changes of colour; the tree climbing 'Kiftsgate' 'Paul's Himalayan Musk', *R. longicuspis* and, of unstated origin, the variety 'Rambling Rector'; that unique offspring of *R. bracteata*, 'Mermaid' and, finally, the comparatively recent result of the use by Wilhelm Kordes of *R. spinosissima* as a parent, 'Maigold'.

Every rosarian of long experience will have developed an affection for one or more of these varieties of vintage quality and some growers may feel that one of their own personal favourites has been unjustly omitted from my selections. Perhaps it is as well that we should not all agree on what is and what is not meritorious. If we did, the list of Climbers and Ramblers available to each new generation of gardeners might be even more limited than it now is.

Using Climbers and Ramblers in the Garden

It is commonly accepted that a climbing plant is one that, in the garden, will be provided with suitable natural or artificial supports up which to climb or be trained to climb. Rambling plants, in their natural habitat, tend to spread more laterally than upwards and, in the artificial environment of the garden, may sometimes be required to proceed in directions they would not normally follow. The object in using and training these two types of roses in the garden is to exploit their potential for furnishing the 'third dimension' of our outdoor living space. The training programmes necessary to achieve this objective could, if the habits of growth of individual varieties are not taken into account, result in less than attractive or practical features being created.

On walls and fences

Almost every private garden has one or more boundaries in the form of walls or fences and, just as we furnish the walls of our rooms with coverings, drapes, pictures or other suitable decorations, so we should consider treating similarly the physical boundaries to our gardens. The less attractive the boundary structure might be, the more the satisfaction and pleasure that can result from clothing it with appropriate varieties of climbing and rambling roses (Fig.11.1).

The life span of a rose can be upwards of 30 years, so it is wise to spend a little time assessing what is available and selecting the varieties that will be happy in each particular situation. The aspect of the structure is the first consideration, together with the micro-climate of the garden as a whole.

In districts where cold winters are experienced, it will be advisable to avoid varieties that have a reputation for being somewhat tender, particularly where the wall or fence faces north or east. This consideration may limit the choice of varieties to some small degree, and the choice could be further reduced by the need to balance the colour of the flowers with the background colour of the wall or fence.

Next, it is important to select varieties whose habits and lengths of growth permit them to fit comfortably into the space available, neither failing to give adequate cover nor having to be cruelly treated to keep them within their allotted domain. The size of the clusters or blooms carried by the plants will be more important in some instances than their form; the more distant the points from which they will be viewed the larger should be the clusters of individual flowers to achieve sufficient impact. Then there is the scent; where the wall or fence is adjacent to a sitting-out area or a

Fig. 11.1 The dullest of walls can be given colour with a well grown climber.

walkway, the more desirable it may be to select roses that are noted for their fragrance.

A possibility that is seldom given sufficient thought is that of planting to achieve a change of scene. Remontant climbers are very often used to provide what are, in effect, permanent wall coverings, but once-flowering varieties offer the possibility of changing the drapes, so to speak. If the wall space permits, two varieties of matching habits of growth, one a late spring and early summer, the other a mid- and late summer-flowering rose could be planted so that their stems may intermingle to some degree and thus result in the changing scene effect. It often occurs when this option is taken that the flowering seasons of the two roses overlap by a week or so. That likelihood suggests that some care needs to be taken to ensure that their colours are compatible.

At first sight it may appear that the considerations listed above might reduce one's choice to very few varieties or even none at all. In practice this has rarely been known to be the case, there being a sufficient range of climbers and ramblers available to result in a list of 'probables', that might leave one wishing that one could use them all!

When planting a rose at the foot of a wall or fence it is of course important to consider the aspect and the extent to which the site becomes a water meadow in winter or a dried out desert in the summer. The former needs to be remedied by improving drainage or raising the soil level. The latter carries the threat of exposing the roses, even the most disease-resistant varieties, to foliage disfiguring attacks by mildew, and indicates the need to make the soil more moisture retentive. It also helps, in this instance, to plant the roses at some distance, say 45cm (18in) from the foot of the wall or fence and to mulch the area quite heavily before the soil dries out in spring.

A rose planted at the foot of a wall or fence will, if left to its own devices, tend to grow upwards and, most probably, away from the wall. To be persuaded to spread along the wall it will need training and tying to the structure. Fortunately, there are numerous devices available to assist the gardener to do this, ranging from simple wall nails and straining wires to more sophisticated panels of open mesh trellis. Whichever device is used, it is important to guide into place and secure strong new growths at some time in late summer or autumn before they become too stiff to accept training.

If it is desired to clothe the walls of, say, a two-storey dwelling with climbers or ramblers, it is wise to check the progress of new growths and to take steps to ensure they do not obstruct guttering or begin to penetrate beneath roof shingles.

On 'see-through' screens

In gardens where the design incorporates two or more areas that are very different in concept, for instance, formal and wild garden sections, it may be desired to separate the divisions in a physical way. Solid hedges or fences may be thought inappropriate but one of the many forms of rigid, open structured, 'see through' screen that modern technology has made available to us, could suggest an attractive alternative. Made from an increasing range of materials, including wood and plastic-coated steel, they make splendid supports for climbing roses and provide the opportunity for the structure thus clothed to become a delightful composition in its own right. The open mesh design allows for a free flow of air through and around the screen which is of benefit to the health of the roses, reducing, in particular the risk of mildew attacks. It also has the considerable advantage that the grower can tie in the rose stems at almost any desired point without difficulty. Similarly, should spraying become necessary, good coverage can be obtained by applying the spray from both sides.

The choice of varieties to grow on a see-through screen is limited only by the length of the structure and the degree to which the garden is subject to damaging winter frosts. The screen being open, the background will always be visible to some extent and this should be a consideration when choosing the roses to plant. Of course, one does not have to plant against one side of the screen only, both sides can be used thus varying the effect from the two aspects. Selecting this option presents something of a challenge to one's artistic vision; the two sides of the screen will present different pictures, each having the roses on the other side peeping through as part of its composition. Fortunately, there are so few climbing roses of garish and difficult hues that screaming clashes of colour can easily be avoided.

On pillars

Growing climbing roses on pillars to provide a third dimension to uninteresting flat areas has long been practised. In modern times it has been made easier and the decorative possibilities greatly enhanced by the introduction of a wider range of shorter growing, remontant, free-flowering varieties. The range now includes flower forms of all types; Hybrid Tea, Floribunda, 'old fashioned' and single forms, many offering some degree of fragrance. If pillars are positioned so as to be easily approachable from all angles, maintenance activities such as training and tying in (and spraying should this be necessary) are made quite easy. To ensure that this is so, it is wise to limit the height of a pillar to the maximum that the gardener can reach with ease, an untidy mass of loose shoots breaking out of the top of an otherwise neatly decorative feature can ruin the picture.

As is the case with screens, several ideas using modern materials have recently been introduced that greatly assist the gardener in the training and management of 'pillar' roses. We are all familiar with the spectacle of roses growing on pillars constructed of brick or, more simply, merely a single substantial pole. Two of the newer forms of support are a 'wigwam' or tripod (Fig.11.2) and a vertical open cylinder. The former usually consists of three poles reasonably widely spaced at ground level and converging to meet at the top. This offers the choice of planting just one rose at the centre of the tripod base or three roses, one in each space between the legs. The open cylinder support, usually of very wide mesh plastic-coated steel, is most often employed to support two or three roses planted equidistantly round the base of the cylinder. Both of these designs of 'pillar' make for easy management, offering greater facility for persuading stiffer

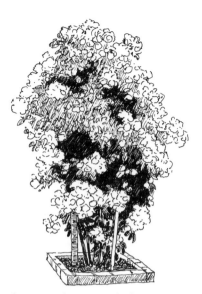

Fig. 11.2
A well structured tripod will support many varieties of climber, particularly the slower growing types.

growths to twine round the support and providing numerous points for attaching the necessary ties.

Whichever structural form you choose, bear in mind that a pillar is a vertical object beyond which there is a background landscape of some kind. The pillar is, in effect, the dominant subject in a three-dimensional picture. To create a pleasing artistic effect, the pillar and the background should relate both in proportion and colour balance. An experienced landscape designer once recommended that, before committing oneself to the permanent erection of a pillar and the selection and planting of the roses, one should proceed as follows; decide on a possible site and temporarily erect there a thick pole, attaching to it a few cut flowers of the preferred colour. View this from all possible positions in the garden and, if in every instance it looks 'right', go ahead with the actual erection and planting of the chosen form of pillar. If it does not seem 'right', change the colour of the flowers or the siting of the pole (or both) until a satisfactory effect is achieved. Following this excellent advice can avoid the probability of making bad mistakes.

Pillars can, where space is available, be used in one or more pairs to suggest a direction of traffic movement through a garden or even in lines, perhaps linked by ropes, to flank a path or grass walk. The possibilities for imaginative design and colour harmonization are considerable and every such possibility should be given careful thought. Those that emerge as likely candidates can then be put through the 'try it and see' method of assessment before the committal of time, labour and expenditure, to the construction and planting of the feature.

On arches
An archway is historically ingrained in the human mind as marking the point of entry or exit from one area to another of a different character as, for example, the gateway to a city. Thus, on approaching a rose-bedecked arch in a garden, the human eye is conditioned to expect a new experience on passing through it. Keeping this concept in mind when siting the arch and selecting the roses to train on it should result in the creation of a beautiful and satisfying feature.

The physical construction of an arch should not present a problem, as there is a wide range of designs available in complete, kit or DIY forms in a selection of appropriate low-maintenance materials. The arch, being a 'see-through' feature as well as being a thing of beauty in its own right, imposes the need to select the roses to grow on it such that, in addition to producing immediate impact, there is colour harmony with the view beyond.

It will be apparent that, to achieve sufficient coverage, the varieties chosen will grow tall enough to reach and partially cross the top. Crossing over the top implies, also, that their growths should be flexible enough to make training over the highest point a practical proposition. Keeping an arch looking neat, attractive and, very importantly, safe at all times, does impose the need for fairly frequent attention, especially during periods of rapid growth. Suffering facial injury from hanging, wind-blown, wayward growths does not increase one's enjoyment of a garden!

In a sufficiently spacious garden, the addition of open screens (q.v.) on either side of the arch greatly increases both the entrance gateway effect and the opportunity for really imaginative plant selection.

Graduations of colour and form of flowers from the arch across the wings can result in a delightful picture being created.

On pergolas and tunnels

The great gardens of the world (see Chapter 13) contain some remarkably clever and very beautiful examples of rose covered walk-through tunnels and pergolas. Visits to these gardens or a study of photographs taken in them might easily fill one with enthusiasm to create scaled-down versions of them in one's own garden. But, take care, for these are space-gobbling constructions and, if not carefully designed and sited, could so easily turn out to be heavily disproportionate monsters. That warning having been given, many gardeners will, with lightness of touch in design and in choice of materials with which to build it, succeed in creating a rose tunnel or pergola of delicate beauty (Fig.11.3).

As with arches, tunnels and pergolas should be seen as decorated highways going from some area of interest in the garden to another and vistas and backgrounds will also be involved. Having the added dimension of length, they provide a wide range of variety selection possibilities. Combinations of remontant and once-flowering varieties can be considered and thought might be given to those roses that produce attractive hips in the autumn and winter, thus extending the season during which the feature presents a colourful picture.

Fig. 11.3 Well-designed and planted pergolas can add a new dimension to the garden.

The considerations relevant to the training and pruning of roses on tunnels and pergolas are similar to those applying to roses on arches. It is advisable not to crowd the plants too closely together, not only to make the work less difficult but to ensure that an impression of elegance and airiness is achieved. This latter point is also relevant to the health of the plants, overcrowding tending to encourage mildew and the rapid spread of any other fungus diseases that might strike.

On arbours

The romantic connotations of the rose arbour have inspired many generations of poets and artists. An arbour is at once a retreat, a sanctuary and a place of pleasurable relaxation. Through the ages the poetic vision has mostly been of a structure clothed on three sides and roofed over with sweetly scented and delicately hued climbing plants, usually roses. The modern world has not yet engineered the romance out of our lives and, where the situation suggests it, a rose arbour can be a most delightful place in which to rest and be relieved of life's stresses.

The design of an arbour may reflect the personality of its owner and his or her inner sense of what is appropriate to the garden as a whole. It could be totally rustic in concept or could mirror feelings of sympathy for classical Greek or Roman styles. There is no shortage of variety in the materials available; these range from natural wood through to real or artificial stone. For the most satisfying effect, the roses chosen should be seen to have an affinity to the style of the arbour and the materials from which it is constructed. A rustic structure would seem to ask to be clothed in roses of lighter hue while the adoption of a classical style in stone would suggest varieties of soft warm red colouring, perhaps combined with the occasional pale yellow or cream rose.

The nature of this place of, hopefully, idyllic contentment obviously implies that the roses used should fill the air with scent and this, in turn, suggests that care should be taken to ensure that the fragrance is of the kind that one finds attractive. Some roses offer the renowned Damask perfume, others are fruity and suggestive of apples or peaches. It is therefore of some importance to choose varieties that offer the kind of fragrance that one can live with and enjoy for several hours at a time.

In selecting and planting roses on an arbour, it should be remembered that the object is to create a sanctuary not a prison. The roses, and any other plants used should be spaced and trained so that at no time do they give the occupants the feeling of being shut in. Care taken in these matters will also be reflected in the health of the plants and the ease with which the necessary training and tying in can be effected.

Up trees
In the wild it is the nature of some kinds of roses to creep and scramble up and through the cover of other shrubs and trees so that their flowering shoots emerge from the darkness below into the light they need to ripen their seed-bearing hips. In the garden we can mimic this phenomenon by planting those same kinds of roses near to suitable trees and then assisting them to climb and flower up to whatever heights they can reach (Fig.11.4). Very attractive examples of these uses of roses can be seen in the Royal National Rose Society's 'Gardens of the Rose' at St. Albans in England and are models well worth studying.

It is sometimes recommended that large old, even dead trees can be beautified in this way but there are two dangers to avoid. The skeletons of dead trees present the risks of their being felled by gales and their roots of playing host to honey fungus, a much-feared enemy of the ornamental garden. Most kinds of healthy tree can be attired with one or more roses so long as the top cover is not so high and dense that the roses would have little chance of stretching up to the sunlit world above. Many of the most successful combinations are those of long-reaching roses such as 'Kiftsgate' and 'Rambling Rector' being trained up and through columnar coniferous trees. The majority of the roses suggested in the A–Z list as probables for this treatment bear

Fig. 11.4
Provided a rambler is given a good start it will quickly cover the most unpretentious trees.

white or cream, often scented, flowers which, peeping out from the green of the trees, present really delightful spectacles. These varieties are usually mid-season flowering but, occasionally, may produce a few blooms later in the summer or richly coloured small hips in autumn.

Planting
When planting a rose to be trained up into a mature tree, it is important to ensure that the young rose does not immediately have to compete for nutrients with the roots of the tree. A method used successfully by a wise old gardener is to dig out the planting hole 1–2m (3–6ft) away from the tree, making it 1m (3ft) wide and 45cm (18in) deep.

Line the vertical sides of the hole with several thicknesses of newspaper or plastic dustbin liners, then plant the rose in fresh soil in this hole. The purpose of the paper or plastic wall lining is to form a barrier to the tree roots which, though temporary, will last long enough for the rose to establish itself. To train the rose into the tree, ropes or 'ladders' of wide mesh plastic-covered steel panels can lead from the rose up to and into the heart of the tree. Tied to this support, the rose can be guided as far up the tree as it has capacity to reach – which could be 10m (33ft) after several years of growth. At a number of levels, the rose's flowering shoots will reach out into the sunlight where the clusters of bloom and their fragrance will be a midsummer delight.

Clearly the training and the subsequent occasional removal of dead growths, probably about every four years, are tasks for the fit, able and to some degree, skilled. As with any garden operation, personal safety should be at the top of one's list of priorities. It is difficult to enjoy a garden from the confines of a distant hospital bed!

As weeping standards

The growing and training of roses as weeping standards has been practised for more than a century. At first, there was a very limited choice of suitable varieties, mostly those arising from the Ayshires, Boursaults or *R. alpina* hybrids. Then, in the early decades of the twentieth century, the arrival of numerous *wichuraiana* hybrids such as the famous 'Excelsa' (1909) inspired a surge of interest in this technique of rose culture. When budded on stocks at up to 2m (about 6ft), the lax growths of these roses tend to hang down and, as was reported by a rose expert of the time, 'readily adapt themselves to form the umbrella shape in which it is generally desired to train them'. Unfortunately, this rise in popularity was relatively short lived. Today, as we look back over more than half a century of time, we can only guess at the factors that mitigated against their continued success; a wait of two or more years after planting for any worthwhile display to appear,

the fact that the varieties then used gave only one short, if splendid, flush of bloom and, perhaps most damaging of all, the intervention of World War II. Then, after hostilities ceased, there came a rush of new kinds of remontant climbers to compete with them for a place in the pleasure gardener's affections. Despite their fall to minority status in the popularity stakes, weeping standards of these lovely old hybrids are still grown by a few connoisseurs and beautiful pictures they present in mid-summer. Even the discovery that the lovely remontant Climber 'New Dawn' can be persuaded to develop into a satisfactory weeping standard failed to stir more than a ripple of interest in this use of climbing roses.

Although what can be termed the traditional form of weeping standard has apparently lost much of its appeal for ever, a new star has appeared in the firmament and is now captivating rose lovers all over Europe. This takes the form of what rose catalogues describe as the 'speciality' weeping standard and the roses used are mostly procumbent varieties of the kinds first introduced as Shrub or Ground cover roses. Budded on standard stocks at a range of heights up to 1m (about 3ft), they develop their umbrella shape quite quickly with little or no training. The most widely available varieties so far are 'Ballerina', 'Nozomi' and 'The Fairy', but their predominance in the field is being challenged by a host of newcomers such as 'Suma' and 'Swany'. On the evidence of the results of recent international trials, the choice of varieties will expand rapidly and, because of their compactness, generally dense foliage and their free and repeat-flowering qualities, they are likely to make an irresistible appeal to a great many gardeners.

These delightful little weeping standards can be used as 'third dimension' dot features in even quite small gardens and, with an increasing range of colours appearing, present few problems of colour balancing. Requiring little or no maintenance, they must surely figure prominently in the gardens of the future.

An A–Z of Repeat-flowering Climbers

'Agatha Christie' (Kormeita, Ramira); Kordes 1990. Pink, fully double large and shapely blooms which shed their petals cleanly. Having strong but not excessively long growth with glossy green foliage, it is suitable for growing on pillars, screens and walls. Slight but tantalizing scent. Named to celebrate the centenary of the famous writer of murder mysteries. The aura of this rose seems most appropriate to memorialize the creator of those intriguing fictional sleuths, Miss Jane Marple and Hercule Poirot.

'Alister Stella Gray' (Golden Rambler); Gray 1894. Roundish buds open to an appealingly untidy, almost quartered flower; a deep yellow in the centre and paler towards the edges of the petals. The flowers are rather small and appear in moderate size clusters. This variety has the unusual reputation of tending to carry more and better flowers in early autumn than in high summer. Growth is somewhat stiff and bears matt mid-green foliage. Not a rose for cold, exposed places, it should give pleasure when grown on a warm wall where its musky scent can be appreciated.

'Aloha' Boerner 1949. A rose and salmon-pink confection displayed in fully double blooms of moderate size produced singly and in small clusters. Rather short growth with dark green slightly glossy foliage which has the reputation of being relatively resistant to disease. Its reasonably continuous succession of strongly scented blooms makes it a good choice for growing on pillars, or any other site where its fragrance can be enjoyed.

'Altissimo' Delbard Chabert 1966. Bright red single blooms with yellow centres; quite large and distinctive when fully open. Short growth with medium-green foliage; its continuous flowering suits it to growing on pillars where its weak scent is its only fault. A variety that has achieved world wide popularity.

'Antique' (Kordalen, Antike '89); Kordes 1989. Deep rose-pink large fully double flowers with paler pink reverse have an Old Garden rose look about them. They come in small clusters on strong growth which is clothed with dark green foliage. With some scent, it should do well on pergolas, screens and walls.

'Autumn Sunlight' Gregory 1965. Orange vermilion, fully double, large and shapely flowers come singly and in small clusters. Free-growing, short enough to be grown on pillars and enhanced by glossy green foliage and a moderately strong scent.

'Bantry Bay' McGredy 1967. Rather light rose-pink coloured semi-double, moderately large flowers in clusters. Growths are long enough for use on arches and pergolas and are clothed with bright, slightly glossy dense green foliage. Not much scent.

'Blaze' Jackson & Perkins 1950. Bright scarlet, medium-size blooms of good form freely produced, usually in small clusters. Has a reputation for freedom of blooming throughout the season. With an acceptable scent, this improved form of a variety bred by Kallay and introduced in 1932 has a considerable following in the US. Its amenable habit of growth and good foliage has enabled gardeners to use it successfully on pillars, screens, walls and fences.

'Breath of Life' (Harquanne); Harkness 1982. Pink and apricot double flowers of good size and form; produced singly and in small clusters. Stiff growth of moderate length is suited to training on a pillar, screen or wall. Grow it where its scent can be enjoyed. Named in the UK for that country's Royal College of Midwives.

'Casino' McGredy 1963. The buds are deep golden yellow which becomes softer as the fairly large fully double blooms open. Moderately strong growth but the deep green foliage could be more abundant. With good scent, it is suited to growing on walls and pillars but, preferably, not in cold districts.

'Compassion' (Belle de Londres); Harkness 1973. Pink and apricot shades which vary in intensity in response to changes in weather and season. The large flowers are shapely and appear in small clusters in almost unbroken succession until quite late in the autumn. The strong hardy growth clothed with large dark green foliage makes this a fine rose for pillars, screens and walls. The scent is strong enough to suggest that this rose should be planted where its fragrance can be enjoyed. Named for a UK welfare organization.

'Coral Dawn' Boerner 1952. Deep coral, very large and well-formed flowers produced singly and in small clusters. Of moderately strong growth with good foliage and having a good scent, this can make an attractive pillar rose. Comes into bloom earlier than most and continues through the season.

'Crimson Cascade' (Fryclimbdown); Fryer 1991. Crimson. Moderately large blooms of good form produced singly and in clusters. Moderately strong growth carries a good covering of reputedly disease-resistant foliage. Although not the most strongly scented of red roses, it should give pleasure if planted against a light-coloured wall where its colour can show to good effect.

'Danse Du Feu' (Spectacular); Mallerin 1954. Orange-scarlet double blooms of medium size in large clusters. Short growths with dark green glossy foliage. Usually grown on a pillar but will succeed on a north wall. Little or no scent.

'Dortmund' Kordesii; Kordes 1955. Crimson single blooms each with a white eye. Medium-size clusters. Fairly short, stiff, stems clothed with dark green foliage. Negligible scent. Has a reputation for health and hardiness and is popular in Australia. Good for pillars and walls.

'Dreaming Spires' Mattock 1973. Golden yellow, large and well-formed, fully double flowers appear singly and in small clusters. The growth is rather upright and bears dark green foliage. With its quite strong scent it makes a good subject to grow on a pillar close to a path or against a dark background where its golden colour will stand out.

'Dublin Bay' McGredy 1976. Bright crimson large, well-shaped, double blooms borne singly and in small clusters. Growth rather short but branching with glossy foliage. Popular in Australasia as well as in Europe, it can be grown on pillars, walls and screens.

'Galway Bay' McGredy 1966. Salmon-pink double, medium size, blooms in small clusters. A fairly short grower with mid-green foliage, it is suitable for growing on pillars. It could do with having a stronger scent.

'Gloire de Dijon' Noisette; Jacotot 1853. One of those difficult-to-describe colours, it is a sort of buff yellow fading to creamy yellow at the edges of the petals. The medium-size double flowers open rather flat. The growths are moderately long but the foliage is somewhat less than luxuriant. A rose must have a rather special 'something' to remain as popular as this one has for almost 150 years. Generally thought best grown on a south-west-facing wall, where its doubtful hardiness does not get put to the test, but where its strong fragrance can be appreciated. Has the reputation for becoming bare at the base and under-planting may be desirable.

'Golden Showers' Lammerts 1957. Large double golden yellow blooms which tend to fade quickly to a pale butter yellow in hot sunshine. Free-flowering through a long season on quite strong wood. The leaves are slightly glossy but less numerous than some would like. This rose has become a firm favourite world wide, its merits far outweighing its minor faults. Hardy and tolerant of degrees of ill-treatment, it makes a good pillar rose in temperate zones and a spreading climber for fences, screens and walls in warm climates. When I grew it, I did wish the scent was stronger.

'Grand Hotel' McGredy 1972. Bright, almost scarlet, red blooms; fully double and of good size, shapely when young. Strong growth of moderate height with dark green foliage. Some feel that this is best grown on a pillar in an open site where disease attacks are less likely. Only a weak scent.

'Handel' McGredy 1965. Large, beautifully formed, creamy white blooms with a rose-pink flush towards the edges of the petals. Flowers in moderately sized clusters non-stop throughout the season. Strong growth with glossy large and rather dark foliage. I freely confess my intense love for this rose, a love that seems to be shared by rose connoisseurs right across the world. Grown on a wall or screen where the sun can shine across its petals, its beauty is heart throbbing and its rather weak fragrance is easily forgiven. In some years it gets black spot, in others, it remains healthy but, either way, its vigour appears to be unaffected.

'Highfield' (Harcomp); Harkness 1981. This butter-yellow variety is a sport from 'Compassion' (q.v.), differing from it only in the colour and in producing a slightly less full flower. Its fragrance is as good as that of 'Compassion' and some may prefer the self-colour. As with many sports, the occasional cluster may revert to the original colour.

'High Hopes' ('Haryup'); Harkness 1992. Rose-pink double blooms of true Hybrid-tea form produced singly and in small clusters. Its full potential has yet to be explored but it looks to be a candidate for pillars, fences and screens and should be planted where the scent can be enjoyed. Named to mark the 50 years of endeavour of the famine charity, Oxfam.

Fig. 11.5 Many of the recurrent flowering climbers can be beautiful shrubs.

'Joseph's Coat' Armstrong and Swim 1964. With a confection of hues of orange and cherry red on a golden yellow base, this rose is aptly named after the biblical owner of the 'coat of many colours'. Lots of semi-double flowers in medium-size clusters right through the season. Rather stiff branching shoots of sufficient length to train on a fence or wall to give brightness to a dull background. Tough dark green glossy foliage. There is a slight fragrance but its joyful colours are its main attraction.

'Kathleen Harrop' Bourbon; Dickson 1919. Light pink semi-double, quite large, flowers come in loose clusters very early in the season and carry on intermittently deep into autumn. Growth is thornless and similar to that of 'Zéphirine Drouhin', from which it is a sport. With similar light green foliage, it can be attractive as a pillar or on an open screen where its susceptibility to disease may be more easily combatted. Its terrific fragrance can make one forgive it a few black spots.

'Lady Waterlow' Nabonnand 1903. Variable salmon pink to pink semi-double blooms, initially of hybrid tea shape, with a moderate scent. Opinions differ about its vigour and, therefore, about how best to use it. Some suggest it makes a fine pillar rose, others would put it on an east facing wall. Either way, it is a venerable old rose of some intrinsic merit.

'Laura Ford' (Chewarvel); Warner 1990. Small, semi-double yellow blooms appear in clusters without a break all through the season. I watched with increasing excitement as this rose, along with its stable mate 'Warm Welcome' (q.v.), went through its three-year test growing on pillars in the Royal National Rose Society's International Trials at St. Albans, England. With its very small but beautiful dark green foliage, this was something new. Generally referred to as a Miniature climber, it possesses just sufficient scent to satisfy those who think that a rose without fragrance is not a rose at all.

'Lavinia' (Tanklewi, Lawinia); Tantau 1980. Fairly large double blooms of a pleasing shade of pink, which may appear both singly and in clusters. The short, firm growths make 'Lavinia' a candidate for growing on pillars in an open site. Happily, it is blessed with a good scent.

'Leaping Salmon' (Peamight); Pearce 1986. Salmon pink large double blooms of good shape, produced singly and in clusters. Growth a little on the stiff side with good foliage. Can look good and smell good on a pillar, arch or wall.

'Leverkusen' Kordes 1955. Lemon-yellow, semi-double, medium-size flowers in fairly large clusters. Fairly short growth with small glossy green leaves. Flowering early in the season, it is sometimes rather sparing with its late season crop of blooms. Not much fragrance.

'Madame Alfred Carrière' Noisette; Schwartz 1879. Fairly large, fully double white in small clusters. Long growth, with not too many thorns and light green foliage. With its fine fragrance, it is a rose for a warm wall where its continued popularity after more than a century will be seen to be justified. It is very likely to need protection from attacks of mildew.

'Malaga' McGredy 1971. Salmon pink double flowers, often showing a darker hue on the reverse of the petals. Fairly short grower with large semi-glossy deep green leaves. Its *R. kordesii* origins suggest that it should make a hardy pillar rose. Blessed with a good Sweet briar scent, one would have expected it to be more widely grown than it is. Perhaps the colour is too quiet for some tastes.

'Marechal Niel' Pradel 1864. Long pointed buds open to large many petalled bright golden yellow blooms of classic Hybrid-tea form; at one time it was considered the almost perfect exhibition flower. Unfortunately the growths are so tender that, in England, it can be expected to succeed only in warm and sheltered sites. It is often recommended that it should be trained across the inside of a roof of a cool greenhouse with the roots planted outside. Thus grown, both the blooms, which tend to hang down on weak stems and their strong fragrance can be enjoyed to the full. Growth is quite strong and the plant seems to appreciate being given space in which to spread itself. With its lovely form, colour and numerous petals, it makes a good rose to cut for indoor decoration. A wonderful old variety that is really for those who can provide the conditions and the cosseting necessary for it to give of its best.

'Mermaid' Bracteata hybrid; Paul 1918. This lovely rose, once seen, will never be forgotten. The large creamy yellow single floppy petalled flowers with their amber stamens are unique and, happily, are freely produced without a break throughout the season. The main growths are usually very long, stiff and rather brittle, well furnished with glossy, deep green foliage. Should be grown in mild districts where, after a slow start, it can rampage over high walls with cheerful abandon. Its moderate scent is an almost unnecessary bonus for this very popular visual delight.

'Morning Jewel' Cocker 1968. The large semi-double bright pink blooms appear in small clusters in mid-summer and continue fitfully through to the autumn. Short growing but with ample foliage, it is a good candidate for growing on pillars. There is some scent.

'Mutabilis' (*Rosa chinensis* 'Mutabilis', Tipo Ideale). From China towards the end of the nineteenth century. The flowers are single, initially of an apricot-yellow colour which is overpainted by an Old Rose hue that spreads inwards from the edges of the petals as they age. The first blooms appear early in small clusters and continue in varying numbers deep into the autumn. Very often catalogued as a Shrub rose, its relatively short dark stems carrying almost coppery young leaves, are amenable to training on a warm wall, in which position its simple beauty shows to advantage. With a reputation for being slow to start but long to live, it is well worth the exercise of a little patience. Not noticeably scented.

'New Dawn' (The New Dawn, Everblooming Dr W Van Fleet); Somerset Roses 1930. The elegant long-pointed, pale pink, thinly double blooms produced in clusters all through the summer possess a charm that has endeared this variety to millions of rose lovers across the northern hemisphere. It's easy-to-train long growths with healthy glossy green foliage, coupled with the rose's lovely fragrance, have made this a rose for almost every situation. This beautiful rose is also famed as being the progenitor of a significant proportion of our modern garden climbing roses.

'Night Light' (Poullight); Poulsen 1982. Deep yellow large flowers of good form appear sometimes singly but mostly in clusters. Usually blooms in mid-summer and repeats through to the autumn. The growth is strong but not exceptionally long and is clothed with ample foliage. With only a slight scent, it is a rose that can provide a refreshing contrast to a dark background.

'Parade' Boerner 1953. The moderately large, Hybrid-tea shaped, fully double, carmine-pink flowers come in small clusters in mid-summer and repeat until the late autumn. Rain may make the heavy blooms bow their lightly scented heads. Stiffish and rather short growths with dark green foliage suggest its use on pillars as well as walls. If one likes the colour and its rather odd scent, its reputed health and hardiness should have a strong appeal.

'Parkdirektor Riggers' Kordes 1957. With bright red, semi-double, medium-sized flowers regularly produced in small clusters, this hardy rose of stiff growth makes a first class subject for growing on a pillar. On a wall, disease may attack its dark green and slightly glossy foliage. Regrettably there is not much fragrance.

'Phylllis Bide' Bide 1923. A colour that invites argument; some describe it as pale yellow flushed pink, others as carmine pink shaded yellow – I am not taking sides. The bloom is double but the petals are rather small. Growth is short and the foliage is on the small side, too. Having 'Gloire de Dijon' as a parent, its ability to withstand severe winters must be suspect – as I found when I grew it many years ago. But, given a short pillar to support it in a reasonably sheltered situation it can exude both charm and a pleasing scent.

'Pink Perpétué' Gregory 1965. The thinly double pink blooms, which show a darker colour on the reverse of the petals, appear in large clusters from mid-summer to the end of the season. Medium-length, rather stiff growths, are well endowed with leathery foliage. With a reputation for being hardy enough for chilly sites, it is seen doing well on pillars and walls. If only the scent was stronger!

'Rosalie Coral' (Chewallop); Warner 1992. The semi-double, light orange blooms, showing yellow at the base of the petals, come in small clusters all through the season. Growths pliable but rather short with deep green small foliage. Another of the newer Miniature climbers that should make an attractive pillar rose. Unfortunately, no scent is detectable.

'**Rosy Mantle**' Cocker 1968. Large and fully double rose-pink flowers of good form that keep coming all through the season and offer a reasonable but not exciting fragrance. A short grower, skimpily dressed with rather dark foliage, it can give good service grown on a pillar.

'**Royal Gold**' Morey 1957. Its large Hybrid-tea shaped blooms in a rich golden yellow colour are produced both singly and in small clusters. Of fairly short growth with adequate glossy foliage, it is not the most vigorous or hardy of climbers. In the less cold parts of the world, where it grows more strongly, it has, aided by its noticeable scent, deservedly attracted large numbers of admirers. So, the message is clearly that a little cossetting should reap handsome dividends.

'**Schoolgirl**' McGredy 1964. The apricot-shaded pink blooms are large and rather loose when past the half open stage. Inclined to bloom in spasms, it will nevertheless continue until well into autumn. The growth is of medium length and reasonably amenable to training. The mid-green foliage is adequate and the moderate scent is best described as slightly fruity. Should be grown on a pergola, screen or wall rather than restricted to a pillar. This variety needs under-planting with something that will hide an inevitable bareness at the base.

'**Souvenir de Claudius Denoyel**' Chambard 1920. Crimson blooms which possess only just enough petals to justify the description 'double' and which have a tendency to hang their heads so that the observer needs to be able to look up into their strongly scented, rather cup-shaped and colour-fast hearts. The growth is moderately strong but the rather dull and spare foliage is a weak point. It is one of those roses that is best trained so that its blooms come at least at head height where its qualities of form and scent can be appreciated. Perhaps a pillar or pergola should be considered as a suitable support for this undoubtedly delightful variety.

'**Sparkling Scarlet**' (Iskra); Meilland 1970. Bright and cheerful small semi-double red flowers come in small clusters and repeat through the season. The growth is moderately strong with adequate foliage. Perhaps the somewhat weak scent has prevented this variety from becoming more popular. There could be a risk of disease in a bad season.

'**Summer Wine**' (Korizont); Kordes 1984. The individual blooms, not quite semi-double, are of a fascinating hue; deep pink with a yellowish centre, which is enhanced by the display of red stamens. The colouring varies with the weather and the age of the flower. To appreciate this rose, plant it where its subtleties can be appreciated close up. Scent is only average. The quite strong growths with slightly glossy dark leaves are, in my view, best spread out on a screen or pale-coloured wall so that the delicate hues are not swamped by an intrusive background.

'**Swan Lake**' (Schwansee); McGredy 1968. This rose is a teaser. It produces very full and very shapely Hybrid-tea type exhibition quality, weather-resistant pure white flowers, usually in small clusters. Its outstanding beauty is captivating but its susceptibility to defoliation by black spot is disappointing. I find its growth rather short and its scent and freedom of flowering less than satisfying. If one passionately desires its undoubted beauty, notwithstanding it being a disease addict, that is fine; otherwise, avoid it.

'**Sympathie**' Kordes 1964. Deep red large and shapely exhibition quality Hybrid tea-type blooms that tend to come in two waves, first in mid-summer and then in early autumn, with a scattering between. Offers a less strong scent than one would like in a red rose of this beauty. It grows strongly and possesses good dark green foliage. Growers differ about its resistance to black spot. Looks marvellous grown against a light-coloured wall.

'**Warm Welcome**' (Chewizz); Warner

1991. A fascinating sort of orange-red colour with a yellow base to the petals, this Miniature climber, along with its sister variety, 'Laura Ford' (q.v.), created a considerable stir when it appeared in the Royal National Rose Society's International Trials in England. The agitation was justified for the rose seemed never to be out of flower and, with its dark foliage, looked very good indeed on the pillars on which it took its test. It took the highest award with some ease. A new and welcome development in Climbing roses, there will soon be more of the kind appearing.

'White Cockade' Cocker 1968. Moderately large, fully double Hybrid-tea shaped, creamy white flowers that appear singly and in small clusters. Offering a very weak version of 'New Dawn' scent, this is an attractive white Climber that, while lacking the visual appeal of 'Swan Lake' (q.v.), is much healthier and more reliable as a garden plant. The short growths clothed in large dark green leaves indicate that it should look good grown on a pillar or used as a rose to put a bright face on a dark wall or fence.

'William Allen Richardson' Noisette; Ducher 1878. This is another of those roses that give catalogue writers colour blinding headaches – bright orange to yellow seems to be the most accurate of the various attempts to describe the only barely double but large and shapely blooms. The scent and the foliage are also confusingly differently described, ranging from strong to moderate and from glossy to matt respectively. It is best to see this great centenarian for oneself before deciding to offer it a sheltered and somewhat shady (the flowers bleach in hot sun) place of honour in one's garden. As is common with Noisettes, there is a strong tendency to suffer from black spot.

'Zéphirine Drouhin' Bourbon; Bizot 1868. The cerise-coloured semi-double flowers of medium size appear in large clusters relatively early in the season and exude a strong scent. It is advisable to dead-head

the first flush of bloom with some alacrity to ensure a good supply of flowers later in the season. The growths, dark in colour and almost free of thorns, are moderately long and carry deep green foliage. It is easy to train on pillars, pergolas, walls or in almost any way one fancies. This long-standing old favourite has one failing, it is susceptible to mildew, black spot and rust if not adequately protected – but it is worth the trouble.

An A–Z of Once-flowering Climbers and Ramblers

'Albéric Barbier' *wichuraiana* hybrid; Barbier 1900. Creamy-white, medium-size, fully double flowers produced in profusion in small clusters during mid-summer. Moderately vigorous of somewhat rambling habit and suitable for clothing arches and pergolas. Scent is fruity; some feel it to be similar to that of ripe apples. An old favourite that has stood the test of time.

'Albertine' *wichuraiana* hybrid; Barbier 1921. Salmon-pink buds opening to light pink, medium-sized, double flowers very freely produced in clusters in mid-summer. With plentiful, very thorny, growth clothed in small green foliage, which can become afflicted with mildew, it is generally felt to be best grown in an open site on arches, pergolas and similar supports rather than on walls. It has the kind of scent that can pervade the air on a still summer evening.

'Alchymist' Kordes 1956. Fully double flowers that are perhaps best described as a confection of yellow, orange, pink and red, the relative dominance of the different shades tending to change with the weather. Moderately tall grower with glossy slightly bronze foliage and a good scent. Some gardeners like to grow it against a drab background so that its bright colours attract attention, others allow it to grow as a tall shrub – my own preference is the former. Mid-summer flowering.

'**American Pillar**' *setigera* hybrid; Van Fleet 1902. Carmine with a clean white eye; the blooms are single and rather small but, being produced with great profusion in mid-summer, it makes a great show for a few weeks. Strong growth carries bright green foliage which is very subject to mildew later in the season. Will produce large hips which most growers recommend should not be allowed to develop for fear of reducing the next season's growth and flower. Despite the inclusion of the word 'pillar' in its name, its long thorny growth make it more appropriate to grow it on a fence or screen where it can spread as far as it wishes. Unfortunately, there is no detectable scent.

'**Banksian White**' (*R. banksiae* 'Alba-Plena', White Banksian); Banksian, Kerr from China 1807. The small, double white flowers are freely produced in spring. They appear in large clusters and are blessed with a reasonable scent. Making very long, almost thornless growths, which bloom on laterals produced in the second

year, this variety's dubious hardiness demands that it be grown in a sheltered site. Sometimes allowed to grow as a loose, untidy shrub, the best examples that I have seen were those somewhat loosely trained on reasonably warm walls.

'**Banksian Yellow**' (*R. banksiae* 'Lutea', Yellow Banksian); Parks from China 1824. In many respects similar to Banksian White, the flowers have, to me, that indefinable quality that proves to be the stronger attraction. Perhaps it is the strong butter yellow colour or the greater abundance of flower that gives it the edge. It is certainly not the scent which, though quite acceptable, is less demanding of attention than that of the white form. It has an almost identical habit and the same lack of hardiness and so, is also a candidate for a spacious site on a warm wall (Fig. 11.6).

'**Blairii Number Two**' Bourbon; Blair 1845. Pink double flowers which pale towards the edges. Blooms are moderately large and appear in small clusters in mid-

Fig. 11.6
'Banksian Yellow' will flower very early in the season on a warm wall.

summer. There is a good scent reminiscent of the Damask roses. Growth is quite strong in temperate areas and bears lightish-green foliage. Reputed to dislike hard pruning, it will often reward the grower with a few blooms later in the season.

'Bobby James' *multiflora* hybrid; Sunningdale 1961. Creamy-white, semi-double, small flowers produced in large clusters in early to mid-summer. Very long rambling growths that will happily reach up into tall trees. It has the merit of possessing a strong pervasive scent.

'Chaplin's Pink Climber' *wichuraina* hybrid; Chaplin 1928. Bright semi-double, medium-sized flowers which display bright golden stamens as they open. The abundant and large clusters of bloom almost hide the glossy dark green foliage during the short mid-summer display. A good rose for a background wall or fence where its lack of scent will not be noticed.

'Crimson Shower' *wichuraiana* hybrid; Norman 1951. Crimson, small double blooms in large clusters which first appear in mid-season and continue for several weeks, sometimes into early autumn. Moderately strong growth with light green glossy foliage. Easy to train and often recommended for arches and pergolas. Unfortunately, there is little scent.

'Dorothy Perkins' *wichuraiana* hybrid; Jackson & Perkins 1901. Rose-pink, small, semi-double, blooms freely produced in large clusters in early to mid-season. Long pliant growths with bright green foliage make it easy to train. An old favourite usually grown on arches or pergolas rather than on walls where it can be attacked by mildew. Only slight scent.

'Elegance' Brownell 1937. Large and shapely deep yellow blooms with paler edges borne freely on good stems. Very thorny growths and glorious foliage. A personal favourite, I grew it over a wide arch where I could enjoy its lovely scent. It is best not to grow it in very cold districts.

'Emily Gray' *wichuraiana* hybrid; Williams 1916. Golden-yellow, small, double blooms which come in large clusters for a few weeks in mid-summer. Its reasonably long arching growths with glossy green leaves are easy to train and it looks lovely when grown on a pergola or against a south-facing mellow-red brick wall. In cold areas it can suffer die back and if the soil is allowed to dry out, it is likely to suffer from mildew. With a moderate scent, this old favourite is still worth its place in a favourable site. Be sparing with the pruners.

'Excelsa' (Red Dorothy Perkins); *wichuraiana* hybrid; Walsh 1909. Small rosy-crimson, double blooms borne in profusion in large clusters in mid-summer. Long, easy-to-train, pliable growths with small leaflets make this 'grandma's rose', suitable for pergolas in open sites where mildew is less likely to strike. There is only a very slight scent.

'Félicité et Perpétue' (Félicité Perpétue); *sempervirens*; Jacques 1827. The many petalled white flowers (with a hint of pink), are small and of rosette form. Produced in numerous large clusters they make a fine display for a few weeks from mid-summer. The very long growths carry small, attractive and almost evergreen glossy foliage. A good rose for growing up into tall trees. The accepted story behind the name is that the raiser named the rose for his twin daughters who, in turn, were named in memory of two early Christian martyrs; St. Felicitas and St. Perpetua. There could be a risk of winter damage in cold districts.

'Francois Juranville' *wichuraiana* hybrid; Barbier 1906. Salmon pink fairly large double flowers in large clusters in mid-summer. Occasionally, may produce some more flowers later in the season. Of rather long rambling growth with glossy green foliage, it can be encouraged to cover a pergola or wander up a mature tree. Just a little scent.

'Goldfinch' Paul 1907. Apricot to yellow, long, pointed buds open to semi-double small flowers that fade to plain white very quickly. The quite large clusters usually appear in mid-summer on almost thornless quite long growths. Its deliciously strong scent and its freedom of flowering justify its continued appearance in nursery catalogues.

'Guinee' Mallerin 1938. Dark red, quite large, blooms of good double form which open to display bright golden stamens. Growth is quite strong making it suitable for growing on a wall or fence where the sun can highlight the unique colour. Prized for this quality and its very good fragrance, this rose blooms freely in mid-summer with, sometimes, a second but lesser flush of bloom later: regard a second flowering as an unexpected bonus.

'Kiftsgate' (*R. filipes* 'Kiftsgate'); synstylae; Murrell 1954. Small creamy-white single blooms in large clusters appearing in early to mid-summer. Its long rambling shoots will quickly ascend into trees. Has the merits of strong scent and, usually, a good crop of red hips in autumn.

'Lawrence Johnston' (Hidcote Yellow); Pernet-Ducher 1923. Bright yellow semi-double flowers, which tend to hold their colour almost to petal fall, come in considerable quantity in early summer and, in some gardens, may appear in ones and twos later. A very strong grower with ample glossy green leaves, it can rapidly cover wide expanses of wall or fence and will fill the air with its strong fragrance. Its hardiness may be suspect in very cold areas. It is recorded that the raiser did not introduce this rose; the only plant being bought by Major Lawrence Johnston and planted in the famous gardens of Hidcote Manor, Gloucestershire, England. Its merits led to its eventual introduction in the UK and the USA, in both of which it found favour.

'Madame Grégoire Staechlin' (Spanish Beauty); Dot 1927. With its thinly double but large clear-pink blooms being produced in great quantity early to mid-season, this lovely rose is seen to have been aptly named. The long flexible growths with good green foliage need careful training to avoid the plant becoming bare towards the base. A fine rose to grow on a wall, its great summer display and a strong scent will repay the small effort required.

'Maigold' *spinosissima* hybrid; Kordes 1953. Bright yellow, large, semi-double, flowers appear in considerable quantity very early in the season – a quality for which it is much appreciated. The strong growth is well endowed with sharp thorns as well as deep green leathery leaves. Although usually regarded as a once-flowering variety, it may surprise one with a second, if much lesser, flush of bloom in late summer. Its strong scent contributes to its popularity. Generally considered to be above average for hardiness and health, it is a fine rose for a pergola, wall or screen.

'Meg' Gosset 1954. Large semi-double pink and apricot flowers of exceptional beauty come in small clusters in mid-summer. Very prompt dead-heading may result in more blooms in early autumn. Vigorous stiff and thorny growth make training this beautiful though lightly scented rose a task to be undertaken with care.

'Paul's Himalayan Musk' (Paul's Himalayan Rambler; Paul's Himalayan Double Pink); Synstylae; Paul 1916. This rapid growing pale lilac-pink scrambler with hooked prickles and slightly glossy foliage can be expected to reach high into tall trees. Mid-summer blooming in clusters with a very good scent, it has made many friends during its long life. Being allegedly descended from *R. moschata* and *R. multiflora*, it could interest those who like to grow a page of rose history (or, possibly, fiction?) in their gardens.

'Paul's Lemon Pillar' (Lemon Pillar); Paul 1915. This variety's very well-formed large double primrose-yellow to cream blooms was once favoured as an exhibition rose despite its short flowering season. Perhaps better suited to growing on a wall than on a pillar, it has notable fragrance and large but not plentiful leaves.

'Paul's Scarlet Climber' Paul 1915. The cheerful mid-summer display of bright red, medium-size, semi-double blooms profusely produced in such numerous clusters ensured the popularity of this variety. Growth is long enough to make it a good subject for a pillar or pergola. Because it is likely to get mildew, it may be wise not to plant it on a dry wall site. It may sometimes produce a few blooms later in the season. In spite of being sadly lacking in fragrance, it has a strong following in countries south of the equator.

'Rambling Rector' Origin not known; early twentieth century. A great climber of trees with large clusters of white semi-double and strongly scented white flowers. Blooms in early summer and, on occasions, gives a scattering of flowers later. Usually bears small red hips in the autumn. A deservedly popular old-timer.

Rosa longicuspis (*R. lucens*) from China or Assam, possibly circa 1900. Single white, rather small flowers, produced in large clusters during early to mid-summer. It has a delightfully strong scent. This really lovely vintage rose makes very long and pliable green shoots lightly armed with slightly hooked thorns. As with many roses of this type, the green foliage is not as closely packed as one might wish. But this is not usually considered a serious weakness because the use generally recommended is for growing into tall trees. The biggest question mark concerns its suitability for growing in very cold districts.

Rosa wichuraiana (Memorial Rose). The wild rose collected by Dr Wichura in Japan around 1860. The flowers are small, single, white with pale yellow centre and are produced in large clusters. They usually appear just after mid-summer, offering a good scent and are followed by small dark red hips. The growth is long and lax and is clothed with glossy green almost evergreen foliage. Left to itself, it will wander across the ground but is easy to train over a pergola or up a tree. A rose to interest those who would like to possess the original from which a substantial number of our Modern garden Climbing roses emanated, as well as being beautiful in its own right.

'Sander's White Rambler' *wichuraiana* hybrid; Sander 1912. Large clusters of small, rosette-shaped, double white blooms make a fine show in mid-summer. The growth is, as the name suggests, rather long and rambling and is enhanced by bright glossy foliage. Being amenable to training, it deserves to be allowed to spread itself rather then be restricted. Its virtues include a quite strong scent.

'Seagull' (Polyantha) Pritchard 1907. Masses of small single white, yellow-centred flowers come in large clusters. They appear fairly early in the season and go on for a few weeks. With quite long pliable growths, it looks wonderful on a pergola. Less rampant and with less fragrance than 'Kiftsgate' (q.v.), it is a good scrambler up moderately tall trees. Still going strong after almost a century in commerce, it should remain popular for years to come.

'The Garland' (Wood's Garland); Wells 1835. Pale salmon pink, semi-double flowers that fade quickly to off-white appear in upright clusters in early summer. Strongly scented and free flowering for a short period, its long green shoots can be trained into small trees. Alternatively some growers prune it fairly hard and grow it as a free standing shrub where its upward facing flowers and its strong scent can be better appreciated. An old stager that is still worth considering.

'Veilchenblau' (Violet Blue); *setigera* hybrid; Schmidt 1909. The name of this old rambling rose is rather misleading as the blooms are usually a pale lilac in colour with a white eye. They are small, semi-double and come in clusters around mid-summer, releasing a scent that some liken to apples. The growth is long, flexible and mercifully almost free of prickles so that it is easy to train. To those with a taste for the colour it could give much pleasure. I note that writers tend to disagree about whether it is best to grow it in full sun or partial shade. My own feeling is that a few hours of light shade on a summer's day is no bad thing.

'Violette' Turbot 1921. Variously described as deep violet or a sort of purplish mauve, the small flowers are only semi-double. They are produced in large clusters in mid-summer and the plant has the merit of being almost free of thorns. Growth is moderately strong but is considered to be somewhat shorter than that of 'Veilchenblau' to which it bears a superficial resem-

blance, the two having common distant origins. This rose, too, needs some degree of shade to prevent the fleeting colour from fading before its delicate 'olde-worlde' charm can be enjoyed. Not much scent.

'Wedding Day' *sinowilsonii* hybrid; Stern 1950. Small yellow buds open to a creamy-white that sometimes acquires a pale pink blush as the flowers age. The scent is strong and, as the clusters are extremely large, it is a pleasure to eyes and nose alike. Very long scrambling growths with glossy foliage make this a lovely thing to grow up tall trees or to train over ugly outbuildings. Said to have derived its name from the fact that it opened its first blooms on its raiser's wedding anniversary. Another of Mother Nature's many happy gestures!

An A–Z of Weeping Standards

The roses named in this list are all described in detail in other A–Z lists in the book. The information in parentheses following each name shows you where to find the full description of the variety.

'Alberic Barbier'	(once-flowering Climbers and Ramblers A–Z)
'Albertine'	(once-flowering Climbers and Ramblers A–Z)
'Ballerina'	(Miniatures, Patio and Ground cover A–Z)
'Bonica 82'	(Miniatures, Patio and Ground cover A–Z)
'Canary Bird'	(Species, Old Garden roses and Modern Shrubs A–Z)
'Crimson Shower'	(once-flowering Climbers and Ramblers A–Z)
'Dorothy Perkins'	(once-flowering Climbers and Ramblers A–Z)
'Emily Gray'	(once-flowering Climbers and Ramblers A–Z)
'Excelsa'	(once-flowering Climbers and Ramblers A–Z)
'Francois Juranville'	(once-flowering Climbers and Ramblers A–Z)
'New Dawn'	(repeat-flowering Climbers A–Z)
'Nozomi'	(Miniatures, Patio and Ground cover A–Z)
'Sander's White'	(once-flowering Climbers and Ramblers A–Z)
'Suma'	(Miniatures, Patio and Ground cover A–Z)
'Swany'	(Miniatures, Patio and Ground cover A–Z)
'The Fairy'	(Miniatures, Patio and Ground cover A–Z)

An A–Z of Climbing Sports of Bush Roses

The varieties listed below are all climbing sports of bush or shrub roses and those that are described in detail in A–Z lists in other chapters of the book are designated as such.

'Allgold'	(Floribunda – yellow)
'Arthur Bell'	(Bush roses A–Z)
'Blue Moon'	(Hybrid Tea – blue)
'Caroline Testout'	(Hybrid Tea – rose pink)
'Cécile Brunner'	(Species, Old Garden roses and Modern Shrubs A–Z)
'Crimson Glory'	(Bush roses A–Z)
'Ena Harkness'	(Hybrid Tea – scarlet pink)
'Etoile de Hollande'	(Hybrid Tea – crimson)
'Fragrant Cloud'	(Bush roses A–Z)
'Iceberg'	(Bush roses A–Z)
'Lady Hillingdon'	(Bush roses A–Z)
'Lady Sylvia'	(Hybrid Tea – pale pink)
'Masquerade'	(Bush roses A–Z)
'Mrs Herbert Stevens'	(Hybrid Tea – white)
'Mrs Sam McGredy'	(Bush roses A–Z)
'Orange Sunblaze'	(Miniatures, Patio and Ground cover A–Z)
'Queen Elizabeth'	(Bush roses A–Z)
'Shot Silk'	(Bush roses A–Z)
'Spek's Yellow'	(Bush roses A–Z)
'Super Star'	(Bush roses A–Z)

CHAPTER 12

Miniatures, Patio and Ground Cover Roses

MINIATURE ROSES

There is a certain appeal in small or miniature things, whether it be an ornament, a piece of jewellery or a flower. Miniature roses, certainly, have never been more popular than they are today, not only in the UK but particularly in the USA. Their origins are surrounded in mystery but most authorities agree that they came originally from China and are a form of *Rosa chinensis*. According to *The Rose Directory*, a publication of the Royal National Rose Society, they arose as seedlings of *Rosa chinensis semperflorens*. Other authorities attribute them to *Rosa chinensis minima* and *Rosa chinensis* 'Pumila'. It is all a little confusing but it would seem that the true Miniature rose never existed in the wild but appeared by chance as a result of a mutation or as a seedling in China. Some people think that it came to England via Mauritius – on the trade routes from China – at the beginning of the last century. One of the earliest Miniatures is delightfully portrayed in Curtis's Botanical Magazine of 1815, bearing the name *Rosa sempervirens minima*.

The popularity of Miniature roses grew, not only in the UK but on the Continent, being introduced into France by that great rosarian Louis Noisette. At that time they were highly fashionable as pot plants for indoor decoration. New varieties were raised in a range of colours from white to pink and red. Gradually, interest in them declined, particularly as a result of of developments with other exciting new rose forms.

Roulet's Rose

The present day Miniature roses would not exist had it not been for the discovery of a new kind which had, apparently, been grown in two Swiss alpine villages for a very long time. There are all sorts of stories about its discovery but the true one, which is well documented, shows that a Colonel Roulet, a doctor in the Swiss army, found this tiny miniature rose growing as a pot plant in the windows of the inhabitants. They did not have a name for it but said that it had been grown for a very long time. The colonel told a friend of his, Henry Correvon from Geneva, who was a keen horticulturist, about the rose. They both went to see it, only to discover that the village had been burned down. Fortunately, they heard that the rose was also grown in another village nearby and M. Correvon was able to obtain some cuttings. What made them excited about the rose was that it was a real midget, growing only 5cm (2in) tall, and producing its tiny pink, scented double flowers for most of the year. All this happened in about 1917 and M. Correvon soon built up a stock of the rose which he introduced in 1922. As it had no name he decided to call it *Rosa rouletii* after Col Roulet who rediscovered it. He also found that, although it had been treated as a window sill plant in the alpine villages, it was perfectly hardy. He grew his plants in the open to increase his stock as quickly as possible and also found that the plants grew taller. The new rose aroused great interest and was soon being grown in France, England and America.

Several years were to elapse before nurserymen realized the potential of the tiny rose for breeding. A Dutch grower in the famous nursery district of Boskoop, Jan de Vink, crossed it with a polyantha rose and produced a new Miniature which he called 'Peon'. It had red flowers with white centres. It did not seem to attract much attention until Robert Pyle of the famous Conard-Pyle rose nursery in the USA spotted it and realized its potential. He did not think it had a good 'selling' name and changed it to 'Tom Thumb'. It was launched on the market in 1936 and was in great demand.

Realizing that Miniature roses had a future, Pyle went in search of more varieties and introduced many more raised by Jan de Vink. Working mainly with polyantha roses and 'Cécile Brunner', he produced 'Baby Bunting', 'Cinderella' and 'Red Imp'. At the same time his roses were being introduced to England by Thomas Robinson of Nottingham.

Much breeding of Miniatures was also being carried out in Spain by Pedro Dot who had a nursery near Barcelona. He crossed *R.* 'Rouletii' with Hybrid Teas and came up with 'Baby Gold Star', 'Rosina' and 'Pour Toi', among many others.

Soon other rose breeders were at work, including famous names such as Meilland in France who launched 'Starina' in 1965 and Tantau in Germany with 'Baby Masquerade'.

Whenever Miniature roses are being discussed you will hear the name of Ralph Moore from California. Although starting with *R.* 'Rouletii' as one parent he brought in other types of rose, including Climbing and Rambler roses, in his breeding programmes. Over the past 30 years he has produced hundreds of exciting new Miniatures and today they are grown throughout the world. One of his earliest successes was 'Easter Morning', a white miniature with Hybrid-tea type flowers which appeared in 1960. 'New Penny', 'Little Buckaroo', 'Stacey Sue' and 'Sheri Anne' are a few others raised by him. Some are more suited to the Californian climate than the UK and several of his yellow varieties, such as 'Rise 'n Shine' and 'Yellow Doll' are, unfortunately, prone to disease in the UK.

Another of his developments has been the breeding of Miniature Moss roses. This is no mean achievement as Moss roses are difficult to breed because of sterility problems. Among his successful varieties are 'Dresden Doll' and 'Mood Music'. The

development of the Miniature rose is a fascinating story. From the pink 'Rouletii', the colour range has expanded to include a wide variety of shades from red to white, yellow, orange and pink. So, too, has the height of the plants increased. Breeding has also meant that some varieties are prone to disease. 'Rouletii' has survived for a great many years and unless we can breed varieties with a similar constitution the present popularity of Miniatures is bound to decline once again.

A matter of size

Many people expect Miniature roses to be really small or a few centimetres tall. Not all fit into this category and as a result of modern breeding there has been a tendency for them to increase in size and become more like low-growing, cluster-flowered or patio roses (see page 183).

The official classification for Miniatures states that the diameter of the flowers can be: small, 25mm (1in); medium, 30mm (1–1½in); fairly large, 40mm (1½–1¾in); large, 50mm (1¾–2in); and very large, over 50mm (2in).

Heights can also vary from 150mm (about 6in) to 460mm (18in or more) for tall varieties. There are also intermediate groupings of short, 230mm (9in); medium 300mm (about 12in); medium to tall 380mm (about 15in). Because of this variation in size it is very important to find out the dimensions of a variety before buying it to ensure that it is suitable for the intended purpose. Plant one of the real Miniatures among taller plants and it could soon be smothered.

Climbers and standards

Apart from miniature bush roses, mini-climbing forms have also developed as sports or by hybridizing. Several breeders have promising varieties coming along and they are being looked at with great interest. Ideally, they should be able to climb to about 1.8m (6ft) tall, have slim stems and small flowers about 5cm (2in) in diameter. One of the latest, bred by Chris Warner in England, is 'Warm Welcome'. It has certainly been welcomed by the judges as it won the Gold Medal and President's International Trophy at the Royal National Rose Society's trials in 1988. 'Laura Ford' is another bred by Chris Warner which has received a Certificate of Merit from the RNRS. 'Nozomi' is a Japanese rose listed as a Miniature Climber but which is often grown as a Ground cover rose (see p. 194) and as a standard. 'Suma', which was bred from 'Nozomi', and Climbing 'Orange Sunblaze' are two other good Miniature Climbers.

These small climbers have great possibilities as they are ideal for today's small gardens and can fit in where larger climbers would be overpowering. They can be trained to fences, walls and pillars, just as ordinary climbers would be treated, without the fear of them growing beyond their allotted space.

Miniature standards

In America standard roses are called 'tree roses' and in miniature form they make delightful pot plants or add interest to a bed of Miniature roses in the open garden. Miniature varieties such as 'Baby Masquerade', 'Orange Sunblaze', and 'Colibri' are grafted on the top of a rose stem about 45cm (18in) high. In the States they have even smaller standards with stems 15cm (6in) tall. Weeping miniature standards are particularly attractive with varieties such as 'Nozomi' and 'Snow Carpet'. They are widely available from most rose nurserymen and are becoming popular at garden centres.

Miniatures in pots

Vast quantities of Miniature roses are sold as pot plants in florists, multiple stores and garden centres. They are available at most times of the year and can give the impression that they are tender house plants. They can certainly be enjoyed indoors for a short time but the truth is that they are perfectly hardy and are best grown outside. If you buy a plant out of season it has probably been forced under glass and in artificial conditions of supplementary lighting. The growth will be soft and tender and the plant will not like being put out in the cold. To keep a plant of this sort for as long as possible stand it in a light place in a room with little heating. It will not like the hot, dry air in a centrally heated room. To provide some moisture around the plant, stand it on a tray of pebbles that are kept moist. Plants will be happy in a greenhouse or conservatory for a while but once the weather is mild it is best to plant them outside in a window box, trough or in a rock garden.

Miniatures are not good as permanent indoor plants. As a result of dry air the foliage invariably drops because of red spider mites and the plants soon perish.

Where to grow miniatures

Modern, miniature roses are such adaptable little plants that they can be grown in a variety of situations. At one time it was felt that they should be confined to a Miniature rose garden. This is all very well but laid out at ground level it is difficult to appreciate the roses without stooping and bending. The answer is to lift them up on raised beds at waist height. Grown in this way they are delightful subjects to grow for people who are confined to a wheelchair or who have difficulty in bending.

Formal beds

The taller Miniature roses, such as 'Angela Rippon', 'Pallas', 'Pour Toi', 'Magic Carousel' and 'Rise 'n Shine', are excellent as bedding plants, particularly in small gardens. It is more effective if separate varieties are grown in beds on their own and perhaps edged with a low-growing blue viola. To give extra height to a bed, one or two dwarf or Patio half standard roses could be grown with the Miniatures.

Terrace beds

One of the best ways of growing Miniatures can be seen at the gardens of the Royal National Rose Society at Chiswell Green, St. Albans. Here a sunken paved area is surrounded by raised terraced beds supported with brick walls. The beds are arranged at different levels so that the tiny bushes of flowers can be admired at close quarters. Grown in this way the plants are also easy to attend to for general care and maintenance. Few people with small gardens can devote such a large area to Miniature roses but, with a little ingenuity, it is suprising how they can be accommodated in most gardens. One way of tackling a steep bank is to terrace it. If the different levels are filled with Miniature roses it becomes a delightful feature in the garden. It is important that the roses are grown in good light; they will not do well if the beds are shaded by overhanging trees.

Window boxes and containers

Miniature roses are excellent plants for growing in containers. In window boxes choose the shorter-growing varieties as some of the taller ones can obscure the windows too much. They can be grown on their own or mixed with other small plants to provide interest when the roses are not flowering. Small bulbs such as crocuses and Miniature daffodils could be grown with them for flowering in early spring before the roses start to bloom. Almost any sort of container or ornamental pot can be planted with Miniatures (Fig.12.1). It is vital that there are drainage holes in the base for surplus water to escape. Cover the holes with broken pieces of pot or rubble and plant the roses in a good potting mixture. Do not use ordinary garden soil as it will not give good results. Instead use a mixture such as John Innes Potting Compost No.3. Do not fill the container to the rim but leave space at the top for watering. During the winter it should not be necessary to do any watering but in the spring and summer, when temperatures are higher and the plants are in full growth, watering must not be neglected. In very hot weather the compost in the container can dry out rapidly and water may have to be given two or three times a day. If the roses dry out they could lose their leaves and become more prone to pests and diseases.

Feeding in containers

Roses in containers soon use up most of the goodness in the potting compost and to keep the plants growing healthily and flowering well, supplementary feeding is required. It is not necessary to feed until the plants are well established in the container but liquid feeds of a general fertilizer can then be given at frequent intervals through the summer. It is best not to feed after mid-summer to give the growth time to become hardened before the winter. If feeding is continued soft, sappy growth will form which is likely to die back in the autumn. To save time in giving regular feeds at intervals through the growing season, a single application of a slow-release fertilizer such as Osmocote Plus can be given in the spring. It will keep plants in containers growing well for the whole

Fig. 12.1 Very free flowering Miniatures are useful to plant in pots.

season without any other feeding being necessary.

Before the end of March overhaul roses in containers so that they get off to a flying start in the spring. First attend to pruning (see page 52) and clear away any dead leaves. Using a hand fork carefully remove most of the surface soil from the container and top dress with fresh potting compost firming it well in. Once new foliage appears, spray with a rose insecticide and fungicide (see page 56).

Hanging baskets

Miniature roses are not often seen in hanging baskets but there is no reason why they should not be grown in them. The main problem is that the soil in baskets dries out very rapidly in hot weather in the summer and to overcome the difficulty it is probably a good idea to use the modern plastic baskets fitted with a water reservoir. Also, choose a large basket as small baskets cannot hold enough soil for the needs of the plants.

Another way of solving the watering problem it to fit up a system of small bore pipes so that the soil in the baskets is kept moist on a drip system.

Choose roses for a basket carefully. Upright-growing kinds would hardly be seen in a basket. Choose trailing varieties which will clothe and cover the basket effectively. Good varieties are 'Nozomi', 'Red Cascade', and 'Snow Carpet'.

Use a good potting compost, such as John Innes Potting Compost No.3, for filling the baskets. If a slow-release fertilizer, such as Osmocote Plus, is added to the planting mixture, it should keep the roses growing happily throughout the summer without supplementary feeding being necessary.

Rock gardens

Although the specialist alpine gardener may not agree, Miniature roses can look charming in rock gardens. The best way to grow them is to devote small beds or pockets of soil for them, putting a number of plants together in a single group. As in containers, give them a good soil mixture and

after planting, top dress the bed with grit, which helps to smother weeds and keeps the soil moist. Most varieties can be grown in a rock garden but the smaller kinds are probably more in keeping with the size of other alpine plants. *Rosa* 'Rouletii' – the original miniature – is still available from alpine specialist nurserymen and other small varieties are: 'Snowball', 'Red Imp', 'Pot Black', 'Peon', 'Bit o' Gold' and 'Cinderella'.

Hedging and edging

Another way of using Miniature roses is as low hedges and as edging plants for a border in the way that lavender is often used. They can be grown as an attractive edging for a border of larger rose, provided due care is taken in choosing the right colours to blend with the taller roses. They must also be given plenty of room, otherwise the taller varieties could crowd them out.

For low hedges choose the more vigorous varieties growing about 45cm (18in) tall. A hedge of one variety only is more preferable to a mixture of varieties which could vary in height and colour and look a mess. Space the plants about 23cm (9in) apart.

Planting

The soil in open borders intended for Miniature roses must be prepared as well as if you were planting Hybrid Tea or Floribunda roses. Good results cannot be expected unless the soil is fertile. Never plant in ground that has grown roses for the past two or three years. This is because the soil will have become 'rose sick' and the new plants will not flourish. Dig over the soil to the depth of a spade and incorporate well-decayed compost or manure. Prior to planting, scatter a slow-acting organic manure, such as bonemeal or hoof-and-horn meal, over the soil.

Miniature roses can be purchased in pots or with bare roots. The latter will have been budded on a rose rootstock and can be planted only in the dormant season between late autumn and early spring, provided the soil is not too wet or frozen. As with larger types of rose, take out holes large enough to accommodate the roots comfortably and keep the graft union just below soil level. Grafted plants tend to grow a little taller in the garden than similar plants grown from cuttings in pots.

Plants purchased in pots will, normally, have been grown from cuttings and be on their own roots. They can be planted at most times of the year but in summer special care has to be taken to ensure that the soil does not dry out around them. Space the plants approximately 38cm (15in) apart. This does depend on the size the bushes will grow and the very small varieties can be planted closer.

To help conserve soil moisture, mulch the surface of the soil around the bushes with a thick layer of decayed compost, manure or other organic manure. It does make all the difference to good plant growth in the summer.

Pruning

It should not be necessary to prune pot-grown Miniature roses after planting but the stems of bare-root plants should be cut back to within a few inches of soil level. This is to stimulate strong basal shoots. Always use sharp secateurs and cut just above a bud, making a sloping cut away from it.

Annual pruning of established bushes is best carried out in early spring. All they need is a light trim. First, cut out dead and diseased wood. Shorten the rest of the shoots by about one third of their length.

General care

Just like their larger relatives, Miniature roses respond to feeding with a good rose fertilizer. Give the first application after pruning in early spring and follow up with two or three more feeds during the spring and summer. It is not wise to feed later than mid-summer, otherwise soft sappy shoots will be made that do not ripen before the winter.

Thick mulches of organic matter around the bushes each spring after pruning will help keep the soil moist, but in very dry weather in the summer, watering may be necessary.

Pests and diseases

Miniature roses, unfortunately, are affected with the same pests and diseases as Hybrid Teas and Floribundas. Black spot, mildew and rust are the three common diseases and greenfly is the most common pest. Details on controlling disorders are given in Chapter 5. Some varieties are more prone to diseases than others and it is as well to check their health rating when selecting new varieties. Many yellow varieties seem particularly prone to disease.

Propagation

Miniature roses are increased in a variety of ways. Specialist commercial growers use a technique called micro-propagation for the mass production of Miniature pot plants. This involves growing microscopic sections of a rose in nutrient solutions in laboratory conditions. Thousands of plants can be produced economically by this system but it is not something that is of practical interest for amateur gardeners.

Nurserymen also bud Miniature roses on a rose rootstock and if you buy bare-root roses they will in all probability have been budded. In the garden these tend to make larger plants than Miniatures raised from cuttings. So, if you want to have true Miniature roses, obtain plants raised from cuttings.

Having purchased a Miniature rose which is particularly pleasing, you may want to have more plants of the same variety. The easiest way to do it is to take cuttings from it. They are not difficult to root and no special equipment is needed. They can be rooted through spring and summer but late summer is probably the best time. Select firm shoots that have finished flowering and make the cuttings about 15cm (6in) long. Trim each one with a sharp knife just below a bud at the base and above a bud at the top. Remove the lower leaflets. Insert the cuttings around the edge of a small pot filled with a gritty soil mixture. A soilless seed mixture can be used if extra coarse grit or Perlite is added. Fill the container with the mixture and cover it with a layer of Perlite. When holes are made with a dibber for the cuttings, some of the Perlite trickles down to the bottom and assists the base of the cutting to form roots. Although not essential, the base of the cuttings can be dipped in a hormone rooting powder. As each cutting is inserted, firm the soil mixture around it with the fingers. Give the cuttings a good watering and enclose each pot in a polythene bag to conserve moisture. If you should have a propagating frame the cuttings can be put in it instead of being covered with a polythene bag. Stand the cuttings on a window sill or in a greenhouse.

After a few weeks, signs of new growth on the cuttings is an indication that roots are being made. At this stage pot the rooted cuttings individually in a good potting mixture. If you don't want to be bothered with pots, try inserting the cuttings in a sheltered spot outside. Put some coarse sand or Perlite in the base of the planting holes and press the soil around each cutting firmly. Plant the cuttings so that a glass jar can be put over them as a mini propagator.

Layering

Another simple way of increasing Miniatures with a lax or pendulous habit is to layer the shoots. This often occurs naturally on a whole range of plants if a stem touches the soil. All you have to do is to make a slit part way into the underside of a stem. Keep the tongue that is made open with a sliver of wood and dust the wound with hormone rooting powder. Peg the layer into the soil to which has been added plenty of coarse sand to assist rooting. Roots should form where the cut was made. Leave the layer undisturbed for about a year. At this stage lift it carefully with a fork. Sever the rooted part with secateurs and replant it in its new home.

Seeds

Raising Miniature roses from seed is, primarily, of interest to the hybridist or breeder. However, some seedsmen offer seed of Miniature roses under a variety of interesting names including *Rosa chinensis minima* 'Angel Rose' and *Rosa polyantha* 'Angel Rose Mixed'. These are said to produce plants about 30cm (12in) tall and with single and double flowers. They are really mystery packages as you can never be quite sure what the results will be. However, it can be fun growing them and there is always the possibility that you may produce a particularly good new Miniature rose. Sow the seed in pots in a greenhouse in early spring. Once the seedlings can be handled, pot them separately in small pots and grow them on in the greenhouse. Before the end of the summer they should be flowering. Some may not be particularly attractive. Discard these and keep the ones that take your fancy. Once they have flowered they can be planted in the open garden.

Exhibiting Miniatures

As the popularity of Miniature roses has increased, special classes for them have been introduced into many rose shows. The Royal National Rose Society held its first show for Miniatures in August 1991 and it was highly successful, attracting exhibitors from all over the UK as well as from the States where there is great interest in growing and showing Miniatures. Another show was held in 1992 and it is now planned as an annual event with great hopes of attracting more overseas exhibitors.

One big advantage of showing Miniatures, compared with their larger relatives, is that they are so easy to transport. It is surprising how many blooms can be packed in a small plastic box. Classes at the show included single and multiple stems in vases, boxes, artist's palettes, bowls, baskets and the interesting 'three-stage blooms' class. Three stems of one variety are required with one bloom at the bud stage, another at the 'perfect' stage and the third at the 'full bloom' stage. The classes are split into divisions according to the number of roses grown by the exhibitor.

What do the judges look for? For a start the flowers and foliage have to be Miniature in all respects. The blooms must be fresh, of good colour, true to the variety and free from blemishes. In box classes the blooms should be matching and of equal size. The foliage must be fresh and clean and without blemishes. Each stem should have at least two sets of leaves. They can be wiped over with water but leaf shines must not be used. You can be sure that if there are two entries with almost perfect blooms but one has poor foliage, the other is bound to win. In vases and baskets the arrangement of the Miniatures can also gain extra points.

Many exhibitors grow their Miniatures in large containers so that they can give them the best possible soil and treatment. Regular feeding through the summer will encourage good sturdy growth and special attention must be paid to pest and disease control by regular spraying. Blooms in tight bud can be picked several days before the show if necesssary and stored in the warmest part of a refrigerator. They will continue to develop but more slowly than if in the open. The best way to store them in the fridge is to place the stems in glass or plastic tubes stood in a small rack.

It is best to cut the blooms either first thing in the morning or in the evening when they are turgid and full of moisture. Cut the stems a little longer than will be required and stand them immediately in a deep pail of tepid water in a cool place; any that should go limp can be recut under water. Some exhibitors add a little 'flower preserver', obtainable from florists, to the water to keep the blooms in peak condition. It is wise to take more blooms than are required to the show so that you have a choice for each class you enter. Give yourself plenty of time for staging and make sure you read the schedule thoroughly. If a class calls for five stems make sure you have put the right number in the vase! If you happen to have four or six blooms in the vase you will find the entry card marked 'nas' or 'not according to schedule' by the judges. Always label the roses with the name of the variety. Do this neatly on a plain card. It should not be obtrusive but large enough to be read without difficulty. You can always recognize a good showman by his neat labelling.

Finally, choose your varieties carefully. Some, although excellent in the garden, may not have exhibition potential. The best way to choose suitable varieties is to see what is winning on the show benches and talk to winning exhibitors. Anne and Maurice Grosse from Suffolk are among the most successful exhibitors of Miniatures in this country and, currently, their 'Top Twenty' Miniatures for showing are shown in Table 12.1. You cannot go far wrong if you grow some of them.

Table 12.1 Top Twenty Miniatures for showing

'Arizona Sunset'	yellow blend
'Dreamglo'	red blend
'Jade'	dark red
'Jean Kennealy'	apricot blend
'June Laver'	yellow
'Longleat'	red
'Luis Desamero'	medium yellow
'Magic Carousel'	red blend
'Minnie Pearl'	light pink
'Party Girl'	yellow
'Peaches 'n' Cream'	pink blend
'Pink Petticoat'	light pink
'Rainbow's End'	yellow blend
'Red Ace'	red
'Red Beauty'	dark red
'Rise n' Shine' (syn. 'Golden Sunblaze')	yellow
'Snow Bride'	white
'Starina'	orange
'Winsome'	mauve
'Yellow Sunblaze'	yellow

An A-Z of Miniature Roses

There are hundreds of different varieties of Miniature roses and new ones are appearing each year. The following is a selection of some of the best for use as garden plants and for exhibition. Climbing Miniatures are included at the end of the main list. The varieties suggested for exhibition are based on the recommendations of Maurice Grosse, one of the country's most successful exhibitors of Miniature roses.

'Air France' (Meifinaro, Rosy Meillandina, American Independence); Meilland 1982. A variety growing 30cm (12in) tall. The pretty, double pink flowers have an old fashioned look and are carried in clusters, opening to reveal yellow stamens in the centres. The dark green leaves resist diseases well.

'Angela Rippon' (Ocaru, Ocarina); De Ruiter 1978. One of the best selling Modern Miniatures in the UK but not so well known in America. It is good for both garden decoration and showing. The deep pink double flowers are produced in abundance on healthy bushes up to 30cm (12in) tall.

'Baby Darling' Moore 1964. This is one of the top rated Miniatures in America but in the UK it does not do well in cold districts. The small flowers are orange-pink in colour and bushes grow to 25cm (10in) tall. It is often grown for exhibition.

'Baby Masquerade' (Baby Carnaval); Tantau 1956. Although this miniature has been around for some time, it is still one of the best for garden display. The flowers are yellow at first and gradually turn pink and red. Bushes grow to about 45cm (18in). Spraying may be necessary against mildew.

'Baby Sunrise' (Macparlez, Gold Fever); McGredy 1984. The coppery-orange/yellow blooms are well formed and produced in clusters on bushes of 30cm (1ft). It is a pretty rose suitable for garden display in a border or container.

'Black Jade' (Benblack); Bernardella 1985. One of the most successful Miniatures in America with almost unique crimson-black flowers of good shape.

'Blue Peter' (Bluenette, Azulabria); De Ruiter 1982. Named after the well known television programme, the flowers are not a true blue but more of a purplish shade. Plants grow about 30cm (12in) tall. It is also available as a Miniature standard.

'Bush Baby' (Peanob); Pearce 1983. This is one of the real Miniatures growing not much more than 15cm (6in). The flowers are a delicate shade of salmon-pink and have some scent. It is a healthy rose with resistance to disease.

'Cinderella' De Vink 1992. A real Miniature that has stood the test of time having been bred by the Dutch pioneer of Miniatures. The tiny blooms, of Hybrid-tea shape, are white with a faint tinge of pink and appear throughout the summer. Bushes, almost free of thorns, do not usually exceed 25cm (10in) in height.

'Colibri '79' (Meidanover); Meilland 1979. This variety should not be confused with 'Colibre', another Miniature raised by Meilland. Both are good the latter having golden-orange flowers tinged pink, 'Colibri '79' grows to about 25cm (10in) and has pale yellow flowers, flushed with pink and orange.

'Darling Frame' (Meiluca, Minuetto); Meilland 1971. A popular rose with orange-red flowers and growing to about 45cm (18in). It is good for showing and can be picked for a vase or buttonhole. The foliage is susceptible to disease and spraying is necessary against blackspot, rust and mildew.

'Debut' (Meibarke, Douce Symphonie, Sweet Symphonie); Meilland. Highly thought of in America, this is a fine bedding rose growing to only 36cm (14in). The Hybrid-tea shaped flowers are cherry-red at the tips of the petals blending to creamy-white at the base. It flowers all summer and it has good resistance against disease.

'Dreamglo' Ernest Williams 1978. Another Miniature highly rated in America. The red and white flowers are produced on upright bushes.

'Dresden Doll' Moore 1975. The American raiser is well known for his work in breeding Miniature Moss roses and this is one of his early varieties. The double, cup-shaped flowers are a delicate shade of pink and have an old world charm. They are surrounded by 'moss' covered buds. It is a charming rose growing to about 38cm (15in). The fading flowers can be unsightly and need removing. Mildew may also be a problem.

'Dwarfking' (Zwergkonig); Kordes 1957. Despite its age this is still a good deep red Miniature. The small, semi-double flowers are cup shaped and have a faint scent. Plants grow to about 30cm.

'Easter Morning' (Easter Morn); Moore 1960. One of the best white Miniatures as the blooms are not spoilt by rain. The flowers are fully double and are of typical Hybrid-tea shape. Growth of the plants is upright to 38cm (15in)

'Fire Princess' Moore 1969. The scarlet flowers appear on upright bushes up to 45cm (18in) tall. The foliage is dark green and healthy. A useful variety for a low hedge. Flowers are good for cutting.

'Gold Pin' Mattock 1974. Producing masses of golden-yellow flowers this is a bright little rose growing about 30cm (12in) tall. The flowers are slightly scented but, as with many yellow varieties, it is prone to disease and needs spraying.

'Gourmet Popcorn' (Weopopi); Desamero 1986. This is becoming highly regarded in this country. It is a sport from the white 'Popcorn', to which it is very similar although larger.

'Green Diamond' Moore 1975. The very small, double flowers are greenish-pink and are not particularly showy in the garden. The flower arrangers, however, like it. Plants grow about 25cm (10in) tall.

'Hollie Roffey' (Harramin); Harkness 1986. The first Miniature raised by Jack Harkness, one of the leading British rose breeders. The small flower rosettes are rose-pink in colour and are good for cutting. The dark foliage is healthy and bushes grow to about 38cm (15in).

'Jean Kenneally' (Tineally); Bennet 1984. This is regarded as one of the best Miniatures in America. It has beautifully formed apricot flowers and is an excellent variety for exhibition.

'Judy Fischer' Moore 1968. Another highly rated Miniature in America and also popular in the UK. The double, deep pink flowers do not fade in the sun and are produced freely on bushes growing to 30cm (12in) tall.

'Juliet Ann' (Harvissa); Harkness 1990. A new British Miniature not to be confused with the orange-red 'Julie Ann'. The primrose-yellow flowers appear all summer and into autumn on rounded bushes 38cm (15in) tall. It is a good rose for garden decoration and for cutting.

'June Laver' (Lavjune); Laver 1989. One of the most beautifully formed, golden-yellow Miniatures of undoubted hardiness. The colour of the flowers fades to cream as the blooms age. It was raised in Canada and, although the stems are short, it has great possibilties as a Miniature for exhibition.

'Lady Sunblaze' (Meilarco, Peace Sunblaze); Meilland 1989. One of a group of Miniatures named by the raisers as 'Sunblaze' roses. They have all been very successful and noted for their hardiness and freedom from disease. They are nearly always in flower and are excellent for growing in pots and containers. This variety has masses of pink pompon flowers and is available as a Miniature standard.

'Lavender Lace' Moore 1968. A true Miniature growing no more than 30cm (12in) tall. The small pointed flower buds are lavender in colour backed by small, shiny leaves. The flowers are also pleasantly fragrant.

'Little Buckaroo' Moore 1956. Although it has been around for over thirty years it is is still a good Miniature rose. The colour of the double flowers is red with white centres. They have a light fragrance. Plants grow to about 45cm (18in).

'Little Flirt' Moore 1961. Still a popular variety after over thirty years. Growing to about 38cm (15in) the small flowers are double, orange-red in colour, and with a yellow reverse to the petals. Growth is robust but the flowers have only slight scent.

'Luis Desamero' (Tinluis); Bennett 1989. One of the newer varieties from America and highly recommended for showing. It produces high pointed flower buds in plenty on vigorous bushes. It is classified as a yellow variety but the colour tends to be a pale cream.

'Magic Carrousel' (Morroussel); Moore 1972. Although it has been around for twenty years it is still a popular variety. The high pointed flowers are basically white with deep pink edges to the petals. Plants grow to 38cm (15in) tall and are upright in growth. The foliage is good and healthy. There is only a little scent. It is a good variety to grow for cut flowers.

'Mini Metro' (Rufin, Finstar); De Ruiter 1980. Growing to about 38cm (15in) the flowers are small and double. Salmon-orange in colour they open to show attractive yellow stamens in the centres. Scent is only slight.

'Minnie Pearl' (Savahowdy); Saville 1982. Another highly rated American variety and a top Miniature for showing. The high pointed flowers are, as the name describes, white with a tinge of pink. Having long stems it is a good variety for cutting but it also does well when used as a garden plant.

'Orange Sunblaze' (Meijikatar, Orange Meillandina); Meilland 1982. Another variety in the 'Sunblaze' series producing large clusters of reddish-orange flowers. It is a hardy, reliable variety resisting disease well. Plants grow to 25cm (10in). There is also a climbing form.

'Over the Rainbow' Moore 1972. One of the top rated American Miniatures, the high centred flowers are red and yellow bicolours. Plants grow to 30cm (12in) tall and the foliage is healthy. Scent is only slight.

'Pallas' (Harvestal); Harkness 1989. An attractive variety with pretty, double flowers in peach-pink on plants growing 38cm (15in) tall

'Pandora' (Harwinner); Harkness 1989. Very similar rosette-type flowers to the preceeding variety but the colour is pale yellow at the edges, deepening towards the centres. Plants grow to 38cm (15in).

'Party Girl' Saville 1979. Another fine variety and one of the top rated Miniatures in America. The high pointed, apricot-yellow flowers are excellent for showing and the long stems are good for cutting. Plants grow to 25cm (10in) tall.

'Peaches 'n' Cream' Ernest Woolcock 1976. Officially described as a pink blend Miniature the flower colour is almost white. It is a first class variety, particularly for exhibition.

'Phoebe' (Harvander); Harkness 1989. One of a series of four introduced by the raiser in the same year, the others being 'Pandora', 'Pallas' and 'Phoenix'. All are compact in growth to about 45cm (18in) and have double flowers in attractive colours. This variety has small flowers in soft rose-pink. All four varieties do well in troughs and containers.

'Phoenix' (Harvee); Harkness 1989. This is the fourth variety in the series (see above) introduced in 1989. The colour of the well shaped flowers of this variety is ruby-red.

'Pierrine' (Micpie); Williams 1988. A new American variety very highly rated for exhibition as well as garden decoration. The high centred soft pink flowers are carried one to a stem.

'Pink Petticoat' Strawn 1979. Although popular in America, this Miniature is slowly being recognized in the UK. The flowers look like perfect Hybrid Teas in miniature. Officially described as a light pink Miniature, there is yellow shading at the base of the petals.

'Pink Sunblaze' (Metjidiro, Pink Meillandina); Meilland 1981. Another in the hardy and reliable 'Sunblaze' series. This one has small, double, coral and rose-pink flowers which do not fade in the sun. Plants grow to 45cm (18in). It is excellent for growing in window boxes and containers (see also 'Lady Sunblaze', 'Orange Sunblaze' and 'Yellow Sunblaze'.

'Pour Toi' (Para Ti, For You, Wendy); Dot 1946. One of the very early Miniatures raised in Spain. It is a very beautiful variety having creamy-white, semi-double flowers with yellow centres and is grown throughout the world. Plants grow only 23cm (9in) tall. It is a good variety for showing and cutting.

'Rainbow's End' (Savalife); Saville 1984. Another highly rated Miniature in Great Britain and America. Officially, it is described as a yellow blend. The odd thing about it is that the tips of the petals become red in a sunny position but in a more shaded situation they are all yellow. It is an excellent Miniature for showing and cutting as well as for garden decoration.

'Red Ace' (Amruda, Amanda); De Ruiter 1982. A very popular Miniature for exhibition in Britain and also good for garden decoration. It produces dark crimson flowers in clusters on bushes growing 30cm (12in) tall.

'Red Beauty' Williams 1981. It is certainly a beauty. The perfectly shaped flowers, like miniature Hybrid Teas, are deep red in colour. It is a highly rated Miniature but, sadly, it appears to be prone to mildew.

'Rise 'n' Shine' (Golden Sunblaze); Moore 1977. One of the best yellow Miniatures that has stood the test of time. The colour is a bright and vivid yellow. It is excellent for garden display as well as for exhibition. Growing to 45cm (18in) tall it is highly rated in Britain and America. Diseases may be a problem.

'Rosina' (Josephine Wheatcroft, Yellow Sweetheart); Dot 1951. One of the early Miniatures growing only 23cm (9in) tall. The semi-double flowers are yellow but like many varieties of this colour it is prone to disease and needs to be sprayed.

'Rouletii' (*Rosa chinensis minima*); Correvon 1922. The tiny rose that was discovered in Switzerland and started the modern race of Miniatures. It has now been superseded but the semi-double, rose-pink flowers on 23cm (9in) high plants are still charming.

'Royal Salute' (Macros, Rose Baby); McGredy 1977. Named to celebrate the Queen's Silver Jubilee, the large flowers are a deep, rose-pink and have a little scent. It is a good garden variety and is sometimes listed as a Patio rose. Bushes grow to 38cm (15in). The rose was given a Trial Ground Certificate by the RNRS in 1972.

'Snowball' (Macangeli, Angelita); McGredy 1981. A beautiful little variety growing only 20cm (8in) tall. The pure white rosette flowers cover the bushy mounds. It is a good Miniature for growing in containers or in rock garden beds. It was awarded a Trial Ground Certificate by the Royal National Rose Society in 1984.

'Snow Bride' Betty Jolly 1982. Raised in America, this Miniature is highly successful throughout the world and must come in the top ten. It is a very beautiful variety with high pointed white flowers of beautiful form. Excellent for exhibition it is also good for garden decoration.

'Snowdrop' (Amaru, Amorette, Amoretta); De Ruiter 1978. Growing up to 30cm (1ft) the white flowers are freely produced on single stems. Growth is upright.

'Stacey Sue' Moore 1976. Not one of the top Miniatures but still very good. It is one of the smallest varieties growing no more than 30cm (1ft) tall. The flowers are pink and are good for cutting. It is also a good Miniature for rock gardens.

'Starina' (Meigabi); Meilland 1965. Although over twenty years old this is a Miniature highly rated throughout the world. It has large orange-red flowers that are first class for exhibition and cutting. Plants grow to a height of 30cm (1ft).

'Stars 'n' Stripes' Moore 1976. A great historical rose as it was the first stripy rose to be raised by hybridization. It has pretty white flowers marked with red looking like small *Rosa mundi* flowers. Growth is bushy and it is excellent for a small hedge. Plants grow to about 25cm (10in) tall.

'Sweet Fairy' De Vink 1946. One of the early Miniatures growing only 15cm (6in) tall. The soft pink, double flowers, covering the tiny bushes of dark green glossy foliage, are pleasantly fragrant.

'Winsome' (Savawin); Saville 1984. Very highly rated and successful in America. Plants grow a little tall and it is almost a Patio rose. The flowers are mauve in colour and are excellent for cutting. It is equally good for showing and garden decoration.

'Yellow Doll' Moore 1962. A highly thought of yellow rose but which has been superseded by more modern yellow varieties. The flowers are large and fully double but lack form. The plants grow to 38cm (15in) tall. As with many yellow varieties diseases can be a problem unless spraying is carried out.

'Yellow Sunblaze' (Meitrisical, Yellow Meillandina); Meilland 1983. The yellow version in the 'Sunblaze' Series, all of which are tough and reliable. The well formed flowers are a bright yellow and plants grow to 38cm (15in).

'Yorkshire Sunblaze' (White Meillandina, Meiblal); Meilland 1983. An attractive rose with masses of semi-double white flowers on low bushes growing about 25cm (10in) tall.

Climbing Miniature Roses

Although the old rose 'Pompon de Paris' (1839) was once a fashionable, bushy pot plant, it can be grown as a climber up to 2.4m (8ft), if lightly pruned. Its small, pink flowers appear mainly in summer. In recent times breeders have turned their attention to producing new Climbing Miniature roses with some success.

Chris Warner in this country has raised several that are exceedingly good including:

'Warm Welcome' – orange, and **'Laura Ford'** – yellow.

Other miniature climbers are:
'Climbing Orange Sunblaze' – orange.

'Nozomi' – pale pink, often used as a Ground cover rose.

'Suma' – rose-red, sometimes classed as a Patio rose.

Miniature Roses – The Top Ten for Garden Decoration

'Angela Rippon' – pink, excellent garden miniature.

'Baby Masquerade' – red and yellow, an old variety but an excellent bedder.

'Black Jade' – very dark red, almost black, good for exhibition.

'Jean Kenneally' – apricot blend, fine for exhibition.

'**Magic Carousel**' – white and rose-red, good for cutting.

'**Party Girl**' – yellow blend, highly rated for exhibition.

'**Red Ace**' – dark crimson, good for exhibition.

'**Rise 'n' Shine**' – golden yellow, a fine all rounder.

'**Starina**' – orange red, good for cutting and showing.

'**Snow Bride**' – white, one of the best miniatures available.

PATIO ROSES

The first Miniature roses were tiny in all their parts. Once their potential was realized, breeders set to work hybridizing them with their larger brethren, the Hybrid Teas and cluster-flowered or Floribunda roses. As shown on page 171 we now have Miniatures varying considerably in height and flower size. Some have habits that do not fit in with the classification of true Miniatures, as the flowers are too big and they grow too tall. Rose growers set about giving these 'large Miniatures' a new name. Officially they are now called 'dwarf cluster-flowered roses'. This is a clumsy term and as a result they have become popularly known as 'Patio roses'. In America they are called 'sweetheart roses'.

As a guide they should grow between 35cm (14in) and 50cm (20in) tall and have smaller flowers than the compact cluster-flowered roses. Patio roses is not a very satisfactory term as it suggests that plants can be grown only on a patio or terrace which is, of course, not true. However, whatever the pros and cons of the situation, they are becoming very popular as they fit in well with small modern gardens. They also have a place in larger gardens. There is a superb bed of the red-flowered 'Marlena', one of the earliest varieties bred by Kordes in 1964, at the Royal National Rose Society's display garden at St. Albans, which is not at all out of place in its surroundings and which continues to give a good display of blooms well into late autumn.

Patio beds

Patio roses can be grown anywhere in the garden in much the same way as Miniatures. On a terrace, paving slabs can be lifted to form a bed for the roses. As the soil is likely to be poor underneath it pays to excavate most of it down to the sub-soil and replace it with good, imported turfy loam. First fork over the sub-soil to ensure that drainage is good and work in some well-decayed compost or manure before filling the bed with the new soil. Some of the top soil that is advertised is of a dubious nature. Always go to a reliable source and ask to see a sample. Check if it has been analyzed and find out whether it is acid or alkaline. If it is very alkaline roses will not like it and produce chlorotic leaves, a sign of iron deficiency brought about because of the alkalinity of the soil. Small inexpensive soil-testing kits can be purchased from garden centres. If the soil is neutral, pH 7 will be indicated. Any figure above 7 means that the soil is alkaline and figures below 7 show that the soil is acid. Before permanent beds are made in a terrace check that the aspect is suitable. Few roses will do well in a north-facing situation. They must be sited where they will receive direct sunshine for a large part of the day and not be subject to draughts.

The soil in beds close to houses can dry out badly in the summer. If this happens the roses will suffer. In dry spells keep the beds watered. Thick mulches of compost or manure in the spring all over the bed will help greatly in keeping the soil moist. Patio roses can also be grown in formal island beds or borders adjacent to a path or drive (Fig.12.2). Prepare the ground for these as recommended for Hybrid Tea or cluster-flowered roses (see page 24). They do not, of course, have to be grown in beds on their own. There is no reason why they should not be used as part of a mixed border of plants including shrubs and herbaceous perennials. They are plants for the front row and look best planted in informal

Fig. 12.2 Small groups of Patio roses will give pleasing colour in many corners of the garden.

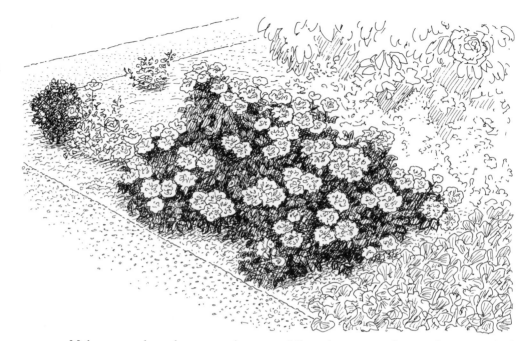

groups. Make sure that they are given plenty of space so that neighbouring plants do not overcrowd them. Plant the roses about 45cm (18in) apart.

Containers

Patio roses are excellent subjects for tubs or containers which can be stood on a terrace. It is important that the container is large enough to allow for good root development and it should be at least 38cm (15in) deep. As described for Miniature roses on p. 173 it is vital that there are holes in the base of the container for surplus water to drain away. Preparation of the containers and general cultivation is the same as suggested for Miniatures. It is also wise to lift the containers on small blocks to ensure the drainage holes do not become blocked. Prune the bushes each early spring, cutting out any dead and diseased shoots. Cut thin, weak shoots back close to their base and shorten the remainder to about 15cm (6in).

Patio roses are also good subjects for low hedges in the same way that lavender and box are used. It is more effective if a single variety is used so that the habit and colour is uniform for the whole length of the hedge.

Like other types of rose, the removal of fading flowers – dead heading – is well worthwhile and helps the plants continue flowering for as long as possible.

Standard patio roses

Most nurserymen offer a range of standard roses including Patio standards. The Patio roses are grown at the top of a main stem of varying height. It is usually about 60cm (24in) but can be up to 75cm (30in). These standards are effective if grown in a large pot or tub on their own or if planted in a formal bed of patio roses to add height to the display. As with all standard roses it is vital that the main stem is adequately supported to a stout stake. It need not be obtrusive and several ties with strong twine or special tree ties should be used to keep the stem supported upright. Do not make the ties too tight as space has to be left for the stem to expand.

Dwarf polyantha roses

It has already been explained that Patio roses are a new grouping for the dwarf cluster-flowered roses that are too big to be called Miniatures. Nurserymen love them because they are something new that they can offer to their customers. Whilst they hold the limelight at the moment, the dwarf Polyantha roses should not be overlooked. They have, in fact, been around for a long time and preceded the cluster-flowered roses. Many varieties grow no more than 60cm (2ft) tall and they have the grace and charm of the old-fashioned roses which is lacking in many of the modern Patio roses. The flowers are produced in clusters like rambler roses over a long season and they are tough compact little bushes. They are due for a return to fashion with the Patio roses and it is good to see some nurserymen encouraging this trend.

They can be grown in exactly the same way as Patio roses. They are happy in small formal beds, containers and window boxes, as well as in the front of borders of mixed shrubs and perennials. Altogether they are excellent for small modern gardens. One that is enjoying a come back is 'The Fairy' which appeared in 1932. It has pale pink flowers and makes a delightful low mound. it can be seen at its best bordering the pond at the Royal National Rose Society's garden at Chiswell Green, St. Albans. Some of the varieties that are still available are: 'Marie Pavie', 1888, pale pink; 'Nathalie Nypels', 1919, rose-pink; 'Coral Cluster', 1920, coral-pink; 'Katharina Zeimet, 1901, white; 'Baby Faurax', 1924, pale purple; 'Margo Koster', 1931, salmon-pink. One of the most modern was raised by Jack Harkness in 1974 who called it, appropriately, 'Yesterday'. It has sprays of scented, pink flowers and is recommended for a low hedge or as a standard. Jack Harkness, in his book *Roses* makes the delightful comment: "Perhaps 'Yesterday' will lead the Polyanthas to their tomorrow". It is more than likely he is correct even if many of them are being called 'Patio' roses!

Dwarf shrub roses

Apart from the Polyantha roses there are also several excellent small shrub roses that can enhance a small garden whether they are grown in borders or containers. One that has great appeal is 'Little White Pet'. Growing about 60cm (2ft) tall it produces its clusters of tiny white, double flowers for most of the summer. Two others that pro-

duce tiny, Hybrid-tea shaped flowers are 'Cécile Brunner', which has pink-scented blooms, and the very similar 'Perle d'Or' which has apricot-pink blooms.

An A-Z of Patio Roses

These, as already explained, are short growing, cluster-flowered roses. There has been an influx of new varieties in recent years and the best of these are listed. Also included are a few that are sometimes known as Polyantha roses. There is some overlap between the taller Miniatures and Patio roses. In certain cases varieties may be listed both as Patio and Miniature roses.

'Anna Ford' (Harpiccolo); Harkness 1980. A variety that has done well on the trials winning Gold Medals at St. Albans, Glasgow and Genoa. It is sometimes classified as a miniature but it grows to 45cm (18in) and is better placed as a Patio rose. The orange-red, semi-double flowers are produced in plenty. The small shiny leaves resist disease well.

'Benson and Hedges Special' (Macshana, Dorola, Parkay); McGredy 1979. The compact bushes grow up to 60cm (2ft) tall and are covered in bright gold flowers over a long season. Apart from garden decoration they are also useful for cutting.

'Bianco' (Cocblanco); Cocker 1983. The compact bushes grow about 45cm (18in) tall and are covered in clusters of pure white, pompon flowers. It is sometimes grown as a small standard plant.

'Boy's Brigade' (Cocdinkum); Cocker 1983. A good, sturdy variety having won a Trial Ground Certificate at St. Albans. The appealing, reddish-crimson blooms appear for most of the summer on plants which keep to a height of about 45cm (18in).

'Bright Smile' (Dicdance); Dickson 1980. Aptly named, the clusters of bright yellow flowers make a cheerful sight backed by shiny, healthy foliage. Bushes grow 60cm (2ft) tall. Unfortunately, scent is only slight.

'Buttons' (Dicmickey); Dickson 1987. The delightful salmon-red flowers resemble Hybrid-tea blooms on small compact bushes growing 45cm (18in) tall. The flowers appear for a long period and it is an excellent bedding rose for small gardens.

'Chelsea Pensioner' (Mattache); Mattock 1982. Almost a miniature, this cheerful little rose has flowers not quite the colour of the Chelsea Pensioners' coats with gold shading at the base of the petals. It is also available as a miniature standard.

'Cider Cup' (Dicladida); Dickson 1988. Making a really bright display, this is one of the best Patio roses. Producing deep apricot flowers for most of the summer, plants grow up to 56cm (22in) tall. The delightful, Hybrid-tea shaped flowers are good for cutting and for buttonholes. Disease resistance is good.

'City Lights' (Poulgan); Poulsen 1992. A new variety commemorating the work of the Church Army Fund, a charity supporting projects in deprived urban areas. The bright yellow flowers resemble miniature Hybrid Teas and have some fragrance. Growth is neat and compact.

'Clarissa' (Harprocrustes); Harkness 1983. One of the best modern patio roses having won many awards including a Trial Ground Certificate from the RNRS. The Hybrid-tea shaped flowers are pale apricot in colour. Growth is tall and upright to 75cm (2½ft) and makes a good low hedge.

'Conservation' (Cocdimple); Cocker 1988. A Scottish rose of great promise. It was named to celebrate the 50th anniversary of the World Wildlife Fund and was a Gold Prize winner in the Dublin trials. The semi-double flowers are pale orange-pink in colour and appear all summer on compact, bushy plants of glossy, green foliage. The flowers are pleasantly fragrant.

'Dainty Dinah' (Cocamand); Cocker 1981. Another Scottish rose with small coral-pink flowers in clusters. The pretty buds open to rounded, semi-double blooms on plants growing 60cm (2ft) tall and spreading out to about the same distance. It has received a Trial Ground Certificate from the RNRS.

'Drummer Boy' (Harvacity); Harkness 1987. Small, rounded bushes become covered in bright crimson flowers over a long season. The richness of the colour contrasts effectively with the bright yellow stamens which are revealed as the flowers open. It can be used for a low hedge up to 45cm (18in) or as a bedding rose for a bright splash of colour.

'Emily Louise' (Harwilla); Harkness 1990. A most unusual rose with attractive, buff-yellow, single flowers which resemble potentilla blooms. They appear against a background of dark, shiny foliage which is resistant to disease. It was named in memory of a little, four year old girl who was tragically drowned in the Herald of Free Enterprise ferry disaster.

'Esther's Baby' (Harkinder); Harkness 1979. Spreading little bushes produce semi-double rose-pink flowers of great charm. Plants grow about 45cm (18in) tall.

'Gentle Touch' (Diclulu); Dickson 1986. A very beautiful rose which was 'Rose of the Year' in 1986 and was the first Patio rose to win this high award. The pale pink flowers resemble miniature Hybrid-tea blooms and appear on strong stems. Plants grow to 50cm (20in).

'Ginger Nut' (Coccrazy); Cocker 1989. A rose which is aptly named as the colour of the flowers is unusual, being orange above and red on the underside of the petals. Plants grow to 45cm (18in) tall and form neat, compact bushes. The semi-double flowers look most effective against the small glossy foliage which is disease resistant. The flowers are also pleasantly fragrant.

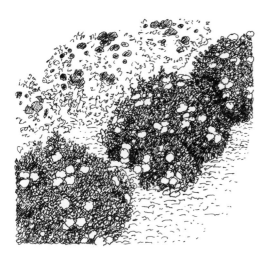

'Guiding Spirit' (Harwolava); Harkness 1989. The rich, rose-red flowers appear in large clusters on compact plants which makes it an ideal bedding rose. Plants grow to about 45cm (18in) tall. The flowers have a pleasant, light fragrance.

'Hakuun' (White Cloud); Poulsen 1962. Had it had a more attractive name this rose would be better known. It means 'white cloud' as the trusses of flowers are borne in profusion and look like a cloud when seen *en masse*. It is a useful rose for blending with varieties in strong colours. Growth is bushy to about 45cm (18in).

'Hello' (Cochello); Cocker 1990. This raiser's roses have a reputation for good health and this new variety is showing great promise. The cheery flowers are crimson with a white eye and appear throughout the summer. There is a light fragrance.

'Honeybunch' (Cocglen); Cocker 1989. One of the best scented Patio roses producing masses of small flowers in yellow and salmon shades over a long period. It is a healthy rose and is also good for cutting.

'International Herald Tribune' (Harquantum, Violette, Viorita) Harkness 1985. The colour of the flowers is unusual being deep violet, edged with purple. Bushes grow to about 60cm (2ft) tall and

the foliage resists diseases well. It has done well in trials in Japan, Switzerland and Italy.

'Jane Asher' (Peapet); Pearce 1987. This is one of the smaller Patio roses growing about 30cm (12in) tall. It has masses of bright scarlet flowers for most of the summer on compact bushy plants. The foliage has good resistance to disease.

'Jean Mermoz' Chenault 1937. An older rose growing only 30cm (12in) tall. It is a pretty little shrub rose with sprays of tiny pink, double flowers which have a light fragrance.

'Kim' Harkness 1973. An attractive rose with yellow flowers, tinged pink, and produced in clusters for most of the summer. Plants grow to 45cm (18in) tall and make compact growth. It is a good rose for cutting. The blooms are slightly fragrant.

'Laura Ashley' (Chewharla); Warner 1991. This rose could be classed as a Ground cover rose as it spreads out to 1.3m (4ft). It has the flowering capacity of 'Nozomi', which is one of its parents with 'Marjorie Fair'. Masses of pretty single magenta pink flowers with yellow centres appear all summer, fading to a paler shade. Bushes grow about 60cm (2ft) tall and can be grown in a variety of ways, in containers, borders or allowed to cascade over a wall. The blooms have a soft fragrance.

'Little Bo Peep' (Poullen); Poulsen 1991. One of the latest varieties having won the President's International Trophy for the best new rose and a Gold Medal. It could be classed as a Miniature Ground cover variety as it has spreading growth which becomes covered in masses of dainty pink blooms. It is equally at home in a container or trained as a dwarf standard.

'Little Jewel' (Cocabel); Cocker 1980. The pretty rose-pink flowers appear on 45cm (18in) tall compact bushes. It is a good rose for bedding or growing in containers. Fragrance is only slight.

Fig. 12.3 'Little Bo Peep' is a new type of Miniature shrub which makes a beautiful round plant about 23cm (9in) high and constantly in flower.

'Little Prince' (Coccord); Cocker 1983. The small orange-red flowers appear for a long time on compact bushes up to 45cm (18in) tall. The small, colourful hips in the autumn are an added attraction.

'Little White Pet' Henderson 1879. Having been around for so long this is a rose that has stood the test of time. Originally it was classified as a Polyantha rose. It produces masses of charming white pompon flowers which have a light fragrance. The spreading habit grows to about 45cm (18in) tall.

'Little Woman' (Diclittle); Dickson 1986. The rose-pink flowers are of true hybrid tea shape in miniature. Plants are of upright growth to a height of about 60cm (2ft).

'Mandarin' (Korcelin); Kordes 1990. A promising new Patio rose with double flowers in shades of pink, orange and yellow. They are produced in compact trusses and appear all summer.

'Marjorie Fair' (Harhero, Red Ballerina, Red Yesterday); Harkness 1978. This is really a short shrub rose but it is some-times regarded as a patio rose. It is very similar to 'Ballerina', having masses of single carmine flowers with white eyes. Plants can reach over 1m (3ft) tall. This very attractive rose received a Trial Ground Certificate from the RNRS in 1976.

'Marlena' Kordes 1964. A first class bedding rose seen at its best in a long bed at the gardens of the Royal National Rose Society at St. Albans. Here the display lasts well into autumn. The blooms are a brilliant scarlet covering bushes which grow about 45cm (18in) tall.

'Minilights' (Dicmoppet, Goldfächer); Dickson 1988. Bright yellow, single flowers cover neat bushes of shiny foliage. Plants grow no more than 25cm (10in) high and spread to 50cm (20in). It is an eye catching rose and an excellent bedding variety.

'Muriel' (Harvool); Harkness 1991. This new patio rose is becoming increasingly popular. The flowers are a light rose-pink and appear on low rounded bushes which grow about 45cm (18in) tall. It is useful rose for edging a border or for growing in a container. It also is a delightful rose

Fig. 12.4
A well-designed series of Patios can contribute to a striking effect when planted with Miniature and Patio roses.

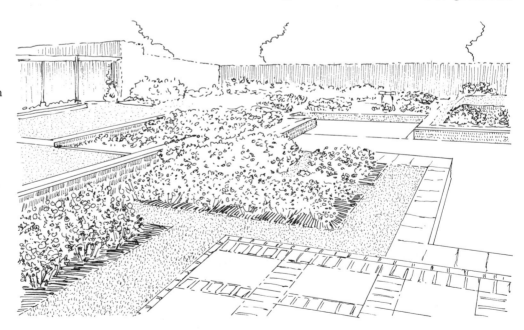

for cutting and has the added bonus of pleasant fragrance.

'Peek a Boo' (Dicgrow); Dickson 1981. Known as 'Brass Ring' in the USA, this is now a popular Patio rose producing graceful sprays of apricot coloured flowers in great quantity. Growing 45cm (18in) tall it is suitable for growing in a rock garden, border or container.

'Penelope Keith' (Macfreego, Freegold); McGredy 1984. An attractive deep yellow Patio rose named after the well known actress. The small flowers are of Hybrid-tea shape and have a tinge of pink in the petals. Growth is compact and it is an excellent rose for small scale beds or for edging a border.

'Perestroika' (Korhitom, Sonnenkind); Kordes 1986. The fully double flowers are a bright golden yellow and look attractive against the dark green, healthy foliage. The habit is compact to a height of 45cm (18in). The flowers are pleasantly fragrant.

'Petit Four' (Interfour); Ilsink 1982. Growing only to 35cm (14in) tall it is an ideal bedding rose. The clear pink flowers, paler in the centres, appear in clusters on compact, rounded bushes.

'Piccolo' (Tanolokip); Tantau 1984. A highly regarded Patio rose producing beautifully formed, coral-red flowers. The foliage is particularly attractive, starting off deep purplish-red and turning to dark green as it ages. It is a good rose for bedding and makes an attractive low hedge.

'Pink Posy' (Cocaneila); Cocker 1983. A little taller than many Patio roses this variety can grow 75cm (2½ft) tall. It is a delightful and unusual rose of polyantha form, producing sprays of small pink, double flowers that are sweetly scented.

'Pretty Polly' (Meitonje, Sweet Sunblaze, Pink Symphonie); Meilland 1989. Regarded as one of the best patio roses having won the RNRS President's Interna-

tional Trophy and a Gold Medal. The soft pink flowers appear in great profusion on neat compact bushes to 45cm (18in) high. It is an excellent variety for growing in tubs and window boxes.

'Queen Mother' (Korquemu); Kordes 1991. This is bound to become a favourite for small gardens as the bright pink, semi-double flowers cover the low bushes for a long period. The foliage is dark and glossy and seems to stand up to wet weather very well. The rose was named to celebrate the 90th birthday of Her Majesty Queen Elizabeth, The Queen Mother in 1990.

'Ray of Sunshine' (Cocclare); Cocker 1988. Growing only 38cm (15in) tall the bushy plants are covered in bright yellow, semi-double flowers which appear in small clusters. The deep green foliage resists disease. The rose was named to celebrate the 70th anniversary of the Sunshine Fund for Blind Babies and Young People.

'Red Rascal' (Jacbed); Warriner 1986. Raised in the USA, the deep red flowers not only stand up to wet weather but they do not fade in the sun. The dark green foliage resists disease and the bushes of neat habit grow to about 38cm (15in) tall.

'Robin Redbreast' (Interrob); Ilsink 1984. This is an attractive little rose with masses of small, dark red flowers, each with a creamy-white eye. The dark green foliage resists disease. It looks most effective when massed as a bedding plant and is also useful for low ground cover. Plants grow 45–60cm (18–24in) tall.

'Rosabell' (Cocceleste); Cocker 1988. Unusual for such a small rose, the flowers have an appealing old fashioned shape and they appear in profusion all summer. Rose-pink in colour the flowers are lightly fragrant. Bushes grow to about 45cm (18in) or less and it is an ideal rose for small gardens.

'Rosy Future' (Harwaderox); Harkness 1991. One of the latest Patio roses and also one of the best for scent. The rose-pink flowers appear in clusters covering the bushes which grow to 45cm (18in) tall. Grow it in containers stood near a door or window so that the perfume can be fully appreciated.

'Rugul' (Tapis Jaune, Guletta); De Ruiter 1973. A very showy variety with bright yellow, semi-double flowers covering compact little bushes about 38cm (15in) tall. It is a useful rose for providing a bright edging to a border or for growing in containers.

'Save the Children' (Hartred); Harkness 1986. The rose is worthy of its emotive name. The deep scarlet flowers are very showy with golden-yellow stamens providing a bright combination. Growth is compact and bushes grow to 45cm (18in) tall. The dark shiny leaves resist disease well.

'Scottish Special' (Cocdapple); Cocker 1987. The pretty peach-pink flowers are produced in abundance covering the low, rounded bushes. The golden yellow stamens add to the attractiveness of the flowers. Bushes grow to 45cm (18in).

'Simon Robinson' (Trobwich); Robinson 1982. With parents of *Rosa wichuraiana* and the miniature 'New Penny' one would have expected to produce a ground cover rose. Growth is certainly spreading to 60cm (2ft) and as much in height. The small, single flowers are produced in attractive sprays backed by healthy foliage.

'St Boniface' (Kormatto); Kordes 1980. The orange-vermilion flowers are beautifully formed and are of typical hybrid tea shape produced in clusters on low growing bushes. The variety was awarded a Certificate of Merit by the RNRS in 1981.

'Sweet Dream' (Fryminicot); Fryers 1988. One of the most successful of the newer Patio roses having been 'Rose of the Year' in 1988. The frilly apricot flowers are produced in good clusters and are most effective for garden display. Plants grow to 45cm (18in) and there is ample glossy foliage. There is only slight fragrance.

'Sweet Magic' (Dicmagic); Dickson 1987. Voted joint 'Rose of the Year' in 1987, the flowers are an appealing shade of golden-orange. The small, Hybrid-tea shaped buds open into semi-double flowers that are pleasantly fragrant. Growth is to 45cm (18in) and the glossy foliage enhances the unusual colour of the flowers.

'Tear Drop' (Dicomo); Dickson 1989. One of the few new white patio roses. The flowers are semi-double and the golden stamens add to the beauty of this delightful rose which is in flower for most of the summer. The flowers are not spoilt by rain and the foliage is healthy. Plants grow to 45cm (18in). It is a most effective rose for bedding and could replace annual bedding flowers.

'The Valois Rose' (Kordadel); Kordes 1990. The fully double flowers are an unusual combination of pale yellow with carmine shading to the edges of the petals. They are produced in clusters on neat, bushy plants with good dark green foliage.

'Top Marks' (Fryministar); Fryer 1992. Launched with great success, being the 'Rose of the Year' in 1992. It is appropriately named as it received the highest points ever in the trial. It has also received Gold Medals at the Hague and at St. Albans as well as a Certificate of Merit in Geneva and Bronze Medal at Baden Baden. This little rose with sparkling vermilion flowers could become an effective permanent bedding replacement for red salvias or geraniums. Despite all its awards it does seem to be prone to disease and needs spraying. Plants grow to 45cm (18in) and the same across. Fragrance is only slight.

'Wee Jock' (Cocabest); Cocker 1980. The bushes form cushions of crimson-scarlet flowers of hybrid tea shape. Plants grow 30–45cm (12–18in) tall with good, glossy foliage. Apart from being an excellent bedding rose, it can be grown in containers and the blooms make good buttonholes. There is only very slight fragrance.

'**Yesterday**' (Tapis d'Orient); Harkness 1974. This charming rose has sprays of dainty pink flowers and grows taller than most Patio roses – up to 120cm (4ft). The raisers recommend it for a low hedge. The variety is often grown as a standard.

'**Yvonne Rabier**' Turbat 1910. Strictly speaking this is an old polyantha rose but it is still well worth growing today as a patio rose. It has charming clusters of small white, double flowers that are pleasantly fragrant. Growth is bushy with good, shiny foliage and reaches to about 115cm (3¹/₂ft) tall. Light pruning is recommended.

Patio Roses – The Top Ten for Garden Decoration

'**Anna Ford**' – orange-red, disease-resistant foliage.

'**Bright Smile**' – yellow flowers on compact bushes.

'**Cider Cup**' – apricot flowers, good disease resistance.

'**Conservation**' – semi-double, pale orange-pink, scented flowers.

'**Gentle Touch**' – soft pink, 'Rose of the Year' 1986.

'**Little Bo Peep**' – pink flowers, highly awarded.

'**Marlena**' – scarlet, long flowering season.

'**Pretty Polly**' – soft pink flowers in profusion, highly rated.

'**Queen Mother**' – pink, stands up to wet weather well.

'**Sweet Magic**' – orange-gold flowers with fragrance.

GROUND COVER ROSES

Forty years ago Ground cover roses were hardly recognized but as interest in labour-saving, ground-covering shrubs and perennials grew it is not surprising that rose growers began to take a long, hard look at the existing ground-hugging roses to see if they could serve a similar purpose. At that time one of the most interesting was a rose called 'Max Graf'. It was raised in America in 1919 and is reputed to be a hybrid between *Rosa wichuraiana* and *R. rugosa*. It is a trailing rose with pink, single flowers which appear only in summer. (Apart from its value as a Ground cover rose it was used by Kordes in Germany to breed a race of tough, disease-resistant climbing roses). Although able to cover the ground for over 2m (6–8ft) and growing 60cm (2ft) tall, it had the disadvantage of flowering only in the summer. It was also too spreading for small gardens.

Another of the early Ground coverers was *Rosa × paulii*. This has white single flowers and the stems creep along the ground for as much as 3m (10ft) and to a height of about 90cm (3ft). Again, it was not ideal for small gardens because of its vigour and disadvantage of flowering only once in the summer. It also has a form with pink flowers.

Apart from these roses, several Rambler roses existed which were often allowed to scramble over banks soon covering large areas. They included 'Dorothy Perkins', 'Albéric Barbier', 'Félicité et Perpétue' and *Rosa wichuraiana*, the parent of many ramblers.

The disadvantage with all these roses was that they were far too vigorous for small modern gardens. What was needed was a rose that was tough and hardy, would form a dense weed-inhibiting cover quickly, have a long season of flower and be reasonably compact. The ideal rose should also be disease resistant and require the minimum of pruning and maintenance. The rose breeders set to work and soon several interesting varieties began to appear. From Japan came 'Nozomi' in 1968. It is a delightful rose with masses of miniature whitish-pink flowers covering the ground to

Fig. 12.5 Modern Ground cover roses are ideal to plant on the top of walls.

about 1½m (4ft) and 45cm (18in) high. It also makes an attractive weeping standard which has been a feature of Harkness's rose exhibits at recent Chelsea flower shows. Between 1984 and 1986 Kordes in Germany introduced three new varieties with bird names. The parents of 'Grouse' and 'Partridge' are 'The Fairy', a charming old Polyantha and *Rosa wichuraiana*. These were followed by 'Pheasant' but all three spread to as much as 3m (10ft). 'Grouse' has semi-double pink flowers, 'Partridge' has white flowers and 'Pheasant' has pink blooms which last through the summer.

Other breeders were also busy and from McGredy came 'Snowcarpet' in 1980. This grows only about 30cm (1ft) tall, spreading to 1m (3ft) and is covered in tiny, fern-like foliage and white flowers. On the Continent, Poulsen and Kordes produced further selections which were introduced by Mattock in this country as their 'County' Series from 1988 onwards. They are all compact in growth and flower for a long period. A dozen roses now bear the name of different counties. 'Kent' won the President's International Trophy in 1990 and 'Northamptonshire' received a Certificate of Merit after trial at the Royal National Rose Society's trial grounds at St. Albans.

There has never been a wider selection of Ground cover roses varying in vigour and suitable for a variety of purposes. Some are prostrate and hug the ground. Others make arching growths and are really dense Shrub roses. These include the delightful 'Raubritter' with small, cupped flowers raised by Kordes. David Austin, a nurseryman who specializes in Shrub and Old-fashioned roses, has also raised several good Shrub roses suitable for ground cover. They include 'Francine Austin', growing 1m (3ft) tall and as much across, and 'Scintillation' which grows even wider.

Some of the older Ground cover roses flowered only once but many of the newer varieties, including the 'County' Series, have an extended flowering period.

The more compact varieties are good for growing at the top of low walls where the roses can cascade over the wall (Fig.12.5). Some of the smaller kinds can also be used

as underplanting in a shrub border. As an alternative to grass or other ground cover plants such as *Hypericum calycinum*, plant some of the stronger-growing varieties, such as 'Grouse' and 'Pleine de Grace' on large banks. Provided it is well drained, they will tolerate poor soil conditions.

Planting

Do not be misled into thinking that because Ground cover roses are recommended for smothering weeds that they can be planted in weedy ground. If you do you will have terrible problems for a long time after. It is no fun trying to get your hands among the thorny stems to extract the weeds. For this reason some people do not like the idea of planting Ground cover roses. To lessen the problem, all pernicious and deep-rooted weeds must be forked out before planting is contemplated. If something like couch grass or bindweed is left in the ground it will be practically impossible to clear it after planting.

Do not expect immediate cover in the season after planting. It can take several years to get a good dense cover. This means that weeds can grow in exposed ground for a couple of seasons and they must be kept under control – it pays to wear strong gloves to prevent being scratched by the stout thorns on some of the roses. Probably the best way to avoid weeding is to lay black polythene over the whole area as a mulch and plant the roses through it. It could save many hours of weeding and at the same time it will help to conserve soil moisture.

Planting is best carried out in autumn and winter although container-grown roses can be planted at most times of the year. If they are planted in the summer, special care must be taken to prevent them from suffering from drought. Mulching the ground with compost or other organic matter or black polythene is essential to prevent this happening.

Cold, north-facing positions are not ideal for Ground cover roses. To grow and flower well give them an open, sunny situation.

Calculating the number of plants that are needed for a given area depends on the spread of the different kinds. A rose spreading to 2m (6ft) can be spaced the same distance apart but the more compact bushy varieties should be spaced much closer. Most Ground cover roses are not fussy about soil and will tolerate poor soil conditions. To give the plants a good start take out a large hole for each one and fill it with a good soil mixture – old potting compost is ideal. Also scatter bonemeal in the planting holes.

General maintenance

Not a great deal of care and attention should be necessary, particularly if the ground has been mulched to exclude weeds. Little pruning is necessary for most kinds. All that should be required is a light trim each spring. Remove any dead and diseased stems together with any that may be in the way. Most of the older ground cover roses are pretty resistant to disease and spraying is not usually necessary. However, some of the more modern varieties, such as 'Warwickshire', can suffer from black spot and remedial spraying may be necessary. Greenfly are always fond of the tips of young rose shoots. Strong growing varieties will suffer little harm, particularly if natural predators such as ladybirds and hover flies are encouraged.

An A-Z of Ground Cover Roses

The following lists describe some of the best roses that can be used for ground cover. They include not only the new varieties specially bred for the purpose but also suitable Shrub roses and Ramblers. As they vary a great deal in habit, they are being listed according to the way they grow.

Prostrate growers for small gardens

'Avon' (Poulmulti); Poulsen 1992. One of the latest in the 'County' Series, it is a neat, ground hugging rose growing about 30cm (1ft) tall and 1m (3ft wide). The buds are pale pink opening to masses of double, white blooms. Apart from ground cover it is a good little spreading rose for containers on a terrace or patio.

'Essex' (Poulnoz, Aquitaine, Pink Cover); Poulsen 1988. One of the 'County' Series having rich pink flowers in large clusters throughout the summer. Growth is prostrate with small, healthy foliage spreading to 1.3m (4ft). It was awarded a Certificate of Merit by the RNRS in 1987.

'Fairy Changeling' (Harnumerious); Harkness 1979. One of several delightful seedlings arising from crossing 'The Fairy' with 'Yesterday'. The pink flowers appear among dense, bushy growth on plants growing 45cm (18in) tall and spreading to 60cm (24in).

'Fairyland' (Harlayalong); Harkness 1980. This is a pretty, pink Polyantha rose, the result of a cross between 'The Fairy' with 'Yesterday', also raised by Harkness. The flower clusters are produced for most of the summer and early autumn on plants spreading to 1m (3ft).

'Fairy Prince' (Harnougette); Harkness 1981. Another Pyolyantha with the same parents as the previous rose. The flower clusters are deep pink on plants spreading to over 1m (3ft).

'Gwent' (Poulart); Poulsen 1992. Another of the latest in the 'County' Series. Masses of double yellow flowers are produced over along season through summer and into autumn.

'**Hampshire**' (Korhamp); Kordes 1989. Neat and compact, growing 30cm (12in) high and 60cm (24in) high, this 'County' variety has masses of bright scarlet single flowers and golden stamens that last all through summer and into autumn. They are followed by attractive orange hips.

'**Hertfordshire**' (Kortenay); Kordes 1991. One of the latest in the 'County' Series producing attractive, single pink flowers all summer. The prostrate growth spreads out to 75cm (2¹/₂ft).

'**Norfolk**' (Poulfolk); Poulsen 1990. Another new variety in the 'County' Series and one of the few ground cover roses with yellow blooms. The double flowers are fragrant, produced on neat plants growing only 45cm (18in) tall and spreading to 60cm (2ft). There is a good second crop of flowers.

'**Nozomi**' (Heiderröslein Nozomí); Onodera 1968. A delightful little rose, excellent for ground cover but also used as a miniature climber. Grown as a standard it makes a graceful weeping specimen for a container. It grows to 60cm (2ft) and spreads to 1.8m (6ft). Masses of pinky-white flowers appear for almost two months through the summer.

'**Rutland**' (Poulshine); Poulsen 1988. Another in the 'County' Series forming low spreading bushes to 30cm (1ft) tall with dark green foliage. The small, five-petalled pink flowers are most attractive appearing through the summer and into autumn.

'**Snow Carpet**' (Maccarpe, Blanche Neige), McGredy 1980. A delightful little rose growing only to 30cm (1ft) tall and 90cm (3ft). It is regarded as a Miniature Ground coverer, producing tiny, white, double flowers for almost four months in the summer.

'**Suffolk**' (Kormixal, Bassino); Kordes 1988. Another in the 'County' Series having bright scarlet, single flowers set off attractively with yellow stamens in their centres. Compact in growth it spreads to 1m (3ft) and reaches about 45cm (18in) tall. Flowers appear for most of the summer. It has received a Trial Ground Certificate from the Royal National Rose Society.

'**Suma**' (Harsuma); Onodera 1989. A close companion to 'Nozomi' but having masses of single rosy-pink flowers which last for a long season. It grows to similar dimensions and apart from being a good ground coverer it makes a fine weeping standard for growing in a tub. It can also be trained up a post as a climber.

'**Sussex**' (Poulave); Poulsen 1991. A new colour in the 'County' Series. The double flowers are of a pleasing shade of apricot and appear all summer. A ground hugging variety, the stems spread out to 1m (3ft).

'**Swany**' (Meiburenac); Meilland 1978. Small, white double flowers are produced all summer. Plants grow 60cm (2ft) tall spreading to 90cm (3ft) forming a carpet of dark, glossy foliage. Attractive in a rock garden or for the top of a wall. It is available as a weeping standard.

'**Warwickshire**' (Korkandel); Kordes 1991. The flowers are quite different to the rest in the 'County' Series. The single rose-red blooms have white centres which *en masse* creates a very pretty picture. Plants grow to 45cm (18in) tall and spread to 7cm (30in). The foliage appears to be prone to disease.

Prostrate growers for larger gardens

'**Chilterns**' (Kortemma, Mainaufeuer) Kordes 1992. One of the newest ground cover roses and the first of a new series, larger than the 'County' Series. Growth is vigorous, hugging the ground and spreading to at least 2m (6ft). The deep red flowers are produced in large clusters for most of the summer.

'**Fairy Damsel**' (Harneatly); Harkness 1981. Another of Harkness's hybrids between 'The Fairy' and 'Yesterday'. This one spreads to 1.5m (5ft) and grows 60cm (24in) tall. The flowers are deep red and the growth covers the ground well.

'Flower Carpet' (Noatraum, Heiditraum); Noack 1989. A newer variety having won a Trial Ground Certificate at the RNRS trials at St. Albans. Growing about 45cm (18in) tall and spreading to 1m (3ft) it has large trusses of double pink flowers for most of the summer. It is noted for its resistance to black spot, mildew and rust. It is also grown as a weeping standard and is suitable for growing in a large hanging basket.

'Grouse' (Korimro; Immensée, Lac Rose); Kordes 1984. One of the 'Bird' Series, it is good for covering a large bank as it can spread to 3m (9ft) but, at the same time, keeping to a height of 30cm (1ft). It has single, pale pink, fragrant flowers in late summer and is resistant to disease.

'Partridge' (Korweirm, Weisse Immensée Lac Blanc); Kordes 1984. Another in the 'Bird' Series. Similar habit and vigour to 'Grouse' but the flowers are white. The glossy foliage is also disease resistant. Awarded a Certificate of Merit from the RNRS.

R. × paulii Paul, prior 1903. This is an old and vigorous rose forming thickets of thorny stems and only for growing in a large informal area. The plants can spread to at least 3m (9ft) and are covered with scented, white single flowers in mid-summer. There is also a form (*R. ×* paulii 'Rosea'–1912) with pretty pink flowers. It is not quite as vigorous as the white form.

'Pheasant' (Kordapt, Heidekönigen, Palissade Rose); Kordes 1986. The third in the 'Bird' Series. A very strong grower spreading to 4m (12ft) and producing trusses of deep pink flowers over a long season. Awarded a Certificate of Merit from the RNRS.

'Pink Drift' (Poulcat, Caterpillar, Kiki Rosé); Poulsen 1986. Growing no more than 30cm (12in) tall, it spreads out to 3m (9ft). The double, pale pink flowers appear in large clusters in summer only among handsome foliage.

'Red Max Graf' (Kormax, Rote Max Graf); Kordes 1984. A *rugosa* hybrid with disease resistant foliage. The single, bright red flowers appear only in summer. It is a vigorous grower spreading to 3m (10ft).

'Running Maid' (Lenramp); Lens 1982. Introduced by David Austin in 1985, the dainty flowers are single and deep pink in colour. Growth is dense and low spreading to at least 1.5m (5ft).

'White Max Graf' (Korgram, Weisse Max Graf); Kordes 1983. A companion to and very similar to 'Red Max Graf', the pure white, single flowers are produced in summer only.

Arching growers for small gardens

'Kent' (Poulcov, Pyrenees, White Cover); Poulsen 1988. One of the most successful in the 'County' Series which won the President's International Trophy of the RNRS in 1990. Large trusses of pure white, scented flowers stand up well to wet weather in the summer. This variety grows to about 45cm (18in) tall and spreads to 60cm. Small hips are produced in the autumn.

'Northamptonshire' (Mattador); Mattock 1990. Another in the 'County' Series with attractive flesh-pink flowers produced in clusters. It grows to 45cm (18in) tall and spreads to about 1m (3ft). It has received a Certificate of Merit from the RNRS.

'Pearl Drift' (Leggab); Le Grice 1980. A free-flowering rose with white and pale pink flowers appearing over a long period. Growth is compact and spreads to over 1m (3ft) wide. It has won a Certificate of Merit from the RNRS.

'Surrey' (Korlanum, Summerwind, Vent d'Ete); Kordes 1988. This 'County' Series rose has masses of handsome, deep pink, double flowers which appear all summer. Growing up to 1m (3ft) tall it spreads to 1.5m (4ft) across. It was awarded a Gold Medal by the RNRS in 1987.

'The Fairy' (Feerie); Bentall 1932. It is often said to be a sport from 'Lady Godiva' but this is, apparently, incorrect, the two parents being 'Paul Crampel' and 'Lady Gay'. This charming rose has already been mentioned under Polyantha and Patio roses but it is also a good ground coverer. An old variety, it has staged a come-back in recent times and has been used as a parent in many more modern varieties. The soft pink double flowers appear throughout the summer and autumn on low arching stems to about 60cm (2ft) and 1m (3ft) wide.

Arching growers for large gardens

'Bonica' (Meidomonac, Bonica 2); Meilland 1958. An attractive shrub rose forming a good thicket when planted closely. The double flowers are pale pink and appear over a long season. The young, coppery coloured foliage becomes shiny and dark green resisting disease well. Shrubs grow to about 1m (3ft) and spread to 1.5m (4ft).

'Candy Rose' (Meiranovi); Meilland 1983. The semi-double flowers are a pleasing shade of salmon pink, fading to pale pink at the centres. They appear in small clusters for most of the summer. Plants can grow 1.2m (4ft) tall and spread to 1.8m (6ft).

'Dentelle de Malines' (Lens Pink); Lens 1986. A rose introduced by David Austin in 1983. It forms a bush 1.3m (4ft) tall covering the ground with dense growth to 1.5m (5ft) wide. The soft pink flowers are produced in small sprays but give only one display in the summer.

'Dunwich Rose' This beautiful rose was found growing on Dunwich beach in Suffolk. Its parentage is not known but it is a good Ground cover rose, spreading by means of suckers, and could have possibilities as a parent in breeding programmes. Masses of pale cream flowers are produced each having attractive golden stamens in the centres. It grows 60cm (2ft) tall and 1.2m (4ft) across.

'Eye Opener' (Interop, Erica, Tapis Rouge); Ilsink 1987. A first class Dutch variety with large trusses of bright red flowers. Each one has a whitish eye and bright golden stamens. Growth is vigorous to a width of 1m (3ft) and 60cm (2ft) tall and the dense foliage is disease resistant.

'Ferdy' (Keitoli, Ferdi); Suzuki 1984. The pink, double flowers open to show cream centres which cover the arching branches in profusion in summer and early autumn. Bushes grow to 1.2m (4ft) wide and 1m (3ft) tall.

'Fiona' (Meibeluxen); Meilland 1979. Spreading out to 1.5m (5ft) and reaching up to 1m (3ft) tall the arching branches are covered in small, semi-double, red flowers among dark green glossy foliage. The hips produced in the autumn are an added bonus.

'Francine Austin' (Ausram); David Austin 1988. The raiser says that 'it has a delicacy and elegance not previously found amongst Ground cover roses'. The white pompon flowers appear in clusters on wiry stems for most of the summer. The strong arching growth reaches up to 1m (3ft) and to 1.3m (4ft) across.

'Frau Dagmar Hartopp' (Frau Dagmar Hastrup); Hastrup 1914. A rugosa rose with handsome, pink, single flowers and prominent yellow stamens in the centres; they are pleasantly fragrant. There is a good crop of autumn flowers followed by bright red hips (Fig.12.6). The dark green foliage is disease resistant. The plants grow about 1m (3ft) tall and spread to 1.2m (4ft).

Fig. 12.6
Although 'Frau Dagmar Hartopp' is recognized as a rugosa shrub its spreading habit makes it a good Ground cover plant.

'Hansa' Van Tol 1905. A tough rugosa rose with large, scented, deep red flowers followed by red hips. It is a rose that tolerates poor soil and is useful for covering an out of the way corner. Growth spreads to 1.2m (4ft) and about the same in height.

'Moje Hammarburg' Hammarburg 1931. A moderately vigorous rugosa rose with large, purple, well-scented blooms, followed by large red hips in the autumn. The typical rugosa foliage resists disease well.

'Nitida' (*R. nitida*); Wildenow 1807. An attractive rose species from North America which is very similar to the Burnet or Scotch roses. It suckers freely and produces small, single flowers with golden stamens on stems covered in prickles. The leaves turn a wonderful shade of red in the autumn and the rounded hips are an added attraction. Plants grow about 1m (3ft) tall and as much across.

'Pink Bells' (Poulbells); Poulsen 1983. The pretty, small, pompon pink flowers appear throughout late summer among the neat shiny green foliage. Growing over 60cm (2ft) tall, bushes spread out to 1.2m (4ft).

'Pink Wave' (Mattgro); Mattock 1983. Plants grow 1m (3ft) tall and spread to 1.5 (4ft) producing a profusion of soft pink flowers for most of the summer. It has won a Trial Ground Certificate from the RNRS at St. Albans.

'Pleine de Grace' (Lengra); Lens, introduced by David Austin 1983. A very vigorous rambler-type rose with stems extending to 4.5m (15ft) and arching upwards to over 2m (6ft). It is an outstanding rose where there is plenty of space for it. The stems are covered with clusters of white flowers in summer only.

'Raubritter' Kordes 1936. A spreading shrub covered in delightful cupped-shaped, silvery pink flowers in June only. Excellent for rambling over a bank or tumbling over a wall. It can spread out to 1.8m (6ft) and grows to about 1m (3ft) tall. Unfortunately it is prone to attacks of mildew in late summer.

'Red Bells' (Poulred) Poulsen 1980. A companion and similar in most respects to 'Pink Bells' apart from its crimson red flowers. It flowers for several weeks in late summer.

'Red Blanket' (Intercell); Ilsink 1979. This Dutch rose has become a popular choice as its small, red, semi-double flowers form a carpet of colour for a long period. It can spread to 1.5m (5ft) and grows to a height of 90cm (3ft). The glossy foliage resists disease well and lasts into the winter.

'Rosy Cushion' (Interall); Ilsink 1979. From the same raiser as 'Red Blanket', this variety is very similar to it apart from its rose-pink single flowers. It is also a vigorous grower.

'Scarlet Mediland' (Meikrotal); Meiland 1987. One of a series of vigorous ground cover roses that are popular in America, being marketed by the Conard-Pyle Company. They are notable for their long season of bloom and disease resistant foliage. This variety grows at least 1m (3ft) tall and over 2m (6ft) wide. The scarlet flowers are borne in large clusters. Others in the same series are: 'Red Meidiland' (Meineble) 1989, 'Pink Meidiland' (Meipoque) 1984,' Alba Meidiland' (Meiflopan) 1989,' Pearl Meidiland' (Meiplatin) 1989 and 'White Meidiland' (Meicoublan) 1989. The red and pink varieties have the added bonus of attractive hips in the autumn. Two fungicidal sprays a year are recommended against diseases.

'Scintillation' David Austin 1967. An excellent shrub rose for covering a bank and spreading to 2m (6ft). The flowers are fragrant but there is only one flowering which lasts for many weeks. The semi-double pale pink flowers appear in large clusters.

'Smarty' (Intersmart); Ilsink 1979. This variety completes the trio with 'Red Blanket' and 'Rosy Cushion' from the same Dutch raiser. The large, deep pink, single flowers can be as much as 5cm (2in) across, produced on vigorous arching stems covered in healthy, glossy foliage.

'Tall Story' (Dickooky); Dickson 1984. One of the few ground cover roses with pale yellow flowers. They are semi-double and pleasantly fragrant, appearing throughout summer and autumn. Growth is spreading to about 1m (3ft) and the glossy foliage is disease resistant.

'Temple Bells' Morey 1971. A pretty rose with small white flowers that appear in abundance among the small, shiny and healthy leaves. One of its parents is the vigorous *Rosa wichuraiana*. Growths spread to 1.3m (4ft) and reach a height of 60cm (2ft).

'White Bells' (Poulwhite); Poulsen 1983. This Danish rose is a worthy companion to 'Pink Bells' and 'Red Bells' having the same parents – 'Mini-Poul' × 'Temple Bells'. The growth covers the ground well spreading to 1.3m (4ft) and the flowers appear all summer.

Ground Cover Roses – The Top Ten for Garden Decoration

'Essex' – clusters of pink flowers, prostrate growth.

'Flower Carpet' – trusses of double, pink flowers, spreads to 1m (3ft).

'Grouse' – pale pink, fragrant flowers, good for covering large banks.

'Kent' – trusses of white flowers, highly awarded variety.

'Northamptonshire' – flesh-pink flowers, arching growth spreading to 1m (3ft).

'Nozomi' – pink and white flowers, spreading growth.

'Partridge' – single, white flowers, glossy, disease-resistant foliage.

'Pheasant' – deep pink flowers in trusses, strong grower.

'Snow Carpet' – tiny, white double flowers, glossy, disease-resistant foliage.

'Suffolk' – scarlet, single flowers for most of the summer, spreads to 1m (3ft).

CHAPTER 13

Where to see Good Rose Gardens

The regular visitor to gardens will very often be bemused by the descriptions that various owners are capable of giving to their masterpieces. What will be accepted as the epitome of excellence in the matter of a unique collection of a particular genus will sometimes receive such disparaging remarks from a neighbour as not being worth the soil they are grown on. This happens with remarkable frequency no matter where the genus is displayed. Equally when compiling lists, a review of gardens can be extremely misleading and inaccurate if a very strict cognizance is not made of the current cultivation and maintenance. The seasoned visitor will come to recognize that many gardens are distinguished by the dominance of a particular genus, in some instances to the exclusion of any other types of plant. Some are comprehensive in their collections with several genera receiving a high profile and then there is the interesting garden with no particular plant genus dominating but nevertheless famous and justly so for the simple pleasure of visiting a beautiful garden.

Round the world there are many gardens that are completely devoted to the genus *Rosa*. There are probably just as many where roses dominate in some parts but nevertheless have a happy association with other plants, and then there are those gardens which cater for cosmopolitan tastes but to the rose enthusiast evoke strong memories of a particular plant or plants, which leave a lasting recollection of an enjoyable experience.

This list of gardens is compiled with these various criteria in mind. There are, however, some famous rose gardens which have the added bonus of conducting rose trials, evaluating the newest products of the rose breeders' art. It is these gardens we shall discuss first.

The Gardens of the Rose at the headquarters of the Royal National Rose Society, St. Albans, Herts, UK, are justly famous comprising a well grown collection of old and modern varieties beautifully grown and displayed. The pergolas and arches are clothed in an abundance of flower in high summer and the collection of Species and Old Garden roses is extremely comprehensive.

There is an intimate garden of Patio and Miniature types, a small model garden and beautifully laid out large beds of Modern introductions. A 'library' collection is maintained of recent award winning varieties and in an adjoining field a continuing three year programme of trials to evaluate the best of the newest introductions is constantly in progress. Within the garden there are currently demonstrations and experiments including the evaluation of various methods of pruning and disease resistant trials.

The recent acquisition of new ground has encouraged garden designers to display their ingenuity to transform a very ordinary flat meadow into what in due course will be the biggest and finest rose garden in the world.

Westbroekpark, The Hague, Holland, is unique in that it comprises a trial for seedling varieties, a testing ground for established new introductions and in addition a beautiful display of Modern roses which are well grown and maintained. A mecca for every aspiring hybridist in July on the occasion of the 'Hague Trials' there is probably no other garden in the world where modern prize winning introductions can be seen to better effect.

The rose collection in the **Sir Thomas and Lady Dixon Park, Belfast, Northern Ireland**, has benefited greatly from being restructured on the occasion of the World Rose conference in 1992. There is the most interesting display of varieties illustrating the history of the rose, well-planned beds with current varieties, which have been successful in the 'Belfast trials' but of greatest significance are the methods used to accommodate and use to good effect the unconventional rolling structure of the terrain. Not for the Ulstermen is the flat conventional garden but the undulating experience of the emerald isle with an imaginative display of rose varieties. The Belfast trials are unique in that the candidates are all varieties, which have already been introduced onto the market, and are grown in beds of twenty five plants to enhance there presentational potential.

St Anne's Rose Garden, Dublin is a well-designed garden comprising vast beds of modern varieties superbly grown and cultivated to a very high standard. A unique feature is the new part of the garden which has been designed to accommodate a large collection of Miniature and Patio roses. A quiet oasis with a unique interpretation of these newest types of rose. There are trials for new seedling roses.

Other gardens which incorporate famous trials in association or in parallel with beautiful rose gardens are Baden Baden the famous spa town in Germany; Bagatelle in Paris, France; Parc de la Grange in Geneva, Switzerland; The Municipal Rose Gardens in Rome and the Parque de Oeste in Madrid, Spain.

There are two gardens in Europe which are distinguished by the vast collections of varieties which they contain. The **Rosetta Cavriglia, Valdarno in Tuscany** comprises a collection of every conceivable variety of rose which has ever been introduced and which is extant. The collection assembled by Professor Fineschi, a distinguished Doctor of Medicine, has been twenty five years in the making. For his own simple pleasure in addition to his professorial duties (he is a world famous orthopaedic surgeon) he has assembled some 7,500 varieties. From the earliest Gallicas and Damasks to the exuberances of the late victorian wichuriana hybrids and from the first Hybrid Teas to the newest introductions, this collection must be unique in the history of the rose. This is a private collection assembled for his own enjoyment but nevertheless every visitor to Tuscany who is interested in the history of the rose must visit this garden.

As a courtesy it is advised to ask for an invitation which will never be refused. This is a feast of knowledge for the rose lover, not a rose garden, but a collection which must be preserved.

The Rosarium at Sangerhausen, Leipzig, Germany, boasted the largest collection of roses in the world but has had difficulties with maintenance problems in recent years; it is reputed to be still worth a visit.

We now come to famous gardens which have a predominance of roses which are grown in association with other plants. Probably the most famous garden in this category is on the **island of Mainau on Lake Constance in Southern Germany**. With the benefit of a micro climate which can support bougainvillea and many other tropical plants in addition to a wide spectrum of the flora of temperate climates it is unique in its cultivation of the genus *Rosa*. There is an area completely devoted to the rose as a shrub and many old varieties are grown alongside Floribundas and Climbers in a wide range of plant forms. To see old favourites and modern cultivars in unconventional forms is a cultural shock to the conservative rose afficionado. The total park is a wonderful horticultural experience with a comprehensive arboretum and a diversity of plants in season, including fuchsias and dahlias.

To equal the exhuberances of the previous garden is a totally different concept in rose gardens at **Zweibrucken, near Saarbrucken, in Germany**. Very accessible to visitors in the Rhine and Moselle areas, this garden has a tremendous appeal to the rosarian who is interested in the integration of a wide selection of plants with roses combining modern garden designs and structures with a diversity of water features.

In the USA there are three gardens which are worthy of merit with extensive collections. The **Hershey Rose Gardens in Pennsylvania** is a large collection of modern varieties in a well-designed garden that was built in the nineteen thirties and and has been in the top rank of world quality rose gardens since that time. There is also an All American rose trial conducted here annually.

The Huntingdon Botanical Gardens, San Marino, California has an interesting collection of a wide selection of roses new and old. There is of course also a tremendous selection of many other plants, and a considerable library and art collection. The newest garden in the USA is the modern collection of roses which is a designer's experience at **Shreveport in Louisiana**, the headquarters of the American Rose Society.

In the southern hemisphere there are notable collections of Old Garden roses in the **Royal Botanic Gardens, Victoria,** and **Melbourne, Australia** and in **Christchurch, New Zealand**.

Other gardens worthy of note include the collection of Old Garden roses at **Mottisfont Abbey, Hampshire,** UK which has been collected and planted with tremendous care and scholarship under the aegis of Graham Thomas, the doyen of writers on this subject. With the encyclopaedic knowledge that Graham has of a wide selection of plants, there are some pleasing plant associations. This garden has to be visited towards the end of June where the fusion of Gallicas and Damask roses with the Hybrid Perpetuals and wichuraianas is a glorious panoply of colour.

The Royal Horticultural Society has a wide selection of roses planted at Wisley where the extensive gardens are a horticultural experience. There is also a well-planted area of the newest introductions. The Society's newest acquisitions also have good plantings of roses. **Rosemoor Gardens in North Devon** have only recently been developed but are already attracting visitors in their thousands and **Hyde Hall, Nr Chelmsford, Essex** is a feast to the plantsman of roses old and new which had already been planted up by a true rose lover before they were given to the Society.

The visiting rosarian is bound to be somewhat perplexed with the diversity of names given to familiar varieties when visiting foreign countries. This can be a disconcerting experience and a word of explanation is required. Each country or in some cases continent will give an acceptable name which the variety is recognized by. To use one name throughout the world would be the ideal but this is not possible usually because of commercial considerations but sometimes because of linguistic problems which can sometimes be embarrassing. These differences are usually understood and in the descriptive chapters of this book (9–12) the more common synonyms are quoted.

Appendix

Bibliography

The student of roses and rose culture is thoroughly spoilt with an extraordinary wide selection of books which have been written over the years on the genus rosa, There are, however, a nucleus of sources which will prove invaluable and which can be enjoyed for their considerable scholarship and commentary on rose varieties.

Early rose books

The Rose Garden, William Paul 1848 and many subsequent revisions and editions. The book that really introduced to the Victorian gardener the extraordinarily expanding lists of varieties which were becoming available together with much valuable advice on rose culture.

A Book About Roses. S. Reynolds Hole, 1870. A collector's volume, the script is pure poetry and very revealing of the early formation of the rose societies and showing.

The Genus Rosa, E. Willmott in two volumes, 1914. An extraordinary collection of illustrated monographs of many varieties of rose, which is now a collector's item.

Recent rose books

Rose Growing Complete, E. B. le Grice 1965, Written by a highly respected professional rose grower who was also a successful breeder. There are some very informative chapters on the genetics of rose breeding and a very erudite discourse on the history of the RNRS.

The Old Shrub Roses, *Shrub Roses of Today* and *Climbing Roses Old and New*, Graham Thomas. Three books published in the last thirty years but subsequently recently revised are extremely comprehensive and have been well researched

Roses. Roger Phillips and Martyn Rix, 1988. An illustrated photographic encyclopedia illustrating a vast number of varieties old and new many of which have probably never been photographed before.

There are two important sources of information when endeavouring to trace varieties:

Find That Rose. Compiled by the British Rose Growers Association and now in its eleventh edition it gives sources for some 2,500 varieties in the UK, Published annually it is obtainable from The Editor, 303 Mile End Road, Colchester, Essex, CO4 5EA, UK.

The Combined Rose List. An American publication which lists some 7,000–8,000 cultivars with sources both in North America and many other rose growing areas of the world. Available from Peter Schneider, PO Box 16035, Rocky River, OH 44116, USA.

Some Useful Addresses

The Royal National Rose Society
Chiswell Green,
St. Albans
Herts AL2 3NR   England

The Royal Horticultural Society
80 Vincent Square
London SW1P 2PE   England

American Rose Society
PO Box 30,000
Shreveport
LA 71130   USA

The Rose Society of Northern Ireland
10 Eastleigh Drive
Belfast BT4 3DX
Northern Ireland

Verein Deutscher Rosenfruende
Waldestrasse 14
7570 Baden-Baden
Germany

Index